YALE STUDIES IN ENGLISH
LXXXI

THOMAS SOUTHERNE DRAMATIST

BY

JOHN WENDELL DODDS

Assistant Professor of English in the
University of Pittsburgh

NEW HAVEN: YALE UNIVERSITY PRESS
LONDON: HUMPHREY MILFORD
OXFORD UNIVERSITY PRESS

MDCCCCXXXIII

COPYRIGHT 1933 BY YALE UNIVERSITY PRESS
PRINTED IN THE UNITED STATES OF AMERICA

All rights reserved. This book may not be reproduced, in whole or in part, in any form (except by reviewers for the public press), without written permission from the publishers.

PREFACE

THE flood of literature which in the last decade or so has been rediscovering the Restoration stage for the modern reader has left untouched, strangely enough, one of its most striking figures. Thomas Southerne is of course a dramatist of the second order of excellence, particularly in comedy, where his light glows feebly beside the brilliance of his great contemporaries. And in tragedy, Otway, who preceded, and Rowe, who followed him, have pretty well absorbed the attention of modern critics. Indeed, only one play of his (and that of lesser importance) has been edited since 1774, and except in two brief and perfunctory German dissertations he has been the object of no special study, biographical or critical. In a sense, then, anything that may be said about Thomas Southerne will be "new," in the humorous phrase of scholarship.

It is therefore with some surprise that one discovers, in an impartial reading of Southerne's plays against the others of their time, how favorably his tragedies compare with the best of their kind. Sometimes he approaches Otway in tragic power, while frequently he more than matches Rowe on his own ground. His significance is not altogether an intrinsic one; the distresses of his heroines would draw few tears today. But an understanding of Southerne's two best tragedies is vital to one who would interpret the continuity of English drama. The course of the eighteenth century sentimental theatre was in no small measure directed by *The Fatal Marriage* and *Oroonoko*. Southerne stands as one of the most important links between the old drama and the new.

The nature of this influence may be understood when one considers the stage history of the two plays that made him famous. For nearly a hundred and fifty years after their first appearance, *The Fatal Marriage* and *Oroonoko* were stock plays on the English stage; there were few important tragic actresses who did not attempt the part of Isabella and few tragedians who did not appear as Oroonoko, the royal slave. Such popularity, whether it be deserved or not, is significant. It seems important, in the light of this history, to reappraise Southerne's work and to place it both in reference to the drama of the period and to the later spawn of sentimental tragedy. Such a study, made without the attempt sometimes exerted to create a hero of a man of straw, reveals Southerne as a far more important tragic dramatist than the neglect accorded him by special students of the drama would indicate.

The chapter on Southerne's life and his relations with his contemporaries is the first attempt that has been made to draw from rather dim materials some picture of "Honest Tom" as he was seen by his friends.

It is a great pleasure to express here my gratitude to Professor George H. Nettleton, under whose direction at Yale University I wrote the doctoral thesis from which this book was drawn. To his criticism and encouragement I owe more than I can well say. And without the constant generosity of Professor Roswell G. Ham this book could not have been completed in its present form. I am indebted to him for many details, both in the biographical portion and in the dating of several plays. That my acknowledgments might not become too monotonous, I have merely placed his initials after the notes that I owe to him. To the staff of the Yale University Library and to those friends who so kindly read portions of the manuscript I am happy to express my thanks. And to my wife, who has been my collaborator in more ways than one, I offer the last and by no means the least burden of gratitude.

J. W. D.

Pittsburgh,
December 1, 1932.

CONTENTS

Preface iii
Chronology vii
    I. Biographical Sketch 1
   II. *The Loyal Brother, or The Persian Prince* 28
  III. *The Disappointment, or The Mother in Fashion* . 48
  IV. *Sir Anthony Love, or The Rambling Lady* 63
   V. *The Wives' Excuse, or Cuckolds Make Themselves* 77
  VI. *The Maid's Last Prayer, or Any Rather Than Fail* 89
 VII. *The Fatal Marriage, or The Innocent Adultery* . 98
VIII. *Oroonoka* 128
  IX. *The Fate of Capua* 163
   X. *The Spartan Dame* 176
  XI. *Money the Mistress* 194
 XII. Conclusion 204
Appendix 218
Bibliography 220
Index 229

CHRONOLOGY OF SOUTHERNE'S PLAYS

The Loyal Brother, or The Persian Prince (D.L. February, 1681/2), 1682.

The Disappointment, or The Mother in Fashion (D.L. April, 1684), 1684.

Sir Anthony Love, or The Rambling Lady (D.L. ca. December, 1690), 1691.

The Wives' Excuse, or Cuckolds Make Themselves (D.L. December, 1691), 1692.

The Maid's Last Prayer, or Any Rather Than Fail (D.L. January, 1692/3), 1693.

The Fatal Marriage, or The Innocent Adultery (D.L. February, 1693/4), 1694.

Oroonoko (D.L. December, 1695), 1696.

The Fate of Capua (L.I.F. April, 1700), 1700.

The Spartan Dame (D.L. December, 1719), 1719.

Money the Mistress (L.I.F. February, 1725/6), 1726.

CHAPTER I

BIOGRAPHICAL SKETCH

IN the annals of the Restoration stage there is no dramatist who lived as long as Thomas Southerne, and none who was better liked by those who knew him. It is surprising, then, to discover how thin has been the body of information that would help us see the man as he was. Almost nothing has been written about him and curiously little is known.[1] Born in the very year of the Restoration, and living through the revolution of 1745, he is almost the only writer who bridges the gap between the drama of Charles II and that of George II. The year that young Southerne entered Dublin University, Etherege's Sir Fopling Flutter had just arrived at Lincoln's-Inn-Fields "piping hot from Paris"; when he died, George Barnwell had been instructing London apprentices for fifteen years. Dryden was dramatic king when Southerne wrote his first play, but the younger man lived to see Garrick thrill the crowds at Goodman's Fields with *Richard III*. And throughout his productive years, as one of the most popular and influential playwrights of his day, Southerne had supported Congreve in his first dramatic attempt, had recommended to the patentees Colley Cibber's first play, and had completed for Dryden an unfinished tragedy. Both Swift and Pope he counted among his friends. What memoirs might such a man have left us! But of such memoirs he gave us none, and of letters scarcely any, so that it is hard to trace again the form and pressure of his personality. Unlike most of his fellows in the theatre, he led a quiet life, so universally liked that he was drawn into no bickering controversies, and so circumspect in his private life that scandal had to chatter

---

[1] *Cf.* A. W. Ward's Life of Southerne in the *Dictionary of National Biography,* XVIII, 688-90, for a summary of the facts hitherto collected by literary historians.

at a distance. Upon such a gentle history the biographer, at this distance, feeds but poorly. All that is left is to gather such scattered facts as one may about a long and relatively peaceful life, filling in the picture of Southerne's personality with the references that may be found here and there in the writings of his friends. At all events, it is not unpleasant to find one member of a rather uncertain fraternity living in a precarious age a life that did honor both to himself and to his craft.

Thomas Southerne[2] was born at Oxmantown, Dublin, in 1660,[3] the third son of Francis Southerne,[4] who appears to have been a prominent Dublin brewer. The name of Francis Southerne appears on a petition of October 21, 1670, asking for incorporation for the brewers of Dublin.[5] Francis was to be ordained among twenty others to be "Brewers of Dublin" and was to be named as one of twelve Assistants of the Corporation. The list of petitioners for letters patent included such dignitaries as James, Lord Santry, Chief Justice of the Court of Chief Place [King's Bench], Sir Robert Booth, Chief Justice of the Common Pleas, and John Bysse, Chief Baron of the Exchequer. The corporation had for its philanthropic purpose "the better suppressing and reformation of divers deceipts and other abuses practiced by divers persons who do take upon them without sufficient skill and knowledge to brew ale and beer to sell within the said city . . . to the great damage, hindrance and decay of health of all our loving subjects there." In 1678 the will of "Francis Southerne, St.

---

[2] Sometimes spelled Southern. Southerne himself spelled his name with the final *e*.

[3] I have been able to find no parish record of his birth, but the register of Dublin University states that he was in his seventeenth year when he entered Trinity College, March 30, 1676; and in the Dedication to *The Fate of Capua* (1726) Southerne names his age as 66.

[4] According to the entry in the records of the Middle Temple.

[5] *Calendar of State Papers relating to Ireland. Preserved in the* [British] *Public Record Office, Sept. 1669–Dec. 1670*, London, 1910. Pp. 288–9.

Michan's, brewer" was admitted to probate.[6] The will itself, which might have thrown some light on this now obscure problem of the dramatist's parentage, was lost in the fire in the Four Courts in 1922.

As a child, Thomas attended the grammar school of Edward Wetenhall,[7] who came in 1672 from Exeter to Dublin to teach the free school there.[8] On March 30, 1675/6 he entered Trinity College, Dublin University,[9] the college also of Congreve and Farquhar. He was under Mr. Giles Pooley as College Tutor.[10] Anthony Wood erroneously asserts in his edition of *Athenae Oxonienses*[11] that the dramatist was the son of George Southerne of Stratford-upon-Avon, and was a servitor at Pembroke College, Oxford. In this connection there is recorded for us an interesting letter of Southerne's, written in 1737 to Dr. Richard Rawlinson, who was planning a continuation of Wood's work. The letter is preserved, says Malone, who first quotes it,[12] in Rawlinson's copy of the *Athenae Oxonienses*. The old dramatist is curiously resentful about being described as a servitor of Pembroke.

Sir: I received your letter, with Mr. Anstis's enclosed. This is to assure you, that I had no title to have my name in the ATHENAE OXONIENSES; for I was born in Dublin, and bred up in the college of Dublin, and was never a Servitor, but spent my own money there: many better men have been Servitors, but I never was. Whatever is mentioned of me in the last edition of that book, is scandalously false

---

[6] See Index to the original wills of the diocese of Dublin to 1800, found in the *26th Report of the Deputy Keeper of the Public Records and Keeper of the State Papers in Ireland* (June, 1894), p. 801.

[7] *Alumni Dublinenses,* ed. G. D. Burtchaell and T. U. Sadleir, 1924. (Unless otherwise stated, the books cited in the notes were published in London.)

[8] "Edward Wetenhall, clerke, batchelor of divinities," petitioned the city in 1674 for 160 pounds due him as unpaid salary for two years. *Calendar of Ancient Records of Dublin,* 1895, V, 49–50.

[9] See *Alumni Dublinenses,* p. 769, and Malone's *Critical and Miscellaneous Prose Works of Dryden,* 1800, I, pt. 1, 175–7.

[10] J. W. Stubbs, *History of the University of Dublin,* 1889, p. 345.
[11] Bliss's edition, IV, 750.   [12] *Op. cit.,* I, pt. 1, 176–7.

in fact or circumstance, in every particular: therefore you will do a justice to the truth and me, to leave me out of the edition, and make me some reparation for the abuse done me in that defamatory character. [Southerne here inserts a list of his plays, and a detail about his military service.] If any thing I have said here will be of any use, more than leaving me out of that book, and doeing me justice in my character, you will much oblige, Sir, etc.

There is no B.A. degree recorded for Southerne in the Trinity College records. In the Spring Term of 1696, when he was at the peak of his popular success as a dramatist, he was granted an M.A.[13]

From Dublin, young Southerne crossed the Irish Sea in 1680 to try his fortune in London. On July 15 he was admitted to the Middle Temple.[14] The Inns of Court were, it would seem, assembly grounds for young gentlemen of artistic temperament who were later to desert law for poetry. Shadwell, Wycherley, Ravenscroft, Congreve, Banks, and Rowe each served his apprenticeship at an Inn of Court, and each preferred the stage to jurisprudence. There is no record of Southerne's departure from the Middle Temple, but presumably it was by 1682, when he saw the production at Drury Lane of his first dramatic venture, *The Loyal Brother, or The Persian Prince*. It was two years before his next play appeared on the boards; in April, 1684, *The Disappointment, or The Mother in Fashion* was acted at Drury Lane. Gildon said that the play had "no ill Success, at least with very good Judges."[15] It was performed for the King and Queen on January 27, 1684/5.[16] This was only a fortnight before Charles's death, and the rushing events of the next few months were to take Southerne away from the stage, to which he was not to return until 1690. Like Steele and Farquhar, he was to have his fling at soldiery.

Southerne already stood well in the good graces of James,

---

[13] See *Alumni Dublinenses*, p. 769.
[14] The *D.N.B.* states erroneously that he entered the Middle Temple in 1678.
[15] Gildon's Langbaine's *Lives*, p. 135.
[16] Allardyce Nicoll, *Restoration Drama*, p. 312. Hand-list of plays.

Biographical Sketch

Duke of York, through the elaborate compliment he had paid his Highness in *The Loyal Brother*. Tachmas, the hero of the play and the very soul of noble virtue, was meant to represent James. Therefore when the Duke of York became James II he was ready to pay off the debt with some kind of preferment. When Monmouth invaded England in June, 1685, Southerne left the theatre to take up arms on behalf of his patron. Through Col. Patrick Sarsfield (afterwards Earl of Lucan), an Irishman who later fought for James II in Ireland during the Revolution of 1688, Southerne was recommended to the attention of the young James Fitzjames, later Duke of Berwick, natural son of James II.[17] The young man granted Southerne, on June 19th, 1685, a commission as ensign in the Princess Anne's Regiment of Foot,[18] commanded at that time by Robert Lord Ferrers. On June 1, 1686, his rank was raised to that of lieutenant,[19] and when the Duke of Berwick subsequently took command of the regiment, Southerne was given a company.[20] The Duke was willing to do what he could for the ambitious young Irishman. As Southerne says in the preface to *The Spartan Dame*, "His Grace . . . discovered in a little time, a generous disposition of making my fortune; which, as it would have been no hard matter for a King's favourite son to accomplish, he would probably have finished, had not the changes of the world deprived the country of his service, and his dependants of his support." Thus did the Revolution of 1688 ruin Southerne's political prospects. Before January, 1689, he was out of the regiment.[21] There is no evidence to show that he made any effort to help the sinking cause of James.

[17] See the Preface to *The Spartan Dame*, 1774 edition of the *Plays*.
[18] *English Army Lists and Commission Registers, 1661-1714*, ed. Charles Dalton, 1892-4. II, 29.
[19] *Ibid.*, II, 77.
[20] Preface to *The Spartan Dame*. Dalton gives no record of Southerne's captaincy. In Nov., 1687, he was still listed as a lieutenant. II, 138.
[21] *Army Lists*, II, 77.

We next hear of Southerne in 1690, when he returns to the theatre as author of a rollicking comedy, *Sir Anthony Love, or The Rambling Lady*. Partly because of the superb acting of Mrs. Mountford in the title rôle, this play, unlike the author's previous efforts, caught the favor of the town and became a huge success. Thus encouraged, Southerne produced in rapid succession *The Wives' Excuse, or Cuckolds Make Themselves* (1691); *The Maid's Last Prayer, or Any Rather Than Fail* (1693); *The Fatal Marriage, or The Innocent Adultery* (1694); and *Oroonoko* (1695). The last two are the best, as they were also the most popular, of all his plays. On them his reputation was to rest; for over a century and a quarter they were to draw tears from those whose sensibilities responded to the spectacle of beauty and innocence in distress. With *The Fate of Capua* in 1700 Southerne left off writing, not to return with another production for nineteen years.

There is almost no definite biographical evidence, documented or undocumented, relating to the most active and productive period of Southerne's literary life. Of his friends we know something, and from their report of him we may deduce in part the nature of his personality. But of what he was doing during his unproductive years (and particularly during the long period from 1700 to 1726—for *The Spartan Dame*, in 1719, was only an old play revised) we are in ignorance.[22] Where did he get his money? To be sure, he made more

[22] It is possible that Southerne was engaged in some official capacity to Charles Boyle while the latter was Ambassador to the Low Countries in 1711–13. Professor Ham has called my attention to a life of Congreve in Southerne's hand (British Museum, Birch Ms. 4221). On the back of the Ms. is the note "Memoirs relating to Mr. Congreve written by Mr. Thomas Southern and communicated to me (Dr. Birch) from him by the hand of Dr. Thomas Pellet Jan 12 1735/6." On the same side, in Southerne's writing, is the note: "Brussels Sept 3 1711 Mrs. Peterson, Butler, Porter, Mrs. Barke, The Tallies to be Sold C McHenry Ld. Ossory's order to pay off the . . ." [illegible]
"Pray let the payments be sent over immediately"

money from his plays than did most contemporary playwrights. He was entirely judicious in the selection of patrons. Doubtless he sold his commission well. In addition, he was what Cibber's *Lives* calls "an exact œconomist"[23]—but even this would not have enabled him to die as rich as he undoubtedly did.[24]

The assurance that he made a financially effective marriage would help resolve the problem. Such was perhaps the case, but even here we are left with the most tenuous evidence. He had a daughter, for at his death he left all his property to his "dear daughter Agnes."[25] Although I can find no official record of the marriage, it is definitely referred to in an anonymous satirical poem written in 1703, called *Religio Poetae: or, A Satyr on the Poets.*

> Soft *So*-[uther]-*n's* Pen has something in't so rare,
> His Heroes never fail to please the Fair,
> And Lewdness is drest up with a peculiar Air.
> Tho' *Oroonoko* raves, and stamps, and stares,
> You'd think he'd pull the Sky about his Ears.
> Had he depended solely on the Bays,
> Or on the Income of his two Third Days,
> What might Matter had he got by Plays!
> But wisely he declin'd the starving Herd;
> His brawny Back at length preferr'd the Bard.
> For since the Marriage-Yoke he has put on,
> He drinks *Champaign,* and quits the Helycon.[26]

---

[23] V, 330.

[24] The loss of Francis Southerne's will destroys our best chance of discovering whether Thomas inherited any property from his father. That our poet had some holdings in Ireland may be surmised from the clause in his will which leaves to his daughter all his property "in England or Ireland."

[25] See transcript of Southerne's will in the Appendix. Agnes was drawn into matrimony shortly after receiving her patrimony on her father's death May 26, 1746. See *The Register Book of Marriages, Parish of St. George, London,* ed. J. H. Chapman, 1886. The date of the marriage was Nov. 29, 1746.

[26] Page 9. [R.G.H.]

The last four lines suggest the grounds for Southerne's emancipation from playwriting. That he had planned to abandon the stage is further indicated by the Prologue written by Charles Boyle for Southerne's *Fate of Capua* (1700).

> Our Bard resolv'd to quit this wicked town,
> And all poetic offices lay down;
> But the weak brother was drawn in again,
> And a cast mistress tempted him to sin.

A line in the Prologue to the comedy *As You Find It* (L.I.F. 1703) shows that his retirement was accepted as a fact: "Since S–[outherne] writes no more."

He may have ceased writing, but he certainly did not "quit the town" altogether. In 1704 he is advising John Dennis on his play *Liberty Asserted*.[27] In 1711 Elijah Fenton could address him thus in his *Epistle to Southerne:*

> Yet when you next to *Medway* shall repair,
> And quit the town to breathe a purer air;
> Retiring from the crowd, to steal the sweets
> Of easy life in TWISDEN'S calm retreats;

and by 1719 he is busily engaged in getting permission from the Lord Chamberlain to produce *The Spartan Dame*.

This play, a tragedy, was immediately successful. His next, and last piece, *Money the Mistress* (1726), was a return to comedy, but even his best friends had to admit that the well of dramatic inspiration was now dry. The play was hissed off the stage, and with it departed Southerne's dramatic ambitions.

He lived for twenty years yet—a happy old age spent in making the rounds of his innumerable friends. Now he was in Bath, visiting his friend Martin Killigrew; now in Dublin, dining with Dean Swift; now at Marston with his friend and patron John Boyle, Earl of Orrery. But most of the time he was in London, revising plays for importunate friends and

---

[27] See the Preface to this play, 1704.

Biographical Sketch

faithfully attending worship at Westminster Abbey. Theophilus Cibber says[28] that "a gentleman whose authority we have already quoted,[29] had likewise informed us, that Mr. Southern lived for the last ten years of his life in Westminster,[30] and attended very constant at divine service in the Abbey, being particularly fond of church music. He never staid within doors while in health, two days together, having such a circle of acquaintance of the best rank, that he constantly dined with one or other, by a kind of rotation." He made his home for the greater part of those last ten years with Mr. Whyte, an oilman, in Tothill Street against Dartmouth Street.[31] Tothill Street was the most ancient street in Westminster. Lord Grey de Wilton, Sir George Carew, Edmund Burke, and Sir Henry Herbert are said to have lived there; Thomas Betterton was born there.[32] The number of Southerne's house has been identified as No. 48, formerly 4, on the south side of the street.[33] Sometime before his death, however, he must have moved to Smith Street, Westminster, for the newspaper accounts of his death unite in assigning a house in that street as the last home of Thomas Southerne, "a famous poet," and "possessed of a large fortune."[34]

William Oldys says that he remembered Mr. Southerne "a grave and venerable old gentleman. He lived near Covent-

---

[28] *Lives of the Poets,* V, 331.

[29] "A gentleman personally acquainted with Mr. Southern, who desires to have his name conceal'd." V, 328 n.

[30] He was living in the parish of St. Margaret's, Westminster, as early as 1731, for his will written Nov. 6, 1731, assigns that parish as his, his landlord being one Richard Browne, in little Aumary near Dean's Yard, Westminster. See Southerne's will in the Appendix.

[31] From this place he addresses the letter to Rawlinson quoted above.

[32] *Life and Times of Thomas Betterton, by the Author and Editor of the Lives of Mrs. Abington,* etc., 1888, pp. 5, 6.

[33] G. H. Cunningham, *London, A Comprehensive Survey,* etc., 1927, p. 733.

[34] *The True Patriot,* May 27—June 3, 1746; *St. James's Evening Post,* Tuesday, May 27 to Thursday, May 29, 1746.

garden, and used often to frequent the evening prayers there, always neat and decently dressed, commonly in black, with his silver sword and silver locks; but latterly it seems he resided at Westminster."[35]

Towards the end, as one might expect, his faculties weakened, but in 1737 Thomas Gray found him interesting. In September of that year he writes to Horace Walpole: "We have old Mr. Southern at a gentleman's house a little way off, who often comes to see us; he is now seventy-seven years old, and has almost wholly lost his memory; but is as agreeable as an old man can be, at least I persuade myself so when I look at him, and think of Isabella and Oroonoko."[36] Mason, in his edition of Gray, adds this note to the letter: "Mr. Gray always thought highly of his pathetic powers, at the same time that he blamed his ill taste for mixing them so injudiciously with farce, in order to produce that monstrous species of composition called Tragi-comedy."[37]

At last this long life came to an end, and Thomas Southerne died Monday, May 26, 1746, eighty-six years of age. On May 29 he was laid to rest in St. Margaret's Church, Westminster.[38] The passing of the old dramatist was noticed by the *Gentleman's Magazine* with some anonymous verses *On the Death of Mr. Southern:*

> Prais'd by the *grandsires* of the present age,
> Shall *Southern* pass unnoted off the stage?
> Who, more than half a century ago,
> Caus'd from each eye the tender tear to flow;
> Does not *his death* one grateful drop demand,
> In works of wit, the *Nestor* of our land?

[35] Ms. notes on Gildon's edition of Langbaine's *Lives of the Dramatick Poets,* 1699. Quoted by Richard Ryan in *Biographica Hibernica,* 2 vols., 1821, II, 562.
[36] Gray's *Works,* ed. Edmund Gosse, 4 vols., 1895. II, 10–11.
[37] York, 1775, p. 25.
[38] The entry in the church register is, under "Burials," "May 29. 1746, Thos Southern Esqre G.D." [Great Duty.] Cunningham, p. 168, erroneously gives his burial-place as St. Paul's Church, Covent Garden.

Southern was *Dryden's* friend: him genius warm'd,
When *Otway* wrote, and *Betterton* perform'd.
He knew *poor Nat,* while regular his fire:
Was *Congreve's* pattern ere *he* rais'd desire:
Belong'd to *Charles's* age, when wit ran high,
And liv'd so long but to behold it *die*.[39]

Southerne and his Contemporaries

To trace amid the byways of Queen Anne and Georgian letters the mention made of Southerne by those who knew him is to see a man loved and respected by an extraordinary diversity of people. "Honest Tom" he was called familiarly, and Whig and Tory, noble and playwright, poet and wit alike gave him their affection and admiration. We see a man generous in the extreme to his friends, a boon comrade in his early days and a jovial fireside companion in the long mellow years of his declining age. Dryden was his close friend, and Swift and Pope spoke of him affectionately. There is no more spontaneous tribute to the charm of Southerne's personality, even as an old man, than that held in a letter of John Boyle, Earl of Orrery, written when the poet was in his seventy-eighth year. ". . . I'll pass on to sing of that Nestor of Westminster, Tom Southerne. He still possesses his good humour to roast Beef and Mutton Pye. Whilst we staid at London We had him every Day at our Table. He was in Love with Lady Orrery, or at least, with her Dinners. He even admir'd her Music, tho' he is deaf, and repeated so much of his Plays to her that she became deaf also. Two young Ladies, her Cousins, protest they never heard so many Magic Strains under so comic an appearance since the Hour of their Birth; and for my Part, He has so far infected Me that I speak to my Servants in blank verse, and call for my Buskins instead of my Boots."[40] An amiable guest the old man must have been!

[39] July, 1746. XVI, 378. The lines also appear in the *London Magazine* for June, 1746, 310–11.

[40] *The Orrery Papers*, I, 246. Letter of Nov. 27, 1738, "To the Rev. Mr. Ferrebee."

We may surmise from scattered references that in the days of his youth Southerne had all the dash of the man of fashion; doubtless he too had heard the chimes at midnight. In an epistle to Anthony Hammond, Charles Hopkins refers to the times

> When you, and *Southern, Moyle,* and *Congreve* meet,
> The best, good Men, with the best-natur'd Wit.[41]

In a similar epistolary poem addressed to "Walter Moyle, Esq.," Hopkins commends the convivial life of his friend:

> In full delights let sprightly *Southern* live,
> With all that Women, and that Wine, can give.[42]

Even as late as 1720, Southerne's hearty manner calls forth a comment from John Gay, when, in *Mr. Pope's Welcome from Greece,* he assembles the friends of Pope to welcome him back to England after his spiritual sojourn in Greece with Homer: "See *Digby* faints at *Southern* talking loud."[43]

By 1703, however, sobriety and decorum are descending upon him. In a satirical epistle of Defoe's, published that year, he is described as attempting to live the anomalous life of a pious beau.

> *S*–[outher]–*n,* if such a thing this Age can show,
> Sets up for an instructing sober *Beau,*
> An Air of Gravity upon his Brow,
> And wou'd be Pious too, if he knew how;
> His Language Decent, very seldom Swears,
> And never fails the Play-House, nor his Prayers[.]
> Vice seems to ha' been banish'd from his Doors,
> And very, very, very seldom Whores.

[41] In Charles Hopkins's *Epistolary Poems on Several Occasions,* etc. 1694, p. 10.
[42] *Ibid.,* p. 7. Walter Moyle (1672–1721) was one of the circle at Will's. He was a classical scholar of some ability, and a political pamphleteer.
[43] Gay's *Poetical Works,* ed. G. C. Faber, Oxford, 1926, p. 168.

> His Brother Fops he drags to Church to Pray,
> And checks the Ladies if they talk too Gay:
> But S----n most unhappily has fix'd
> On two Extreams which never can be mix'd;
> For they will all the Power of Art out-do,
> Can join the new Reformer and the Beau.[44]

It is not unlikely that in his old age he repented himself of the immoral tone of his earlier plays, and as the *Biographica Dramatica* says, "used to declare to Lord Corke his regret at complying with the licentious taste of the times."[45] Here at least he is in an honorable tradition. Better writers than he have found time in their declining years to lament the follies of their youthful authorship; Dryden himself had regretted the immorality of his plays.[46]

"Southern was Dryden's friend," said the unknown elegist in the *London Magazine,* and it was with a distinct kindness that Dryden greeted the efforts of the younger dramatist. The two had met as early as 1682, when Dryden had furnished prologue and epilogue for *The Loyal Brother*. Late in 1691, when Southerne's comedy *The Wives' Excuse* was politely damned, Dryden declared to all who would listen that the town had been kind to *Sir Anthony Love,* Southerne's previous comedy, and needed only to be just to this.[47] Southerne soothed his wounded vanity by prefixing to the quarto edition of the play the lines addressed to him by Dryden "On his Comedy, called The Wives Excuse." Here Dryden, with

---

[44] *More Reformation. A Satyr upon Himself. By the Author of The True Born English-Man,* 1703, pp. 11, 12. [R.G.H.]

[45] I, pt. 2, 681. In a letter to John Duncombe in 1734, Southerne praises Duncombe for the "decency" of his epilogue to *Lucius Junius Brutus.* See *Letters by Several Eminent Persons Deceased,* ed. John Duncombe, 2nd ed., 1773. II, 64–5.

[46] *To Mrs. Killigrew,* 1686, and *Letter to Mrs. Thomas,* Nov., 1699. Scott-Saintsbury *Dryden,* XI, 107, and XVIII, 166. *Cf.* also the *Preface to the Fables,* XI, 214.

[47] Dedication to *The Wives' Excuse,* first appearing in the 1713 edition of the *Plays.*

more enthusiasm than judgment, compared Southerne with
Terence, and assured him that although the play failed on the
stage, it would not want readers.

> Yet those who blame the Tale, commend thy Wit;
> So TERENCE plotted; but so TERENCE writ.
> Like his thy Thoughts are true, thy Language clean,
> Ev'n Lewdness is made Moral in thy Scene.

When Dryden fell ill, it was to Southerne's care that he entrusted the half of the last act of his tragedy, *Cleomenes*.[48]
Scott believes that Southerne exercised on the play only the
power of revision and finishing.[49] It is impossible to dogmatize here—without doubt Dryden had outlined to Southerne
the course of the action—but I can find nothing in the verse
of the last half of the fifth act of which Southerne, at his
best, would not have been capable. On the other hand, this
portion of the play lacks somewhat the vigor of phrase and
imagery that was Dryden's. At any rate, Dryden's calling on
Southerne at all for aid shows the degree of intimacy that
had grown out of their friendship, so strangely inaugurated
ten years before.[50]

Pope too paid Southerne graceful compliments on several
occasions. In a note on the manuscript of the *Pastorals*, he
included Southerne's name among those of the people through
whose hands the copy had passed.[51] The *Epistle to Augustus*
names Southerne with Rowe as an admirable delineator of
the passions: "But, for the passions, Southern sure and
Rowe." The same poem includes him with Jonson, Shake-

[48] Dedication to *The Wives' Excuse*.
[49] Scott-Saintsbury *Dryden*, VIII, 209.
[50] The subject of the play is of a distinct Jacobite flavor. It deals
with an exiled monarch who attempts through force to regain his
throne. Such a theme proved distasteful to the court of William and
Mary, and the piece was prohibited by the Chamberlain. Later the ban
was repealed, and the play was produced with great success in 1692.
[51] Elwin-Courthope *Pope*, I, 239.

speare, Cowley, Beaumont and Fletcher, Shadwell, Wycherley, and Rowe in a list of honor:

> These, only these, support the crowded stage
> From eldest Heywood down to Cibber's age.

In 1742 Southerne was invited to dine on his birthday with Lord Orrery, and on this occasion Pope inscribed some cordial lines to the octogenarian dramatist:

> Resign'd to live, prepar'd to die,
> With not one sin, but poetry,
> This day Tom's fair account has run
> (Without a blot) to eighty-one.
> Kind Boyle, before his poet, lays
> A table, with a cloth of bays;
> And Ireland, mother of sweet singers,
> Presents her harp still to his fingers.
> The feast, his tow'ring genius marks
> In yonder wild goose and the larks!
> The mushrooms show his wit was sudden!
> And for his judgment, lo a pudden!
> Roast beef, tho' old, proclaims him stout,
> And grace, altho' a bard, devout.
> May Tom, whom heav'n sent down to raise
> The price of prologues and of plays,
> Be ev'ry birthday more a winner,
> Digest his thirty-thousandth dinner;
> Walk to his grave without reproach,
> And scorn a rascal and a coach.[52]

Southerne's association with Charles Boyle, Earl of Orrery (1676–1731), and later with his son John (1707–1762), was both pleasant and profitable for the dramatist. In 1693 Southerne had sued for the patronage of Orrery in dedicating his *Maid's Last Prayer, or Any Rather Than Fail* to "Mr. Charles Boyl." The dedication is not in Southerne's easiest style; he is obviously awed (at least for dedicatory purposes) by the station of his patron, who was at this time

---

[52] Elwin-Courthope *Pope*, IV, 496–7. (First published in Warburton's edition of 1751, VI, 81–2.)

only seventeen years old. ". . . The distance of your quality and fortune, has made it impossible to come near you, as a friend . . ." he says. Orrery was himself to be an aspirant to literary honors, both as translator of Phalaris in the dispute that led to Swift's *Battle of the Books,* and as author of the comedy *As You Find It.* To Southerne, he was to prove a generous patron. There are no more plays dedicated to him, yet in the dedication to *Money the Mistress* (1726) addressed to John Boyle, Southerne declares: "I take this occasion to confess the obligations that I must ever have to my great benefactor the Earl of *Orrery,* your Lordship's father. It is to his favour that I have now in my old age the reasonable comforts of life, and that I am not straitned in any the conveniencies of it, by what could happen to the play."

There is scanty evidence on the nature of the relationship between Charles Boyle and Southerne, but of the warm friendship of John Boyle[53] for Southerne there is a rich expression in certain letters from the former to the latter, written between the years 1733 and 1737. Southerne was spending much of his time in visiting his friends, both in England and in Ireland. Now we find him regretting that he could not spend the summer with his friend William Broome, now running down for an extended visit to Holme Lacy in Hertfordshire, where Lady Scudamore lived,[54] but returning always to the Orrery estate at Marston, near Frome in Somersetshire. There the old poet was welcomed as to his own home; there he could play with the Orrery children, and regale both Lord and Lady Orrery with his reminiscences. The tone of Orrery's letters to Southerne is one of tender, almost filial affection. He writes intimately of his gardens, his birds, his

[53] Friend of Swift and Pope, and later, of Dr. Johnson; author of *Remarks on the Life and Writings of Swift,* 1751; a translator of the letters of Pliny the Younger, 1751; author of *Letters from Italy in 1754 and 1755,* (published after his death by J. Duncombe in 1774).

[54] See letter from Fenton to Broome, Elwin-Courthope *Pope,* VIII, 80.

dogs, his servants, his children, expressing often the wish that Southerne was at Marston. "Ld. Boyle [Orrery's son] asks me often when Mr Southerne will come home," he writes. "I tell him next Summer."[55] He writes from Cork to urge his "dear Brother Poet" not to venture a trip to Ireland, but to "go and regale thyself amongst my Ancestours at Marston. Pillard shall open my Cellars, and Marston shall be your own House as long as you will think it worth making so. The year following we will both revell there, till then to You and to your Companions I resign It."[56] "Marston looks but half agreable without you," he insists again.[57] "It is an honour to a young Man to boast of the Freindship of one of your Years and Figure in Life. Pope is proud of his Wycherley, lett me be so of my Southerne," is his praise on one occasion.[58]

Orrery's insistence that Southerne should not cross the Irish sea was made in vain. In July, 1733, he is in Dublin visiting Orrery and renewing his friendship with Swift. On July 8, Swift writes to Pope: "Our old friend Southern, who has just left us, was invited to dinner once or twice by a judge, a bishop, or a commissioner of revenue, but most frequented a few particular friends, and chiefly the Doctor, who is so easy in his fortune, and very hospitable."[59]

"A Bawd for the Muses"

"I SEE by the preface to Themistocles that Tom Southerne is still alive and plays the bawd as formerly for the muses," wrote Elijah Fenton to William Broome in 1729.[60] Indeed there is no stronger evidence of Southerne's generosity than the number of times he exerted his influence on behalf of young or obscure playwrights. Not only would he read and

[55] *Orrery Papers*, I, 126.   [56] *Ibid.*, I, 121.
[57] *Ibid.*, I, 123.   [58] *Ibid.*, I, 129.
[59] Swift's *Correspondence,* ed. F. E. Ball, 6 vols., 1910–14. V, 2–3. "The Doctor" is Dr. Delaney.
[60] Elwin-Courthope *Pope*, VIII, 154.

advise changes in a friend's manuscript, but he would carry it to the managers, and frequently secure its production.

It is probable that Congreve's first acknowledged publication was the song "Tell me no more I am deceived," which he contributed in January, 1692/3, to Southerne's *Maid's Last Prayer*.⁶¹ Certain it is that when Congreve had finished his first play, *The Old Bachelor,* he took it to Southerne for advice, and the latter brought it to the attention of Dryden and Arthur Maynwaring. Let Southerne tell the story in his own words:

> Then he began his Play the old Batchelor haveing little Acquaintance withe the traders in that way, his Cozens recommended him to a friend of theirs, [in all likelihood Southerne himself], who was very usefull to him in the whole course of his play, he engag'd Mr. Dryden in its favour, who upon reading it sayd he never saw such a first play in his life, but the Author not being acquainted with the stage or the town, it would be a pity to have it miscarry for want of a little Assistance: the stuff was rich indeed, it wanted only the fashionable cutt of the town. To help that Mr. Dryden, Mr. Manwayring, and Mr. Southern, red it with great care, and Mr. Dryden putt it in the order it was playd, Mr. Southerne obtaind of Mr. Thos: Davenant who then governd the Playhouse, that Mr. Congreve shoud have the previlege of the Playhouse half a year before his play was playd, wh. I never knew allowd any one before.⁶²

The older men were rewarded for their generosity by the play's immediate success. With instinctive unselfishness, Southerne hailed Congreve as Dryden's successor. "CONGREVE appears," he said, "the Darling, and last Comfort of his [Dryden's] Years." He then went on, "But my best Praise is, that I am your Friend."⁶³ Years later, Congreve in a measure repaid his obligation when he wrote a letter to the Lord Chamberlain on behalf of Southerne's tragedy *The Spartan Dame*.⁶⁴

⁶¹ Malone's *Prose Works of Dryden*, I, pt. 1, 227–8.
⁶² Southerne's Ms. notes on Congreve's life (Add. Mss. 4221, B.M.). Quoted by E. Gosse in his *Life of Congreve,* 1924 edition, pp. 175–6.
⁶³ M. Summers' edition of Congreve, I, 163.
⁶⁴ See below, p. 181.

Biographical Sketch 19

Colley Cibber had made his first appearance as an actor in one of Southerne's plays,[65] and now we find Southerne recommending to the managers his first attempt at playwriting. Cibber himself tells the story: "The next Year I produc'd the Comedy of *Love's last Shift;* yet the Difficulty of getting it to the Stage was not easily surmounted; for, at that time, as little was expected from me, as an Author, as had been from my Pretensions to be an Actor. However, Mr. *Southern,* the Author of *Oroonoko,* having had the Patience to hear me read it to him, happened to like it so well that he immediately recommended it to the Patentees, and it was accordingly acted in *January* 1695."[66] In the Dedication Cibber had acknowledged his debt: "Mr. *Southern's* Good-Nature (whose own Works best recommend his Judgment) Engaged his Reputation for the Success," etc.

Love's Last Shift had been dedicated to "Richard Norton, of Southwick, Esq."[67] In that year too there was acted at Drury Lane a tragedy by Norton called *Pausanias, the Betrayer of his Country.* The gentleman-author preferred to remain anonymous, and so Southerne once more played bawd

[65] See below, p. 64.
[66] Cibber's *Apology,* ed. R. W. Lowe, I, 212-3. January, 1695, is of course in the New Style January, 1696.
[67] Of Southwick, Hants., near Portsmouth. Norton, who died December, 1732, was a patron of the stage as well as a modest author. John Dennis addresses a letter to him August 10, 1708, "sent to him by Mr. Booth, when the Players went last down to act at his House." (*Original Letters . . . by Mr. Dennis,* 2 vols., 1721, I, 115.) Dennis praises Norton's encouragement of the "Dramatic Muses" in offering them a refuge and retreat so charming as his place at Southwick, in a time when "an effeminate Musick" is endeavoring to banish the drama from England and to "emasculate the Minds of Men," p. 117. Samuel Briscoe dedicated to him the first edition of Mrs. Behn's posthumously published tale, *The Unfortunate Bride,* in 1698. Norton's will aroused great interest. In it he left his personal estate of £60,000 and the income of his real estate, amounting to £6,000 a year, to Parliament, to be disposed of in charitable uses. (See *Gentleman's Magazine,* Dec., 1732, p. 1125.) The will was cancelled as bearing evident marks of mental derangement!

for the Muses and brought the play on the stage as the work of "a person of quality." There it was promptly damned.[68] When the quarto was published in 1696, it was Southerne again who wrote the Dedication to Anthony Henley, Whig politician and friend to Norton.

Southerne chose his friends upon no party lines. He was no militant Tory, despite his early venture on behalf of James and of his friendship with Dryden. Many of his friends and some of his patrons were Whig. In 1704 we find him, in his amiable capacity of play-doctor, offering fruitful suggestions to John Dennis on his distinctly Whiggish play *Liberty Asserted,* produced that year at Lincoln's-Inn-Fields. Dennis expresses his gratitude in the Preface: "The Design of this Play was much improv'd by the Remonstrances which I receiv'd from my valued Friend Mr. *Southern,* who besides his Zeal to do good to his Friends, and a noble Sincerity, uncommon among the Writers of this Age, by the *ex tempore* Remarks which he made upon my reading this Play to him in a very hasty manner, shew'd at once so much penetrating Quickness, as well as so much Solidity, and so much sureness, as could belong to no Man but one who has a thorough Understanding of Nature, and who has that admirable Talent for touching the Passions which he has shewn in his Tragedies."

When John Hughes (1677–1720) wished to place his play *The Siege of Damascus* in production at Drury Lane but was too ill to give it the necessary attention, it was to Southerne that he turned for help. Southerne had read the play, and now offered to see it through rehearsal.[69] This he did, and the play was performed February 17, 1720, the same night that its author died. Again, the successful tragedy *Mariamne* (Lincoln's-Inn-Fields, 1723) of the scholar and poet Elijah

---

[68] [Chas. Gildon]: *A Comparison Between the Two Stages,* 1702, p. 28.

[69] Letter from Hughes to Robert Wilks, *Letters by Several Eminent Persons Deceased,* ed. John Duncombe, I, 251.

Fenton (1683–1730) was finally produced through the efforts of Southerne,[70] at whose house it was said to have been written while Fenton, pressed with debts, was making his home there.[71] Cibber, on being offered the play, rejected it with the insolent advice to the author to engage himself in some more profitable labor. His "brutal petulance . . . was confuted," says Dr. Johnson, "though perhaps not shamed, by general applause. Fenton's profits are said to have amounted to near a thousand pounds. . . ."[72]

Fenton and Southerne were old friends. In 1711 the former had written and published separately *An Epistle to Mr. Southerne,* a piece of some two hundred and fifty lines,[73] in which the poet traces the history of culture from Grecian times to those of Queen Anne. He pays compliments to Shakespeare, to Beaumont and Fletcher, and would have praised Ben Jonson "Had he not strove to blemish *Shakespear's* name."[74] The supreme tribute, however, is reserved for Southerne. He it is who preserves for Britain the poetic crown, "And mak'st her rival *Athens* in renown." Could Sophocles have seen "The weeping *Graces* on *Imoinda* wait," or have heard "thy *Isabella's* moving moan," only supreme envy could have prevented him from agreeing that "To write by nature were to copy thee."[75] In Dryden's praise, Southerne had been matched with Terence; now he is the rival of Sophocles.

As late as 1729, when he was sixty-nine years of age, Southerne was moving energetically to secure stage representation for a friend's play. In the preface to his tragedy *Themistocles* (1729), Samuel Madden (1686–1765) joins the

[70] Dedication to *Mariamne,* 1723.
[71] T. Evans's introductory account of Southerne in his 1774 edition of the plays.
[72] *Lives of the English Poets,* Hill's edition, II, 260.
[73] Twenty-eight lines were added to the piece on its insertion into the 1721 edition of Southerne's plays.
[74] Southerne's *Plays,* 1774 edition, III, 85.
[75] *Ibid.,* III, 83.

line of those who owed much to Southerne's good-nature. ". . . whatever tolerable Reputation this Piece has got," he announces, "is not a little owing to the warm Declarations, and hearty Zeal, which Mr. *Southern* (my old Acquaintance, and worthy Friend) was pleased to recommend it with, where-ever he came. Be this therefore paid as an honest Debt (and the last I shall ever owe him of this kind) due in Gratitude to his Affection and Friendship, who never forgot the smallest Obligation he received, or remembered the greatest he conferr'd on others."

There remain several scattered references to Southerne by his contemporaries. In his vitriolic *Satyr Against Wit* (1700) Sir Richard Blackmore places Southerne with Congreve and Wycherley as one whose works are marked by excess of false and deficiency of true wit. Yet that judgment is mild compared with that visited upon Dryden.

> 'Tis true, that when the course and worthless Dross
> Is purg'd away, there will be mighty Loss.
> Ev'n *C*-[ongrev]-*e*, *S*-[outher]-*n*, Manly *W*-[ycher]-*ly*,
> When thus refin'd will grievous Suff'rers be.
> Into the melting Pot when *D*-[ryde]-*n* comes,
> What horrid Stench will rise, what noisome Fumes?
> How will he shrink, when all his leud Allay,
> And Wicked Mixture shall be purg'd away?[76]

The Play-house, a Satyr (1709), by Robert Gould, is a violent puritan attack on the immorality of plays and players, and on the lewdness of the audience that attends the theatre. But in the midst of a general and lacerating indictment of the whole stage, he pauses to say a good word for Southerne:

> Besides, of *Writers*, some adorn the *Stage*,
> And *Southern* is the Credit of his Age.[77]

[76] *A Satyr Against Wit*, 1700, pp. 9, 10.
[77] *Works*, 2 vols., 1709. II, 240. In the original version of the poem, in *Poems Chiefly Consisting of Satyrs and Satyrical Epistles*, 1689, Southerne's name is not mentioned. In the 1709 edition, Otway, Etherege, and Wycherley are also granted a fair degree of praise.

Biographical Sketch 23

John Sheffield, Duke of Buckingham, bows generously in Southerne's direction in his poem *The Election of a Poet Laureat in 1719.* Apollo is choosing a Laureate and is overwhelmed with candidates. In desperation, he exclaims "Nay, had honest TOM SOUTHERN but been within Call"—[78] And Southerne enters another satire of contemporary poets in Dr. Daniel Kendrick's *New Session upon the Poets, Occasion'd by the Death of Mr. John Dryden.* Here again the poets who would assume the bays make their pleas to Apollo. D'Urfey, Farquhar, and Congreve are belittled. Of Congrev Apollo says: "You write correct, but *Southern* writes as well."[79]

> Next *Southern* to the Judge himself apply'd,
> With haughty *Oroonoko* by his Side;
> The Ladies Pity, and the Author's Pride.
> *Southern,* who still shew'd Nature on the Stage,
> Not whines his Tender, nor too rough his Rage.
> *Apollo* told him he deserv'd the Bays,
> Had he contented been to write three Plays.
> But since he knew not when he Glory won,
> 'Twas just, that *Capua's* Fate should be his own.[80]

Our opinion of Southerne the man, then, must be formed, in the absence of further biographical material, largely from the reflected light of what those who knew him said of him. Yet our conception of his character need not for that reason be indistinct. There remains a rather clear impression of a man with a great capacity for friendship, unspoiled by a high degree of popular success, and as pleased to help his friends as to advance his own reputation. The one portrait we have of him[81] shows a face strong and somewhat heavy-featured,

---

[78] *Works,* 3rd edition, 2 vols., 1740. I, 200. In the poem, as in life, Laurence Eusden (1688–1730) was the successful candidate.
[79] Found in *The Grove; or a Collection of Original Poems, Translations,* etc., 1721, p. 140. [R.G.H.]
[80] *Ibid.,* 142–3.
[81] In the possession of the Orrery family. It was painted by James

with full eyes, a large nose, and lips that turn up at the corners in a half-smile of good-humored benevolence. A generous double-chin hints that for him at least there were cakes and ale. A good fireside companion he must have been; and if he was fond of cathedral music he was equally fond, we may suppose, of a good story over a steaming pudding. To him was allotted that boon so frequently withheld from his fellow-craftsmen in the disturbing world of the theatre—an honorable old age, free from financial worries and rich in many warm friendships.

We turn now from the man to his plays, to evaluate them both intrinsically and against the background of the late seventeenth and early eighteenth century theatre. But before we begin that examination, there remains one matter of biographical interest. At least a part of Southerne's wealth came out of the theatre, from which, as an "exact œconomist" he drew a greater financial return than most of his fellow-dramatists. What were the rewards of playwriting in those days and how did Southerne help to increase those rewards?

Profits of Playwriting

> . . . Tom, whom Heav'n sent down to raise
> The price of prologues and of plays,

wrote Pope.[82] In an age when Lee and Otway were unable to translate their popularity into terms of pounds and shillings, when the great Dryden himself could declare that "the reward I have from the stage is so little, that it is not worth my labour,"[83] it is significant that Southerne was consistently successful in getting the highest possible return for his labors. There were three sources of income for the playwright at the end of the seventeenth century: the author's benefit

Worsdale and engraved variously by J. Simon, W. Evans, and A. Bannerman.
[82] See above, p. 15.
[83] Preface to *Cleomenes*, Scott-Saintsbury *Dryden*, VIII, 222.

Biographical Sketch

performance, the sale of the copyright to the booksellers, and the gifts from noble patrons and those to whom dedications were addressed.[84] Each of these sources Southerne worked skilfully for its full advantage. He did not hesitate to admit that poetry was his business, and if writing a play once a year "looks very like turning into the Profession . . . let it be the defence of my Writing, that I have nothing else to do."[85]

Southerne is the first dramatist who is known to have received more than one benefit night for a new play. In 1691 in the Preface to *Sir Anthony Love* he thanks "the fair sex" for "so visibly promoting my interest, on those days chiefly (the third, and the sixth) when I had the tenderest relation to the welfare of my play." From that time on, sixth-night benefits were frequently given to the authors of successful plays. Charles Hopkins, in 1697, speaks of the poets who "Dream of a full Third Day, nay, good sixth Night."[86] In 1703, Steele had a sixth-night benefit for *The Lying Lover*,[87] and in 1704 Cibber two for *The Careless Husband*.[88] In 1700, Farquhar, because of the great success of *The Constant Couple* and "in answer to a scandalous Prologue spoken against it at the other house," was allowed still a third benefit.[89] Estcourt mentions a third benefit in the satirical Epistle Dedicatory to *The Fair Example* (acted D.L. 1703; published 1706), addressed to Christopher Rich: ". . . what an open House you

---

[84] Perhaps to these there ought to be added the retaining fees paid at various times by the theatres to popular poets during the period that they were writing for the stage. Such fees seldom exceeded forty shillings a week, however. See A. Thaler: *Shakespeare to Sheridan*, p. 30. Dryden and Lee had been thus retained; Otway and Southerne were not under contract to any theatre.
[85] Dedication to *The Maid's Last Prayer*, 1693.
[86] Prologue to *Boadicea, Queen of Britain*.
[87] Advertisement in *The Daily Courant*, Wed., Dec. 8, 1703.
[88] See the Dedication to *The Careless Husband*, 1705. (Acted December, 1704.)
[89] See Thaler, p. 42, who quotes Genest, II, 166.

have kept for the Author and his Friends on the third Day; nay, some times the sixth or ninth." Times were growing better for the impoverished playwright, and Southerne led the way.

Gildon states that Otway received but a hundred pounds for *Venice Preserved*.[90] Of this amount it is probable that only fifteen pounds came from the bookseller.[91] Malone asserts that from a receipt extant in his day it could be ascertained that Dryden received thirty guineas from the bookseller in 1691 for *Cleomenes*.[92] The usual bookseller's price for a play at the latter end of the century, says Malone,[93] was twenty or twenty-five pounds.

Southerne, however, sold the copyright of his popular *Fatal Marriage* in 1694 for thirty-six pounds, we learn from a contemporary letter quoted by Malone. "Never was poet better rewarded or incouraged by the town; for besides an extraordinary full house, which brought him about 140 l. 50 noblemen . . . gave him guineas apiece, and the printer 36 l. for his copy. This kind usage will encourage desponding minor poets, and vex huffing Dryden and Congreve to madness."[94] In 1715, Addison received fifty pounds from J. Tonson for *The Drummer;* in 1721, Young obtained the same price for his tragedy, *The Revenge*.[95] But in 1719 Southerne had startled the theatrical world by persuading Chetwood to bid one hundred and twenty pounds for *The Spartan Dame*.[96]

---

[90] And a like amount for *The Orphan. Laws of Poetry*, 1721, pp. 37, 38. Quoted by Thaler, p. 40.

[91] *Three Original Letters . . . on the Cause and Manner of the late Riot at the Theatre-Royal*, 1763, p. 21. See Thaler, p. 50.

[92] *Critical and Miscellaneous Prose Works of Dryden*, ed. Malone, I, pt. 1, 455.

[93] *Historical Account . . . of the English Stage*, p. 178 n.

[94] *Ibid.*, p. 180 n.

[95] *Ibid.*, p. 181.

[96] Preface to *The Spartan Dame*, 1774 edition, III, 81. The *Biographica Dramatica* wrongly gives £150 (I, pt. 2, 680), and Nicoll £180 (*Late Eighteenth Century Drama*, p. 47 n.).

Southerne had good connections, which he quite frankly used to bring him revenue. "The secret is," says the *Biographica Dramatica,* "Southern was not beneath the drudgery of solicitation, and often sold his tickets at a very high price, by making applications to persons of distinction."[97] "The favour of great men is the poet's inheritance," was Southerne's way of stating it;[98] nor did he intend to lose his inheritance by default. Says his editor, Thomas Evans, "Mr. Southerne was much respected by persons of distinction, who in return for his tickets usually made him great presents."[99] There is a story to the effect that Dryden once asked Southerne how much he got by his plays. Southerne replied that he was really ashamed to inform him. "But Mr. Dryden being a little importunate to know, he plainly told him, that by his last play he cleared seven hundred pounds; which appeared astonishing to Dryden, as he himself had never been able to acquire more than one hundred by his most successful pieces."[100] In the struggle for financial recognition of the arts, so that poetry need not be its own reward, Southerne played a notable part.

[97] I, pt. 2, 680.
[98] Preface to *Oroonoko,* 1774 edition of the *Plays,* II, 270.
[99] *Plays,* I, 5.
[100] *Biographica Dramatica,* I, pt. 2, 680. Cibber's *Lives of the Poets,* V, 328, gives the same anecdote.

CHAPTER II

THE LOYAL BROTHER, OR THE PERSIAN PRINCE

> *But Plots and Parties give new matter birth;*
> *And State-distractions serve you here for mirth!*
>
> . . . .
>
> *The Stage, like old Rump Pulpits, is become*
> *The Scene of News, a furious Party's Drum.*
> —From *A Lenten Prologue refus'd by the Players*, 1682.

ON February 7, 1681/2,[1] Southerne entered the political arena that was then the stage with his first play, *The Loyal Brother, or The Persian Prince.* The young playwright saw his initial offering acted by a capable cast, with Clark as Tachmas, the loyal brother, and Mohun[2] as the villain, Ismael. Mrs. Cook played Semanthe and the popular Mrs. Anne Guin[3] took the part of Sunamire. The lack of any record would indicate that the piece created no great repercussion in the theatrical world; in the absence of contradictory opinion, we may accept the statement of the *Biographica Dramatica*[4] that it "had but indifferent success on the stage." Southerne himself admitted as much when in the Preface to his next play (*The Disappointment*, 1684) he referred to his

---

[1] The date of production has usually been given as "about March," 1682, but Professor Ham has directed my attention to a broadside in the Bindley folio, Huntington Library, originally in the Narcissus Luttrell collection, which has the Ms. notation "7 Feb. 1682/1" [*sic*]. This early date precludes the possibility advanced by P. Hamelius (p. 53) that Tachmas' triumph in Act II, scene 1, represented York's triumphal return to London in March, 1682.

[2] "Major Moon" in the *dramatis personæ*.

[3] Not to be confused with Nell Gwyn, to whom Genest assigns the part. Nell Gwyn made her last stage appearance as Almahide in *The Conquest of Granada* (1670). See Peter Cunningham: *The Story of Nell Gwyn*, 1852, p. 72 n.

[4] II, 398.

"having hardly escaped the venture of the stage" previously. Doubtless the Tories packed one or two houses to see Shaftesbury vilified, but the popular *Venice Preserved,* produced almost at the same time[5] and satirizing the Earl in a fashion much more pleasing to his enemies, must in any event have divided the attention of the town.

True Tory was *The Loyal Brother,* which saw production under the protecting aegis of Dryden. *Absalom and Achitophel* was still the party anthem of the Tories, and with undiminished vigor Dryden contributed another furious anti-Whig blast in the Prologue and Epilogue to a play itself nicely timed to catch the rising tide of loyal Tory enthusiasm that marked the early months of 1682. The "Damn'd Whigs" are flayed viciously in the Prologue, with particular reference to the refusal of supplies, the petition against the King's guards, and the great Pope-burning. This last ceremony is described with great wealth of satirical detail. The poor Pope

> burns; now all true hearts your triumphs ring:
> And next (for fashion) cry, *God save the king.*
> . . . .
> But after he's once sav'd, to make amends,
> In each succeeding health they damn his friends.[6]

In the Epilogue Dryden, although he bewails the existence of two factions "in one poor isle," castigates the Whig poets as "dull culprits, who have murder'd sense." "Tho' nonsense is a nauseous heavy mass," he says with reason, "the vehicle call'd faction makes it pass."

Our "virgin poet," in Dryden's patronizing phrase, was to become the Laureate's firm friend, but their relationship began with an event which would itself have been sufficient to give Southerne a niche, however small, in the financial history of the theatre. Inadvertently, he was "to raise the price

---

[5] February 9, 1681/2.
[6] The quotations from the plays are uniformly from the only complete edition, brought out in three volumes by Thomas Evans in 1774.

of prologues," as Pope later put it. Southerne first offered Dryden the usual price for a prologue, four guineas. Dryden refused it under six, a demand that the young poet answered by saying that it was more than he had ever heard asked before. Dryden then explained that his request was "not, young man, out of disrespect to you, but the players have had my goods too cheap." This story, says Warburton, in a note published in 1751,[7] was told by Southerne to him and Pope nearly at the same time. The anecdote exists in several forms, differing only in the sum mentioned.

In a flattering dedication, Southerne lays "the first fruits of My Muse" at the door of the ten-year-old Charles Lennox, Duke of Richmond, the son of Charles II and the Duchess of Portsmouth. On January 22, 1681/2, the lad had been appointed Master of the Horse, on the removal of the Duke of Monmouth. "Could my vanity carry me to the hopes of succeeding in things of this kind," writes Southerne, "I am confident my surest way would be, to draw my characters from you, in whom the fairest images of nature are shewn in little: your royal father's greatness, majestic awfulness, wit and goodness, are promised all in you: your mother's conquering beauty triumphs again in you. . . ." What a paragon of childhood! Already the young poet was trimming his sail to meet the wind of patronage.

The Story of The Loyal Brother

SELIMAN, the Sophy of Persia, and his noble and generous brother Tachmas are both in love with Semanthe, who in turn loves only Tachmas. The natural jealousy of Seliman toward Tachmas is inflamed still further by the plots of Ismael, an evil and disappointed statesman whose place as favorite now belongs to Tachmas, and by the schemes of Arbanes, an old general who has been replaced in command by the valorous Tachmas. To the plots of these two against Tachmas are

[7] Pope's *Works*, VI, 82 n.

added the efforts of Sunamire, sister to Arbanes, in love with Tachmas and driven to a frenzy by the knowledge that Semanthe is her successful rival. Ismael influences Seliman to banish his brother and press his own suit to Semanthe. Spurned, the Sophy swears the death of Tachmas, who is saved at the very foot of the scaffold only by the combined pleas of Semanthe and the queen-mother, Begona.

Foiled in their first plot, the conspirators forge a letter in which Tachmas plans his brother's death, and at the same time Semanthe is made to believe that Tachmas is false to her. The Sophy, discovering the letter, again commits Tachmas to prison. The broken-hearted Semanthe visits him there, and with the two lovers in her power, Sunamire confesses the forgery of the fatal letter. The reconfirmed love of Tachmas and Semanthe enables them to face bravely the death that awaits them as the plotters bring in poisoned bowls for them to drink. But through the efforts of a faithful captain of Tachmas', disguised as a servant, the bowls are exchanged, and Sunamire and Arbanes drink the poison instead. As the traitors are dying, Seliman brings in Ismael, who has confessed his villainies and is now ordered to death. Seliman accepts graciously enough the inevitable, and gives the happy lovers his blessing.

The Source

IN the Michaelmas *Term Catalogue* for 1676[8] there was announced a book the title-page of which reads as follows: "TACHMAS / PRINCE OF / PERSIA : / an / Historical NOVEL, / Which happen'd under the / SOPHY SELIMAN, / Who Reigns at this day. / Render'd into English by *P. Porter,* Esq: / London, / Printed for *Dorman Newman,* at the / *King's Arms* in the Poultrey, 1676." Porter, who also translated *Zayde* and the *Life of the Duchess Mazarin,* made in his *Tachmas* a very close translation of a French *turquerie* or

[8] See Arber's Reprint, I, 252.

Oriental tale of similar title published anonymously in Paris the same year.[9] Porter's tale was Southerne's direct source for *The Loyal Brother,* and the kinship in plot and character between novel and play is very close. Even many of the names remain the same: Seliman, Tachmas, Begona, and Sunamire. Arbanes, the "disaffected general," and Osman, Tachmas' faithful captain, who diverts the poison-cups at the last moment, are new with Southerne. Mr. Paul Hamelius, in his edition of the play, draws very detailed comparisons between the action of the play and that of the French novel of which the English novel is almost a literal translation. It is therefore necessary here only to summarize the changes that Southerne has made in shaping his material.

The most obvious difference is in the catastrophe, which Southerne changes from a tragic one in which the heroine takes poison and Tachmas is blinded by his brother, to one better suited to the demands of heroic drama and of the political purpose that lay behind the play. In the play Sunamire and Ismael die ignobly, as is fitting, but as is also fitting in heroic drama, where love and valor are always rewarded, Tachmas the loving and valiant is re-united to Semanthe under the benediction of the chastened Sophy. In general, the sequence of events up to the last scene remains the same. Southerne adds two low-comedy scenes not in his original, for a reason which I shall indicate later.

The characterizations, with one exception, are carried over almost intact. With Southerne, Seliman is hot-headed, jealous, and vacillating in purpose, just as he is in the novel. To fit in with the reformed conclusion, however, he had to be made more definitely generous than the Sophy of the novel,

---

[9] "Tachmas / Prince / de Perse / Nouvelle historique / Arrivée sous le Sophy Séliman / aujourd'hui régnant / à Paris / chez Étienne Loyson, au Palais / à l'entrée de la gallerie des Prisonniers / au nom de Jésus / M.DC.LXXVI / Avec permission." See Hamelius, p. 10. I have not seen a copy of this French source, but I have compared with the English translation such long extracts from it as Hamelius gives.

who was much more capable of blinding Tachmas than of leading him to Negara (the Semanthe of the play). Tachmas himself needed no touching up; he was cut from pattern for the perfect hero. As the novel says, "It is hard to guess whether Tachmas was more obliged to Nature for the Perfections of his Body, or the Excellencies of his Mind, since both these parts of him, so far different the one from the other, equally gained him the admiration of all mankind." Ismael, in each version, is equally malignant—the consummate villain who takes an Iago-like pleasure in his machinations. He too is cut from pattern. But in the characterization of Semanthe Southerne had to make definite changes. In the novel, Negara, moved by the desire to see herself the first lady of the land, accepts for a time the advances of the Sophy. Torn later by remorse, she confesses to Tachmas that she loves only him, and reveals to him the Sophy's plan to marry her. Such a character was too complex to fit the conception of the play, which called for a heroine who could suffer and endure, but on whose faithfulness there must be no stain. The steadfast love of Southerne's Semanthe never wavered; she could spurn a crown without a regret.

As a whole, then, the material of the novel lay close at Southerne's hand for the dramatic effect he devised. The changes he made were those which would adapt the plot to the poetic justice called for by the tradition of the heroic play, which in turn fitted well the political allegory the play was written to support.

Political Significance

IN the history of dramatic literature, *The Loyal Brother* must take its place with the flood of plays poured out to serve the cause of party faction during those politically frenzied years of 1679–82, when all England was in a ferment over the Popish Plot, and the stage furnished a battle-ground for Whig and Tory alike. Of all these plays of party insult and personal defamation only one rose far enough above the purpose of which it was conceived to remain in our anthologies as a work of art. The *Venice Preserved* of Otway arrived on the boards, curiously enough, within a few nights of *The Loyal Brother*.[10] And to understand Southerne's play in relation to its period, we must know something, not only of *Venice Preserved,* but of those other plays born to carry the weight of their own satire.

The political issues of those mad days were clearly enough drawn.[11] On the one side stood the Whigs, led by the Earl of Shaftesbury, making of the terrors of the Popish Plot political ammunition, hoping thereby to exclude from the succession the Catholic Duke of York and to place as heir apparent to the throne the Protestant Duke of Monmouth. On the other side were the Tories, making every effort to secure the succession for York. They were aided by Charles II who, secretly of Catholic sympathies, was covertly drawing on the French for aid and waiting for the political tide to turn in his favor. To a situation delicate at best, the Plot added the nightmare fear of Revolution. In the midst of this excitement the stage reflected the party strife, descending at times to the most virulent of personal attacks.

Even Dryden, with his satire on priests in *The Spanish Fryar, or The Double Discovery* (1680), had laid himself open to the charge of furthering the Protestant cause. But Elkanah Settle and Thomas Shadwell during this period were the chief supporters in the theatre of the anti-Court party. Settle's *Fatal Love, or The Forced Inconstancy* (1680) was a bitter attack on the Papists, and his *Female Prelate: Being the History of the Life and Death of Pope Joan* (1680), dedicated to the Earl of Shaftesbury, was a tragedy of revenge meant to expose the viciousness and cruelty of the

[10] February 9, 1681/2.

[11] For adequate discussion of the political situation see Richard Lodge, *History of England (1660–1702),* 1910; John Pollock, *The Popish Plot,* 1903; Osmund Airy, *Charles II,* London and New York, 1904 (new ed.); Martin Haile, *Queen Mary of Modena,* London and New York, 1905.

Catholic Church. The play has still a kind of crude force, and in 1680 it stirred up a vast amount of enthusiasm among the Whigs. Less viciously, Shadwell joined the Whig forces in 1681 with his *Lancashire Witches and Teague O'Divelly, The Irish Priest,* in which Teague endeavors, by generous application of holy water, to avert the influence of numerous mischievous witches, and ends by being arrested for implication in the Popish Plot.

Yet the Court party was gaining steadily in strength, and most of the political plays produced during the years 1680–82 were of Tory flavor. Since *The Loyal Brother* belongs in that group of Tory plays which centers its attack on Shaftesbury, it might be well to review briefly some of the other dramatic ventures into the field of personal satire. Shaftesbury, as leader of the Whigs and chief advocate of the Exclusion Bill, furnished the best target for such attacks.

As early as 1674, in Nevil Payne's *Siege of Constantinople,* Shaftesbury played the first of his thankless rôles, this time as the crafty and traitorous Chancellor of Constantinople, in league with the Turks against his own Emperor.[12] The satire is largely political, but personal virulence rears its head in the second act when the Chancellor, having declared his purpose to "spend some hours with frolic womankind," has a bawdy scene with some wenches. Ward finds reminiscences of Shaftesbury also in the character of Limberham in Dryden's play *Limberham, or the Kind Keeper* (1678).[13] He is perhaps attacked in Otway's *Caius Marius* (1679), where the elder Marius, delighting in murder and blood, is thus characterized by Cinna:

> Base Ingratitude
> Dissimulation, Cruelty, and Pride,
> Ill Manners, Ignorance, and all the Ills
> Of one base born, in Marius are join'd.[14]

[12] See Genest, I, 167.
[13] *History of English Dramatic Literature,* III, 373 n.
[14] I, 1.

D'Urfey's *Sir Barnaby Whig* (1681), the title character of which is described in the *dramatis personæ* as "a Phanatical Rascal, one of Oliver's Knights; one that always pretends to fear a change of Government, yet does his best to cause one" points clearly at Shaftesbury. His change of policy and his treatment by the town are unmistakably indicated. Ridiculous and cowardly, he is yet thoroughly humorous.

Sixteen eighty-two, and the rise in the political fortunes of the Court party, brought the Tory playwrights raging down on Shaftesbury. In the preface to *The Royalists* (Jan., 1681/2) Tom D'Urfey sneers at Shaftesbury as "the new-elected *warpt* monarch of Poland." Sir Timothy Treat-all in Mrs. Behn's *City Heiress, or Sir Timothy Treat-all* is an obvious caricature of the Whig leader. Sir Timothy, a true Commonwealthman, is tricked by his nephew, Wilding, into believing that Poland plans to elect the knight for its next king. The remaining play of 1682 in which Shaftesbury is pilloried is at once the most famous and the most virulent of all. Of *Venice Preserved* Genest says, conservatively enough, "Otway wrote this play against the Whigs—he evidently means to insinuate that the persons at this time in opposition to the Court were as unprincipled as the Conspirators in his Tragedy."[15] The reference to Anthony Earl of Shaftesbury in the character of the old senator, Antonio, is clear—Antonio's name, his age, his immorality, the reference in the prologue to Poland, all identify him directly. The satire is not so much political as personal. With pitiless strokes Otway ridicules the decayed lust of Antonio, whose sensuality is made only the more obscene by impotence. The famous "Nicky-Nacky" scenes, in which the senile senator barks at the heels of his courtesan, who finally whips him soundly, show political satire issuing in a bitter abuse of character calculated to cheer all stout Tory hearts.

The collapse of Shaftesbury's political and personal fortunes was accompanied by a still further shower of dramatic

[15] I, 353.

fireworks. Crowne returned to the attack with *City Politicks* (1683), in which Shaftesbury is represented as Camillo, the old Podesta. And more than two years after his death he reached a somewhat doubtful translation in Dryden's *Albion and Albanius* (June, 1685). Near the conclusion of the opera is the following description: ". . . the Globe rests on a Pedestal; on the front of the Pedestal is drawn a Man with a long, lean, pale face, with fiend's wings, and snakes twisted round his body; he is encompassed by several fanatical rebellious heads, who suck poison from him, which runs out of a tap in his side."[16]

This was the politico-dramatic world of the theatre that Southerne entered early in 1682 with his *Loyal Brother*. The astute young man had chosen his side well, for the Tories were growing steadily stronger. Although the Duke of York had not yet been recalled from Scotland, Charles, since the Oxford Parliament, was becoming more and more popular, and the Exclusionists were suffering definite loss of prestige. London was still sufficiently under Whig control to prevent the indictment of Shaftesbury on a charge of high treason, but the tremendous stir that *Absalom and Achitophel* had made two months before indicated the direction of the rising Tory power. With Dryden assisting, the moment was ripe for Southerne to try his dramatic wings.

Unlike many political plays of the time, *The Loyal Brother* does not spend all its allegory on denunciation of the enemy. It was conceived as an exaltation of James, Duke of York, who appears as Tachmas, and is exhibited throughout as a monument of virtue and courage. Charles II is shown as the Sophy Seliman, Shaftesbury is Ismael, and Monmouth is Arbanes. Queen Henrietta Maria may be seen in Begona, the

[16] Scott-Saintsbury *Dryden,* VII, 282. "Tapski" was one of Shaftesbury's nicknames. An internal injury received in the overturning of a carriage developed a constant discharge that had to be drained from his side.

queen-mother, and Mary of Modena in Semanthe, but here the parallel grows a little dim, and beyond this it is hazardous to venture.

The picture of York as Tachmas is so noble that we do not wonder that the original, when he reached the throne, gave military preferment to the dramatist who had so flatteringly characterized him. Tachmas is banished by Seliman even as York was banished several times by Charles. When Tachmas is arrested to be taken to his death, the "loyal brother" will not resist, preferring rather to die than from lack of loyalty disobey his king's command! To the very end—the very successful end, of course—his integrity remains unshaken, until even the jealous Seliman can only, in an access of magnanimity, release all claims to Semanthe and place her in the arms of Tachmas. Such a picture of loyalty was meant to flout all reports of James's treachery and present him as the deserving aspirant to the throne.

Ismael fits neatly the Tory estimate of Shaftesbury. Described as a "villainous favorite" who has lost his influence with the Sophy through Tachmas, his one aim is to achieve the downfall of his usurper. To gain this end he concocts elaborate plots, which fail in the end and drag him down to ignominy and death. The comparisons with Shaftesbury are many. Ismael was a deposed favorite; Shaftesbury had been dismissed from his place as President of the Privy Council on Oct. 15, 1679. Ismael, as did Shaftesbury, contemplated an appeal to the City for support:

> I'll steer a different course; grow popular,
> And into the city.[17]

Shaftesbury's supposed ambitions to become King of Poland are mocked in the scene in which the citizens shout to Ismael "Lead us on . . . we'll . . . make you king."[18] Again, Ismael reflects on an ability he held in common with his prototype: "O! there's the pleasure, so to work the crowd."[19]

[17] V, 1.   [18] V, 2.   [19] III, 3.

There is one reference to Shaftesbury's physical incapacity, when Ismael refers to himself as "unfit for fiercer joys."[20] Ismael, though a complete villain, is a rather conventional one. Southerne's pen lacked the scorn and derision that make some contemporary portraits of Shaftesbury so acidly bitter.

Ismael stands to Arbanes as did Achitophel to Absalom in Dryden's poem—the scheming statesman leading the disgruntled and ambitious warrior into conspiracy. In September, 1679, Monmouth was displaced as commander of the forces. Arbanes had suffered similar indignity: "Treachery despoil'd me of those plumes," he says.[21] Arbanes is like Monmouth in that he is impetuous and eager for action. Southerne avoided offensive comparison with the King's son by making Arbanes an old, cast-off general.

The perplexing vagaries of Seliman, constant only to his jealous uncertainty—now banishing, now recalling—would have been, it seems now, dangerously suggestive of Charles's own equivocal position at the time. The characterization is saved by Seliman's essential generosity and his willingness to make amends when the truth is known. The surprising thing is that Southerne should have found in an English translation of a French romance characterizations that with as little change fitted so aptly into his political design.

A good Tory flavor is added to the original story by the addition of two broad scenes involving obviously Whig citizens. Here the satire on the City, which, by rioting, had supported Shaftesbury's policy, is very local and pungent. In the first scene the citizens make drunken holiday while their wives make merry with soldiers.[22] Their pretended obedience to Charles is ridiculed in this speech: ". . . we will be most obediently drunk at the king's charges." In the second scene each of the rabble cries: "I a judge! I a judge!"—a reference to the Middlesex jurymen who turned in an "ignoramus" verdict when Shaftesbury was accused of treason. "Lead us on!" they cry out to Ismael, "we'll fire the palace, depose the

[20] I, 1.   [21] I, 1.   [22] II, 2.

tyrant, make you king." Thus are Shaftesbury's ambitions derided.

The Heroic Ingredient

QUITE naturally, Southerne's first play draws heavily on at least two traditional streams of influence. Of these the more important is the heroic, for *The Loyal Brother,* styled by its author a "tragedy," owes its chief debt to that species of Restoration drama in which love and honor waded through shoals of rhetoric hand in hand with heroes of such gigantic proportion that their success, fortunately, had never to depend upon probability. Our play is a tragedy only in the Fletcherian sense that the hero comes near death; poetic justice is meted out with an uncompromising hand, and only the villains go down to defeat.

The Loyal Brother is in blank verse rather than heroic couplet, for the death-knell of the latter in the heroic play had been sounded when Dryden, in *All for Love* (1677), had deserted rhyme. But the other elements of the heroic play are there: the Eastern setting, the noble personages, the exalted diction, the story of love and jealousy flung against a background of war, and the happy ending, which finds the forces of evil baffled and the hero united with his mistress. The plot follows a conventional channel: the pair of villains (Ismael and Sunamire); the female villain in love with the hero (Tachmas) who in turn is unwaveringly faithful to his beloved (Semanthe); the plot to separate the lovers, which is foiled at the last moment by a device no less unconvincing than opportune. The motive of honor creeps in when Tachmas refuses to resist the arrest ordered by Seliman:

> I must not thus,
> By disobedience to my king's command,
> Rashly forgo my virtue: if he think fit
> To take my life, or make it yet more wretched;
> My loyalty ties up my forward sword,
> And teaches silently to suffer all.[23]

[23] III, 2.

A glance at Dryden's *Aureng-Zebe* (1675) will show the close kinship of plots in heroic plays. There, Indamora, the captive princess, is in love with Aureng-Zebe, and the Emperor is in love with her and jealous of Aureng-Zebe—even as Seliman, in Southerne's play, loves Semanthe and is jealous of Tachmas. Nourmahal, the unworthy lover of Aureng-Zebe, is spurned by the latter just as Sunamire is disdained by Tachmas, and in each play the woman scorned plots to poison the hero. In each play, also, the Emperor resigns the quondam object of his affection to the deserving hero. Thus does Southerne help to perpetuate the history of an imbroglio that only a Tom Thumb was to unravel successfully.

Tachmas is in most respects a hero in the old tradition, honorable, faithful in love, brave in the face of death, and invincible in battle. But in one respect he has suffered a change; he shows signs of an encroaching modesty that would have been scorned as unworthy by any good Almanzor. Nowhere does he threaten to mount and scatter all the gods he hits. He performs highly efficient deeds of valor, only to leave the praises of his victories to others. It is given to Seliman, the lesser hero and the weaker man, to rant in the Cambyses vein:

> Did I not pour upon their foremost ranks,
> Sudden and fierce as lightning, rush among
> Their thickest squadrons, and in glorious heat
> (Like thunder breaking from a teeming cloud)
> Make desolation wait upon my arms?[24]

There is no lack of bombastic inflation in the play. The jealous Sunamire can tear a passion with the best:

> The thunder rages in my breast for vent;
> Here, here it rolls to make its violent way,
> And now it bursts: the flaming bolts are hurl'd:
> See, see! the lovers are dispers'd and scatter'd,
> Whisk'd up into the air, like summer's dust
> By whirlwinds.[25]

[24] I, 1.   [25] IV, 1.

Semanthe, however mild, is able to rant on occasion:

> I am wild,
> Quite mad, distracted, and must rave awhile:
> Rave 'till I burst, and sink down dead with passion.[26]

And even the philosophical Tachmas ascribes heroic powers to the charms of his mistress:

> These beauties will inspire the arms of death,
> And warm the pale, cold tyrant into life.[27]

"O, I cou'd rave for ever," he continues, until we are glad for the five-act limit. Southerne was following his master, Dryden, but afar off.

This was Southerne's first and last venture into the borders of the heroic drama. Reminiscences of the old manner can be traced in the occasional extravagance and bombast of his later plays, but the talent that was to make him popular in his day and significant in dramatic history was to carry him into other and strange waters.

The Debt to Shakespeare

ALTHOUGH Dryden was undoubtedly the chief influence in *The Loyal Brother,* there is discernible here another element that colored all of Southerne's later tragic writing. The reminiscences of an Elizabethan tone join him to one of the main streams of Restoration tragedy, and he finds a certain kinship here with Lee and Otway. With Southerne, this Elizabethan inflection is at its best in the tragic intensity of certain passages and at its worst in an unnatural, hectic coloring of situation and in the introduction of horror. The influence of Shakespeare is the most definite of all; here *The Loyal Brother* proclaims its debt by verbal similarities and in the shaping of at least one character. Ismael is a conventionalized Iago, infinitely less subtle, to be sure, but driven by the same motive, revenge for loss of position. He indulges in frequent

[26] V, 3.   [27] V, 3.

soliloquies on the futility of virtue and the necessity for ruthless cruelty in accomplishing the "ruins that my plots perform."[28] Yet like Iago he is known as "honest."[29] In his crafty ability to turn suspicion upon another while pretending to defend him he is strikingly similar to another of Shakespeare's villains, Edmund.[30] Ismael lacks entirely, however, the grotesque, twisted sense of humor that makes Iago and Edmund incomparably greater creations, and he approaches them only in his ability to insinuate slander and in a relish in his own evil.

The Loyal Brother has frequent verbal echoes of Shakespeare. The sententious reflections of Tachmas in exile are like those of Shakespeare's banished dukes. Driven to the country, he ponders:

> Greatness (the earnest of malicious fate
> For future woe) was never meant a good.
> Baited with gilded ruin, 'tis cast out
> To catch poor easy man.
> What is't to be a prince?
> To have a keener sense of our misfortunes:
>
> . . . .
>
> Had my kind stars design'd my fortune here;
> Bred among swains, with my *Semanthe* by me,
> The conqu'ring beauty of some neighb'ring village;
> What ages of content I might have past . . .[31]

Here he achieves spiritual kinship with Duke Senior in *As You Like It*:

> Hath not old custom made this life more sweet
> Than that of painted pomp? Are not these woods
> More free from peril than the envious court?[32]

---

[28] II, 3.

[29] I, 1. And *Othello*, II, 3, 1. 6 (Cambridge text).

[30] III, 3. In the very process of making excuses for the supposed treason of Tachmas he further inflames Seliman's anger against his brother. *Cf.* Edmund's "defense" of Edgar before Gloucester, *King Lear*, I, 2.

[31] III, 2.   [32] *As You Like It*, II, 1.

And with Belarius, in *Cymbeline,* who before his mountain cave praises the pleasures of the country against the intrigues of court:

> O, this life
> Is nobler than attending for a check,
> Richer than doing nothing for a bribe.[33]

Semanthe's speech upon awakening from a swoon reminds us of Richard II:

Semanthe:
> . . . stand off,
> We'll walk, and tell sad stories round,
> Of injur'd women, and betraying men.[34]

King Richard:
> . . . let us sit upon the ground
> And tell sad stories of the death of kings.[35]

One wonders whether "we'll walk" is an attempt to ring the changes on the Shakespearian passage.

As may be seen from the above quotations, the imitation of Shakespeare is felt more frequently in the tone of a line or the atmosphere of a passage than in clear verbal echo or in a creation of character. Yet it is seen constantly as one of the important strands in Southerne's tragic writing.

The Pathetic Note

INTO the midst of the heroics and intrigues that form the basis of *The Loyal Brother* Southerne introduced almost unawares, it would seem, that quality of characterization that links him with Otway and Rowe in the emphasis on the pathetic as an element of tragedy. The inflation and bombast that pursue heroic drama are touched here at rare intervals by a tenderness and a wistfulness quite foreign to the most of those plays in which even love must assume heroic propor-

[33] *Cymbeline,* III, 3.   [34] *The Loyal Brother,* IV, 2.
[35] *Richard II,* III, 2.

tions. The temper of this change is well-illustrated when Tachmas, on the scaffold, faces imminent death. Nothing is more common to the heroes of such drama than a sublime scorn of death. Tachmas too faces death courageously, but not defiantly. Rather, in a series of long oracular speeches he welcomes it as "the best gift of nature," a

> safe inn, where weary travellers,
> When they have journied through a world of cares,
> May put off life, and be at rest for ever.
> . . . .
> Then why should I delay? or fondly fear
> To embrace this soft repose, this last retreat?
> I? who like blossoms withering on the bough,
> Dy'd in my birth, and almost was born old.[36]

Before he would die, he wishes to remind his executioner-brother that even as he has fought for him in life, so will he die "in dread obedience to your high command," and to his rival's care he entrusts, with a mouthful of melting phrases, the fair Semanthe! Here is no fire-eating hero, flinging defiance into the faces of the angry gods, but a tender philosopher, botanizing almost on his own tomb. The effect, far from being tragic or even heroic, is one of pathos—an appeal to pity based on the tender resignation of one more sinned against than sinning.

In like manner, the scenes introducing Semanthe present an appeal rare to contemporary heroic tragedy. Forlorn and deserted, Semanthe, supposing Tachmas faithless to her, makes a wistful assault on our tenderer emotions. She too wishes for death:

> Why do I wander this wide barren waste,
> Forsaken and forlorn; when a fair prospect
> Of everlasting rest stands right in view?
> This load of woe, that bends me to the ground,
> I can with life put off: yes, I will rush

[36] III, 4.

> Into the arms of death, and shelter there;
>   .   .   .   .
> Tell me some story of my perjur'd dear;
> Tell me he lives, is happy, whilst I sigh
> My spirits out in thanks, and die in peace.[37]

This is the first of Southerne's suffering heroines, who, by bowing nobly under the weight of a misfortune as unjust as it is cruel, make a direct sentimental claim on our sympathy. Already, in this apprentice work, Southerne shows promise of real ability to touch the heart, if not the mind. The scene[38] in which Tachmas, sentenced to banishment, is given a few last minutes alone with Semanthe, touches a note of purity and tenderness meant to wring the very heartstrings. It is at such moments that Southerne strikes the chords he later played most successfully in *The Fatal Marriage* and *Oroonoko*.

Plot and Character

OF these diverse threads, then—political, heroic, pathetic, and Shakespearian—Southerne wove the fabric of his first play. His degree of success was not high. The plot remains stiff and mechanical, and the characters, shaped as they were to a political allegory, are unconvincing. It is the necessity of introducing a political moral, for instance, that drives Southerne to the sorry expedient of making the chief villain, Ismael, as he is about to vanish defeated in the last act, step out of character to address words of Tory wisdom to the audience:

> May lame ambition (for the public good,
> Halting upon the crutches of the crowd)
> Still fall:
>   .   .   .   .
> And last, may all disturbers of the state
> Grow blindly popular, and meet my fate.[39]

[37] V, 1.   [38] II, 4.   [39] V, 3.

The story from which Southerne drew his material had a tragic ending. For his purpose Southerne had to change this, and his lack of dramatic dexterity is displayed in the awkward catastrophe toward which the play creaks. Genest has pointed out[40] the improbability that Sunamire should entrust the management of poison meant for Tachmas and Semanthe to one of Tachmas' officers, merely because he had assumed the disguise of a slave. It is this officer, Osman, who exchanges the bowls so that Arbanes and Sunamire drink the poison instead. But why *four* bowls, and why do Arbanes and Sunamire drink at all? These questions Southerne leaves unanswered.

When Southerne is effective it is usually in a single scene, such as the parting between Tachmas and Semanthe or the scaffold scene, and not in the dramatic integrity of the whole. The play interests us chiefly because of its connection with the political events of the time and because it shows Southerne, thus early, touching briefly on the pathetic, sentimental note that later formed the motif of his most enduring work.

[40] I, 323.

CHAPTER III

THE DISAPPOINTMENT, or THE MOTHER IN FASHION

Alphonso: *And innocence is prov'd: Oh there's the thing.*
Act V, sc. 2.

"HAVING hardly escaped the venture of the stage" with *The Loyal Brother*,[1] Southerne waited two years before once more trying the temper of the town. About April 5, 1684,[2] Drury Lane brought out his *Disappointment, or The Mother in Fashion,* with Betterton as the jealous husband Alphonso and Mrs. Cook as his wife Erminia. Again the young poet's appearance was buttressed by a prologue of Dryden's, spoken by Betterton. I can find no contemporary comments on either the success or failure of the play. That it did not die stillborn, however, may be gathered from the fact that it was played for the King and Queen almost a year after its first presentation.[3]

Southerne calls *The Disappointment* just "a Play," and indeed it is hard to place this drama in any of the convenient pigeon-holes. It is not tragedy, but it is far from comedy in the Restoration sense, and furthest of all from the comedy of manners. Built on an intrigue plot drawn from the *Curious*

---

[1] See the Dedication of *The Disappointment* to James Butler, Earl of Ossory (1665–1745). Butler was born in Dublin Castle. He was no particular friend of James II. After the landing of Orange he joined in the petition which called upon King James to summon a free Parliament, and thereafter he was consistently loyal to William III. Ossory had the reputation of being very generous as well as rich.

[2] The date of a Ms. notation on a broadside in the Bindley folio in the Huntington Library, originally in the Narcissus Luttrell collection. [R.G.H.]

[3] January 27, 1684/5. See Nicoll's hand-list of plays, *Restoration Drama*, p. 312.

Impertinent story in *Don Quixote,* it still has little affinity with the plays of Spanish intrigue that were popular on the English stage. To call it a comedy of romance on the basis of its Florentine setting and love-plot is to minimize unduly its serious qualities. The word tragi-comedy could almost be applied to it in the strict Fletcherian sense that though it wants deaths it yet brings some near death. As a matter of fact, it is a *pot-pourri* of widely diverse elements, showing the young playwright moving somewhat ill at ease among the accepted dramatic forms of the day, uncertain with which to cast his allegiance. Yet in any study of Southerne's work as a whole, *The Disappointment* is extremely significant, for it shows him taking the formulae of Restoration comedy and adding to them something of his own that points forward to his main achievement in the theatre—the development of a sentimental problem drama. To understand this we must first know something of the story he tells here.

The Plot

ALBERTO, a typical Restoration rake, has designs on the virtue of Erminia, wife to the jealous Alphonso. He has been sending her letters as from the Duke of Florence, but finding her chastity impregnable, he plots with her maid Clara to effect by trick what he cannot gain by frontal attack. Alphonso, knowing of the letters, is almost distracted by jealousy, and in spite of the efforts of his friend Lorenzo to convince him of Erminia's honesty, he alternates between belief in his wife and horrible suspicion of her defection. Finally he tells Lorenzo that he will announce that he is leaving Florence temporarily, but will in reality stay close to see what "vigorous lover" will be "bolting at my wife." Even Lorenzo's faith in Erminia wavers when he sees a man coming from her house and recognizes him as Alberto. Alberto himself thinks that he has just completed an assignation with Erminia, when as a matter of fact Clara has duped him. Acceding to the pleas of

Juliana, Alberto's cast-off mistress, Clara has substituted her for Erminia, without Alberto's recognizing the deceit.

To keep Alphonso from rushing off to kill the Duke, Lorenzo (who has been convinced by Erminia's tears that she is innocent and that Alberto must be concerned with Clara in some plot) tells him that Alberto is the man he ought to kill. There is a great reconciliation scene between Alphonso and Erminia, but in the very next act Alphonso's native instability asserts itself, and he forces his wife to receive Alberto while he looks on from hiding to see how the libertine approaches her. Alberto's insinuations to Erminia about the assignation he thinks he had with her the night before convince Alphonso that after all his wife is guilty. He bursts out, wounds Alberto, and follows his wife to kill her too. He is prevented by Lorenzo just in time—the truth comes out, and all ends merrily.

The sub-plot deals with a parallel intrigue of Alberto's against Angeline, young daughter to the humorous old Rogero. In his plans to seduce Angeline he is served as bawd by her supposed mother. Here again, however, he is tricked by Juliana, who substitutes herself for Angeline. In the end it appears that the woman who has passed for Angeline's mother and Rogero's wife is not that at all, but his concubine. Rogero gaily forgives her for bawdry against his daughter. Alberto is so moved by Juliana's affection for him that he repents his evil ways and marries her. Angeline makes it a double wedding by marrying Lorenzo, who has been her faithful and virtuous suitor all the while.

Restoration Comedy Sentimentalized

GIVEN such a situation, imagine how an Etherege or a Wycherley might have developed it. Here are all the elements needed to construct the brittle tissue of a comedy of manners: the gay libertine attempting the virtue of a beautiful wife under the very eyes of her frenzied husband; the cast-off mistress and her deception of her former lover; the bawd-mother and the innocent young daughter; the suspicious father. Horns would be planted and foolish husbands laughed to scorn. Over the whole would be thrown the dry gloss of wit that would make virtue seem as dull as it would be unnecessary.

It is not a little surprising, then, to find in *The Disappointment,* twelve years before *Love's Last Shift* and nineteen years before *The Lying Lover,* a play verging closely on the sentimental, moralizing drama of Cibber and Steele. To be sure, Southerne has formulated no theory of a new drama, but nevertheless he breaks down the world of Restoration dramatic cuckoldry by bathing the old comic motives in the warm light of sensibility. There is in the main plot no striving for wit; the medium is blank verse and the effort no longer for brilliant polish but for poetic softness. The temper of the change may be seen in the character of Alberto, a Restoration libertine if ever there was one, but one whose sensuality is touched with poetry. The play opens with his philosophical defense of rakery:

> The world may laugh at these laborious follies,
> That wear away the day; and so may I,
> When my full veins are ebbing into time;
> When age shall level me to impotence;
> And fleeting pleasure leaves me on the foil.
> Then I may turn a true *Diogenes.*
> Snarl at the pleasures that I cannot taste . . .[4]

Elsewhere he refers to his "dear scene of cuckoldom,"[5] and Juliana puffs him as another Don Juan:

> There's an intemperate devil in his blood,
> That never slips an opportunity
> Where virtue may be bought, or woman ruin'd.[6]

Yet she can excuse him thus:

> If he has left me, 'tis his nature's fault,
> That cannot be confin'd.[7]

[4] I, 1.   [5] III, 1.   [6] IV, 1.   [7] I, 1.

But what happens to this student of debauchery? Instead of duping Alphonso, he is himself tricked by his old mistress. And a fifth-act repentance places him in the company of those later brethren of his, as yet unborn, whose amorous aberrations could not hide the fact that after all their hearts were in the right place:

> Thy story, *Juliana,* has subdu'd
> My wilder thoughts, and fix'd me only thine;
> But oh! instruct me how I shall appear
> Before that injur'd fair, whose innocence,
> To late I find, I have unjustly wrong'd,
> Beyond a hope of pardon.[8]

Another new touch is the love of Lorenzo and Angeline, which is as idyllic as that of any Bevil and Indiana. They have forgotten to banter and have begun to rhapsodize. Lorenzo seems aware of his heresy against the standards of Restoration wooing, for he defends himself from the shafts of a mocking world, thinking of Angeline,

> In whom the infancy of innocence,
> In blushing virtue triumphs o'er again.
> But then the world! why let the babbling world
> Report it as they please. Let interest wed
> The drudgery of a vexatious bed;
> Days without peace, and nights without desire,
> Still toil, and sweat away their youth for hire.
> Whilst, safe in innocence and truth, I taste
> The sweets of love, fresh running to the last.[9]

Angeline, unlike some of her sisters in Restoration comedy, is innocent through inherent goodness rather than through ignorance.

Virtue rather than vice is made attractive in *The Disappointment*. Alberto is not exhibited as any model of perfection; his innate generosity and not his cloak of cynicism is held up for approval. On the other hand, Erminia is the per-

[8] V, 2.   [9] II, 3.

fect wife and heroine. She is wronged but patiently enduring, and faithful to a husband who would cast her out as untrue to him. Never for a moment is there the suggestion of a stain on her character. We think of her much as she describes herself, as one

> Who, wand'ring over a wide, barren waste,
> Views the last circles of the sinking sun,
> Then gazing round, quite destitute of hope,
> Forsaken and forlorn, sits sighing down,
> To mix with night, and entertain despair.[10]

Witness her eloquent distress when Lorenzo accuses her of sinning with Alberto:

> Thus in this awful posture, I invoke
> Heav'n, earth, and men to evidence my truth:
> May comfort never find me, if my heart
> E'er sent a wish to any other man:
> If when my eyes have wander'd, they have fix'd
> On any other object of desire.
> Then why, O why am I thus hardly us'd?[11]

When her husband would kill her on suspicion of treachery and Lorenzo would prevent the blow, she pleads:

> . . . let your fury fall
> Upon my life, and cut me from my woes;
> You think me false, my lord; and in that thought
> Are bury'd all my hopes: high heav'n, that knows
> My bosom'd soul, must witness to this truth;
> Since love and you no more, no more are mine,
> The comforts of this life are mine no more,
> And death alone can be my refuge now.[12]

Alphonso has all the psychological instability of your archsentimentalist. One moment he blows hot, another cold, as his suspicions of Erminia's chastity are aroused or lulled. We first see him raging to Lorenzo, not so much because his wife may have proved untrue to him, but because as a result of her

[10] III, 2.   [11] III, 2.   [12] V, 2.

infidelity he would "know himself a monster," and "stink of cuckold to the world."[13] As soon as Lorenzo tells him that he believes Erminia innocent, Alphonso's bosom immediately is warmed by another emotion:

> My panting heart beats to *Erminia's* breast,
> Struggles and heaves, and fain would be at rest.[14]

Before long, however, he is wrenched by the fear that Erminia may at least be guilty in *thought*. He curses the priest that married them, and says that they must part. Erminia faints, and Alphonso is all melting love again. At least thrice subsequent to this, he perpetrates similar emotional *volte-faces,* until we are ready to sympathize with Erminia for her possession, and not for her possible loss of such a husband.

Dramatic history has too little realized the importance of *The Disappointment* as a fore-runner of the sentimental comedy of the eighteenth century. Already comedy invades the borders of tragedy, calling for tears instead of laughter.[15]

The moral is carefully delineated in the last speech of the play:

> And innocence is prov'd: Oh there's the thing;
> For 'tis a woman's falsest, vainest pride,
> To boast a virtue that has ne'er been try'd:
> —In equal folly too those husbands live,
> Who peevishly against themselves contrive,
> By early fears, to hasten on the day;
> For jealousy but shews our wives the way.

In the Epilogue, the Honorable John Stafford draws a contrast between the virtuous heroine of the play and the vizard masks in front:

> You saw our wife was chaste, yet thoroughly try'd,
> And, without doubt, y'are hugely edify'd;
> For like our hero, whom we shew'd today,
> You think no woman true, but in a play;

---

[13] I, 2. [14] I, 2.
[15] For a further discussion of this point see pp. 213–14.

> Love once did make a pretty kind of show,
> Esteem and kindness in one breast wou'd grow,
> But 'twas heav'n knows how many years ago.[16]

Cross-Currents

THAT Southerne was not consciously attempting to set up a new kind of purged drama is shown by his impinging on this sentimental plot a mingled chime of Jonson's humor and Restoration lubricity. The attempts of the mother-bawd (who gives the play its sub-title) to show the fifteen-year-old Angeline how she may eat her cake and have it too by loving Lorenzo while she accommodates Alberto, are rendered only slightly less nauseous by the revelation that she is not really Angeline's mother. "Poor as I am, I scorn to be a whore," says Angeline.

> Bless me! [replies the mother] how can you expect to thrive with such abominable, ungodly words in your mouth, child? A whore! fy, fy, don't think of the indecent thing; but as I was saying, there will be beauty enough at five and twenty, to throw away upon a husband; then if you should chance to tarnish, or grow rusty in the wearing (as beauty, alas! is but a flower, and flowers will fade), 'tis but the matrimony dip at last, and you appear again as fresh, with as glossy a complexion, as you had never been blown on, and no harm done—[17]

Rogero, Angeline's father, is a garrulous old bustler who represents the humor of the play, and does quite well by it in lusty Restoration fashion. He speaks more lewdly than any of the others, but like Sir Tunbelly Clumsy in *The Relapse*,

---

[16] This Epilogue, given in the 1684 quarto edition as "by the Honourable John Stafford, Esq.," is printed in Dryden's *Poems* (Tonson's Dryden's *Miscellany*, 6 vols., 1727, I, 130) without being designated as belonging to any specific play. The probability is that Tonson, knowing that the Prologue was by Dryden, assumed that the Epilogue was also his. The Scott-Saintsbury *Dryden* does not identify the Epilogue.

[17] II, 3. The scenes involving the mother or Rogero, being on a lower level, are all in prose.

he is very jealous for his daughter's reputation. In his aimless boasting he reminds us of Justice Shallow:

> . . . for I'gad I was a swinger in those days: let me see—I cou'd have done—I don't know what I could have done.[18]

Yet he is shrewd enough to refuse Lorenzo's offer to advance him at court:

> I am not for the court, not I my lord; there's a ruggedness in my nature will not let me sell the freedom of my mind, to feed my body: no, when I see a fool, I must laugh at him; not sooth him in his vanity, nor tickle him 'till he wheeze, and give me an advantage of creeping to his pocket.[19]

And in a scene of vigorous horse-play, it is Rogero who boots off the stage a thoroughly Jonsonian trio—a silly 'Squire who makes advances to Angeline, a Poet who prompts him as he repeats asinine love-verses, and a cowardly Bully who had rather run than fight. As Rogero drives them away the Poet throws back a parting threat: "Let him alone, I am big with *Madrigal,* and will prostitute his daughter to a tinker in my next lampoon."[20]

Shakespeare Again

EVEN more than in *The Loyal Brother* Southerne turns here to Shakespeare for inspiration. The echo of Shallow has been noted. The main thread of verbal influence comes, strangely enough in such a play as this, through *Othello,* and is found in Alphonso's lines. In a number of places the likeness is very close. Alphonso and Othello react similarly under suspicion of their wives' faithlessness:

---

[18] II, 3. Cf. *Henry IV, Part 2,* III, 2:
Silence: "You were called 'lusty Shallow' then, cousin."
Shallow: "By the mass, I was called any thing; and I would have done any thing indeed too, and roundly too . . . you had not four such swinge-bucklers in all the inns of court again."
[19] II, 3.   [20] II, 3.

Alphonso: She might have number'd out the stars in sin;
Fed her hot, lustful appetite with change
Of every high-fed, wanton fool in *Florence;*
Yet I been happy: ignorantly blest,
Like a true marriage tool, I might have sate
Contented, at the lower end o' th' feast,
To welcome all, without a farther thought . . .[21]

Othello: He that is robb'd, not wanting what is stol'n,
Let him not know't, and he's not robb'd at all.

. . . .

I had been happy, if the general camp,
Pioners and all, had tasted her sweet body,
So I had nothing known.[22]

In the second scene of Act II, Alphonso meets Clara's protestations of her mistress's innocence in the same manner that Othello receives Emilia's assurance that Desdemona is guiltless:

Alphonso: Nay, then thou art a praying chamber-bawd.
Othello: This is a subtle whore,

. . . .

And yet she'll kneel and pray; I have seen her do't.[23]

Alphonso, as he tries to stab Erminia, exclaims "O you strumpet down!"[24] Othello strangles Desdemona with "Down, strumpet!"[25] There is a difference, however, between Alphonso's intemperate rage and the almost unbearable poignancy that mingles with Othello's anger. Alphonso would not give his wife "one last repenting hour to save thy soul,"[26] but Othello wakes Desdemona because

I would not kill thy unprepared spirit;
No; heavens forfend! I would not kill thy soul.[27]

Elsewhere, Alphonso baits the uncomprehending Rogero with apparently nonsensical saws, as Hamlet does Polonius. His advice is also the same as Hamlet's:

[21] I, 2.   [22] III, 3.   [23] IV, 2.   [24] V, 2.
[25] V, 2.   [26] V, 2.   [27] V, 2.

> Hast thou a daughter? home, quickly home then: lock up thy doors; let her not see the day; let her not draw the open air; for if there be a pore unbarr'd about her, the bawdy devil will get in, and then, good-morrow grandfather.[28]

Even more directly, Southerne takes part of his plot from *Measure for Measure*. The scheme by which Juliana once more obtains possession of her former lover is the same as that by which Mariana gains rendezvous with her former betrothed, Angelo. Southerne gives the trick a double application: Juliana passes herself off in the darkness, on separate occasions, as Angeline and Erminia. In each play the duped rake marries his deceiver and former mistress.

Plot and Poetry

THE plot of *The Disappointment* moves easily enough, and granted the constitutional inconsistency of Alphonso, is logical in its development. There is one main action, into which the Alberto-Angeline-Juliana-Rogero sub-plot is well tied. All the main characters in one plot touch at some vital place those in the other. Thus even old Rogero, by revealing Juliana's deception, is the instrument to save Alphonso from killing his wife. A crudity of plotting appears, in several instances, in the too-rapid telescoping of time. Alberto enters to enjoy Erminia (really, Juliana) and comes out after exactly ten lines of dialogue have been spoken! Likewise, a dozen lines allow him sufficient opportunity elsewhere to retire and appear again with Juliana when he thinks her Angeline. In each case the assignation apparently reached a consummation!

The Disappointment marks a definite advance in poetic power over *The Loyal Brother*. Southerne has cast aside most traces of the heroic manner, although he occasionally prostitutes a heroic conceit to a sentimental use:

> Her eyes have shot me with a thousand fires;
> A thousand times, the little weeping loves,

[28] III, 1. Cf. *Hamlet*, II, 2.

The Disappointment

> That wanton'd in the liquid crystal there,
> Like *April* showers melting on my cheeks,
> Refresh'd my veins into a wanton spring.[29]

Only Alphonso could speak that and be in character! It is not in such passages that Southerne's power resides, nor in those like the passage of description which opens Act III—lines to which "immature" is the kindest possible epithet that can be applied:

> *Alphonso.* 'Tis late, and I alone: th' hard travell'd sun
>   Now wantons in the bosom of the sea.
>   Whilst amorous clouds steal nearer to the earth,
>   And melt themselves away upon the flow'rs:
>   The beasts in companies to coverts run;
>   And all the feather'd kind, upon the wing,
>   Pair to the groves, and dream the night away.

The failure here to achieve another "Behold the dawn in russet mantle clad" is a painful one.

But now and again Southerne, clearly under an Elizabethan star, writes forcefully and penetratingly. Alberto generalizes on woman-kind:

> . . . there's not a she,
> The coldest constitution of the sex,
> Nay, at the altar, telling o'er her beads,
> But some one rises on her heav'nly thoughts,
> That drives her down the wind of strong desire,
> And makes her taste mortality again.[30]

The dramatist's serious poetic style seldom reached out more powerfully than this:

> Had any broad-mouth'd, sland'rous villain said it,
> I would have turn'd him outward to the sun,
> Display'd th' infected fountain of his thoughts,
> And stabb'd the venom'd lie down to his heart.[31]

[29] I, 2.   [30] I, 1.   [31] I, 2.

As a whole, the blank verse of *The Disappointment* is less bombastic and more evenly capable than that of *The Loyal Brother*.

Don Quixote *and* The Disappointment

SOUTHERNE went to Cervantes for the intrigue of his main plot. The episode of *The Curious Impertinent* in *Don Quixote*[32] concerns two Florentines who are very close friends. The one, who has married a beautiful wife, induces his friend to test her virtue by making love to her. This the friend does, but falls in love with her and finally wins her to his purposes. For a time he conducts his clandestine affair successfully, until one day-break he sees a man slipping away from his mistress's house. The man is a suitor of the wife's maid, but the friend suspects that another is taking his place with the wife, and informs the husband that his wife is false to him. The husband pretends to leave town, but actually secretes himself in his wife's closet. About this time the wife tells her lover the truth about the man he had seen leaving the house. He in turn confesses that in his jealousy he had told her husband to hide in the closet. The wife by a clever trick convinces the hiding husband that his friend has been attempting her virtue but that she had resisted. The husband is overjoyed. Later, however, he discovers the truth and dies of a broken heart.

I list below the situations parallel in novel and play:

Curious Impertinent	*Disappointment*
The setting: Florence.	The setting: Florence.
Anselmo and Lothario very close friends.	Alphonso and Lorenzo very close friends.
Anselmo jealously eager to have Lothario test his wife's virtue.	Alphonso torn by jealousy of his wife.

[32] Part I, bk. IV, chs. 6–8. J. G. Lockhart's edition, 4 vols., 1881.

Curious Impertinent	Disappointment
Lothario sees a man coming from Camilla's house whom he supposes to be Camilla's lover, and Camilla false to him.	Lorenzo sees a man coming from Erminia's house whom he supposes to be Erminia's lover, and Erminia false to her husband. (III, 1.)
The unknown man is the maid's lover.	The unknown man is part of an intrigue promoted by Clara, the maid.
Anselmo pretends to leave town for two or three days, but really stays to observe.	Alphonso *ditto.* (III, 1.)
Lothario, at first instigated by Anselmo, makes love to Camilla.	Lorenzo, to test Erminia, suggests that she prove false to her husband. (III, 2.)
Camilla reveals to Lothario that the unknown man is the maid's lover, not hers.	Erminia convinces Lorenzo that the unknown man is part of an intrigue in which Clara is concerned. (III, 2.)

The differences are important and clear. Camilla, the wife, is false; Erminia remains true. Lothario proves a disloyal friend; Lorenzo is staunch and faithful throughout.

The Curious Impertinent provided grist for the mills of several English dramatists. In 1611 *The Second Maiden's Tragedy* used Cervantes' story as a source. The minor plot of Nat Field's *Amends for Ladies* (1610 or 1611) was culled from the same tale.[33] Crowne's *Married Beau, or the Curious*

[33] A. S. W. Rosenbach, *The Curious-Impertinent in English Dramatic Literature before Shelton's Translation (1612) of Don Quixote.* (*Mod. Lang. Notes,* June, 1902, XVII, 358–67.) Rosenbach also mentions Mrs. Behn's *Amorous Prince; or the Curious Husband* (4to, 1671) as deriving from *The Curious Impertinent.* Mr. M. Summers (Behn's *Works,* IV, 119) says that Behn took the episode of Antonio's persuading Alberto to woo Clarina from Robert Davenport's play *The City Night-Cap* (4to, 1661, but licensed 24 Oct., 1624), which in turn used Greene's *Philomela: the Lady Fitzwater's Nightingale* (1592, 1615, and 1631), rather than Cervantes.

Impertinent (D.L. 1694) clearly draws from *Don Quixote*. Lovely requests his friend Polidor to try his wife's chastity. The plot follows its original much more closely than does Southerne's, for the wife capitulates to the friend's pleas.

The Disappointment is important, not for its intrinsic merit, but for its proof that sentimentalism was articulate as early as 1684. Feeling was encroaching on the territory that wit alone had ruled, although the supreme triumph of the goddess of the woeful countenance lay well around the corner of the next century. Southerne was no special advocate of a strange morality, however. His business, as he saw it, was to hit as accurately as possible the tastes of those who might buy tickets for Drury Lane. And so when he next returned to the theatre, it was with a succession of comedies rich in the style of manners. *The Disappointment* alone among his comedies pointed clearly to the new drama.

CHAPTER IV

SIR ANTHONY LOVE, or THE RAMBLING LADY

Abbé. *Why here's a night of action indeed.*
Act V, sc. 7.

THE beginning of the last decade of the century found Southerne groping through a variety of dramatic forms for the elusive phantom of a popular triumph. Between 1682 and 1688 he had tried the stage with a heroic drama and with a "play" that was neither tragedy nor comedy, and had written four acts of a tragedy (*The Spartan Dame*), which, however, was barred from production because of its political implications. To the one portion of the dramatic field that he had not yet tilled he now turned, and by 1690 was hard at work on the comedy of manners which was destined to establish his reputation as a comic writer. *Sir Anthony Love, or the Rambling Lady,* produced about December, 1690,[1] caught at once the interest of the town and brought the beaux flocking to Drury Lane. Langbaine, within a few months of the first performance, echoed a universal approbation when he wrote: "This Play was acted with extraordinary Applause; the Part of *Sir Anthony Love* being most Masterly play'd by Mrs. Montfort: and certainly, who ever reads it, will find it fraught with true Wit and Humour."[2]

As on so many occasions, Southerne saw his work presented by a very capable cast, representing this time the full strength of the united companies. Undoubtedly, much of the play's drawing power lay in the spirited acting of Mrs. Mont-

---
[1] Its publication was advertised in the *London Gazette* for Dec. 18–22, 1690. In 1698 a second quarto edition was issued when the play was revived at Lincoln's-Inn-Fields. See *Term Catalogues* for Trinity Term, 1698 (Arber's Reprint) for notice of publication.
[2] Appendix to *Account of the English Dramatic Poets,* Oxford, 1691.

ford, strutting about in the title rôle as a girl in breeches and talking like a true rake-hell. While yet Susanna Percival, she had played Juliana in Southerne's *Disappointment,* and five years after *Sir Anthony Love,* as Mrs. Verbruggen then, she was to repeat her success in a similar part in *Oroonoko.*[3] Montford appeared as Valentine and Mrs. Bracegirdle as Charlotte. Anthony Leigh, the famous comedian who had played Rogero in *The Disappointment,* was the wicked old Abbé. The part of the servant to Sir Gentle Golding, containing less than two dozen lines, was entrusted to an ambitious young actor named Colley Cibber, for what was in all probability his first performance on any stage.

In his dedication to Thomas Skipwith (later Sir Thomas),[4] Southerne admitted that he wrote the play with Mrs. Montford in mind, and gave her due meed of praise for her performance. "You know the original Sir *Antony,*"[5] he said, "and therefore can best judge how the copy is drawn; though it will not be to my advantage to have them too narrowly compared; her wit is indeed inimitable, not to be painted: yet I must say, there is something in my draught of her, that carries a resemblance, and makes up a very tolerable figure: and

---

[3] Her husband, William Montford, was assassinated in 1692 by Capt. Richard Hill. Mrs. Montford remained on the stage and later married John Verbruggen, an actor in the Drury Lane Company. She was famous for the comic parts she created. In addition to her other characterizations, she played Mrs. Witwoud in Southerne's *Wives' Excuse* (1691), and Lady Susan Malepert in his *Maid's Last Prayer* (1693).

[4] Skipwith was the son of Sir Thomas Skipwith, an eminent lawyer of Gray's Inn and M.P. in 1660, who died 1694. (See *Lincolnshire Pedigrees: Harleian Soc. Pubs.,* Vol. 52, p. 893.) The younger Skipwith married Margaret, daughter to George, Lord Chandos, and died at Bath, June, 1710. (See J. Le Neve: *Monumenta Anglicana* [1717], p. 207.) He was for a long time the holder of some shares at Drury Lane and together with Rich precipitated the quarrel with the actors which resulted in Betterton's secession. See Hotson, *The Commonwealth and Restoration Stage,* p. 284 f.

[5] The first edition spells the name *Anthony,* the 1774 edition *Antony.*

since I have this occasion of mentioning Mrs. *Montford,* I am pleased, by way of thanks, to do her that public justice in print, which some of the best judges of these performances, have, in her praise, already done her, in public places; that they never saw any part more masterly played: and as I made every line for her, she has mended every word for me; and by a gaiety and air, particular to her action, turned every thing into the genius of the character."

Southerne confessed himself "gratefully sensible of the general good-nature of the town," and made his boast "(though with the most acknowledging respect) of the favours from the fair sex . . . in so visibly promoting my interest, on those days chiefly (the third, and the sixth) when I had the tenderest relation to the welfare of my play." As noted above, this is the first time on record that an author received a second benefit night for a play. All in all, Southerne's first venture into comedy brought him more than satisfactory results.

Sir Anthony Love is the best of our author's three comedies in the manners' style. To that style it belongs, in spite of the fact that its ostensible locale is France. The streets are those of "Montpelier," but the main characters are English and the scene might just as well have been St. James's Park. The wit, the coarseness, the philosophy had been familiar to play-goers for thirty years. Southerne took materials that had been the common property of dramatists for a generation and recombined them without disturbing the fragile texture of Restoration conventions. One looks in vain for any trace of the deliberate morality or emotion that had cropped out in his earlier plays and were to appear even more strikingly later. He gives himself over whole-heartedly to the tradition of Etherege and Wycherley, to which Vanbrugh, Congreve, and Farquhar had yet to contribute the last brilliant examples. It is important to test Southerne's success in this tradition and to see how his play touches the contemporary stream of mannerized comedy.

The plot of *Sir Anthony Love* is so crowded with a multiplicity of actions and so confused with disguise and cross-disguise that it would be impossible to give any close conception of it within reasonable limits. Southerne was not concerned with planning any well-motivated action, but with piling up situation after situation of comic significance. The plot has to shift for itself, and an intricate series of tricks is necessary at the end to bring about even a probable solution of events. His characters might well exclaim as does Flippanta in the last scene of *The Confederacy:* "Then all's peace again, but we have been more lucky than wise." However, from the byways of this play which is as rambling as its title there may be gathered three main threads of story. Sir Anthony Love is a young Englishwoman, Lucia by name, who has robbed her keeper, Sir Gentle Golding, of £500 and has gone colonelling into France disguised as a baronet of £1200 a year on travel allowance from his guardians. She does this in order to be near her dear Valentine, who had admired her as Lucia, and whom she now hopes to make love her. In company with Valentine and Ilford—both Restoration wits and men-about-town—she assumes the airs of an abandoned rake and with her gallantry and charm makes all the women love her, though she must of course always stop short of satisfying them. The love intrigue of the play centers about the efforts of these three English gallants to gain the affections of three French girls, two of them, Floriante and Charlotte, daughters to Count Canaile, who is eager to marry Floriante to the affected Count Verole; the other, Volante, the ward of a licentious old Abbé, brother to Canaile and a boon companion of these Englishmen, whom he is eager to help in their amours. Sir Anthony makes Ilford jealous by capturing the love of the Abbé's ward, Volante, but finally appeases him when she marries Volante and then generously sends Ilford to bed with the bride. Volante accepts the change with a surprising degree of equanimity. Valentine finally marries Floriante, and Charlotte, rather than be sent back to the nunnery, takes for husband the silly Verole.

Another strand of plot concerns the gulling of Sir Gentle Golding by his former mistress, now Sir Anthony. Sir Anthony promises to get Sir Gentle a wench, and when the old knight appears, trembling with eagerness for his appointment, Sir Anthony reveals herself as his own Lucia, and browbeats him into giving her more money. Later, when Sir Gentle thinks that he is marrying Floriante, he finds that his new bride is none other than his old Lucia in Floriante's clothes. To get rid of this unwanted wife he has to settle £500 a year on her.

Palmer, who pretends to be a pilgrim in order to steal, takes a prominent part in the play. Even before she knows him to be a fraud, Sir Anthony plans to make sport of the unctuous fellow. She drugs Palmer and has him carried to the Abbé's for the wits to make sport of. But awakening too soon, Palmer forces his guard, Sir Gentle, to exchange clothes with him. This sets off a series of complicated scenes of mistaken identity.

There was one episode included in the printed copy that was omitted from the representation. Here the degenerate Abbé, supposing Sir Anthony to be a fresh young man, tricks her into a meeting in which he makes suggestive advances. When Sir Anthony reveals her true sex, the Abbé is highly chagrined and disappointed. Soon he recovers his spirits, however, and frisks his way through the rest of the play. Whatever may be said of the immorality of Restoration comedy, it must be admitted that it makes little use of unnatural sex relationships as a comic motive.[6] This is an unsavory attempt of Southerne's to pander to the most depraved tastes of his audience. In the Dedication to the play he explains the reasons for the deletion of this scene in the acting, and makes a feeble gesture to defend it: "The Abbé's

[6] Coupler, in Vanbrugh's *Relapse* (1696) (I, 3), betrays the same perverse desires as does the Abbé.

character languishes in the fifth act for want of the scene between him and Sir Antony, which I plainly saw before, but was contented to leave a gap in the action . . . [rather] than run the venture of offending the women; not that there is one indecent expression in it; but the over-fine folk might run it into a design I never had in my head: my meaning was, to expose the vice; and I thought it could not be more contemptibly exposed, than in the person of a wanton old man, that must make even the most reasonable pleasure ridiculous."

With over a dozen important characters to handle within the limits of a single play, Southerne has hard work to keep the action clear; the summary given above does not begin to represent the dizzying shifts in the course of events.[7] It is with relief that we see the jumble shake down at last, and every Jack get his Jill in the quartet of marriages,—marriages truly Restoration, in the accomplishing of which purpose works to little advantage and love, of course, not at all. Thus the curtain closes on a typical tableau; it is almost as if each man got the woman who was standing next him when it came time for the play to end.

The play is half again as long as it should be, and seven hundred lines had to be left out in the original representation to bring it within the limits of an evening's performance. The first two acts are padded out with an indefatigable display of wit, and the last three acts are loaded with vigorous, not to say boisterous action. It is as if Southerne felt at first the necessity of giving the expected display of witty fireworks; with that out of his system he could settle down to the more agreeable task of devising amusing situations.

It is in the construction of such situations that Southerne's comic talent is revealed. At plotting he shows little ability here, nor does he have Congreve's brilliance, that makes us

---

[7] There are seven scenes in the last act: a house, a bed-chamber, the street, the inside of a house, the backside of a nunnery, the Abbé's house, the street.

forget to ask after the plot. But he does have the knack of getting his characters into situations provocative of real mirth. Such a one is that in which Sir Anthony in petticoats is pursued by Sir Gentle, who does not recognize her as his former mistress whom he loathes and fears. Another occurs when Sir Anthony marries Volante and then sends Ilford into the bridal chamber; Volante is soon convinced that the change is for the better: any man is better than no man, in the Restoration maiden's philosophy. Comedy runs into farce in the third act when Sir Gentle is left to guard the sleeping Palmer. Sir Gentle tickles the pilgrim's nose with a straw to wake him. The pilgrim leaps up, and the two men meet and fall. "Both amazed, raise themselves upon their bottoms, and stare at each other," runs the stage direction. Palmer then presents an ink-horn as a pistol and forces Sir Gentle to change clothes with him, so that he can get past the servants. There follows a farcical scene of mistaken identity when Palmer, mistaken on the street for Sir Gentle, is dunned by a tailor for the very suit he is wearing, and is discovered as an impostor by Sir Gentle's servant (Colley Cibber) who sets up a cry of murder and thievery. It is all very vivacious and lusty, and distinctly English.

The wit of the play is not without its brighter spots, but these are separated by too many arid stretches where there is much that only seems like wit. Sir Anthony palpably awes her companions with her scintillating repartee, until Valentine can only say to Ilford, ". . . We shall neither of us arrive at his wit."[8] Occasionally there are good flashes:

   Sir Anthony. But marriage is the only game, where no body can be the winner.[9]

. . . .

   Abbé. I love to be wicked myself too sometimes, as often as I can decently bring it about.[10]

. . . .

[8] I, 1.   [9] IV, 4.   [10] V, 5.

Abbé.	I am contented to . . . make the most of a good conscience and good company.
Ilford.	A good conscience is good company indeed.
Abbé.	I mean sir, I'll make a conscience of good company[11]—

Contemporary audiences doubtless delighted, too, in the impudently bawdy remarks given to Sir Anthony throughout the play. Wit, however, was not Southerne's best faculty; the effortless, rapier-like thrusts of Etherege or of Congreve were well beyond his reach.[12] Nevertheless his prose style is fluent and vivacious and is buoyed up by a surge of rollicking animal spirits that carries the reader over those places where the epigram is labored and the horn of wit runs dry.

The Pattern of Character

ONE does not turn to the conventionally mannerized comedy of the Restoration for any significant analysis of character or subtlety of motive, and *Sir Anthony Love* is no exception to the rule. There is nothing in the character of any of its gay people that he who runs may not read. No claim of novelty and no number of actresses in pantaloons can conceal the fact that these witty persons bear the stamp of a well-worn comic formula. But to the critic of Southerne even such conformity to the established pattern is important.

Amidst all this hodge-podge of wit, intrigue, and disguise Sir Anthony rides the crest of every wave. She is the mistress of every situation, the instigator of most of the tricks, and the only one who seems to know what it is all about. All the others, sooner or later, come within range of her ingenuity. She baits the foolish and cowardly Count Verole, tricks the Pilgrim, leads on the jealous Ilford, gulls Sir Gen-

---

[11] II, 1.

[12] Cibber's *Lives* (V, 329–30) quotes Colley Cibber on Southerne's comic style: ". . . it might be denominated Whip-Syllabub, that is, flashy and light, but indurable; and as it is without the Sal Atticum of wit, can never much delight the intelligent part of the audience."

tle, and plays with Valentine. It is she who lays the plot whereby Ilford gains Volante as his bride while Volante thinks she is marrying Sir Anthony. It is she also who, disguised as Floriante, allows Sir Gentle to seize and marry her. All this is done with a high-spirited, swaggering impertinence that suggested to the audience how much this emancipated female was enjoying herself. "Anything to be wicked, gentlemen," she exclaims. Satire is Sir Anthony's natural form of expression, and the English frequently the butts of her wit: "You must make your conversation necessary sometimes, as well as agreeable, to preserve a friendship with an *Englishman*."[13] "Thou wou'dst have had me," she protests to her confidante Waitwell, who wonders why she does not declare her love to Valentine, "with the true conduct of an *English* mistress, upon the first inclination, cloy'd him with my person, without any assurance of his relishing me enough to raise his appetite to a second taste."[14] A shrewd, immensely capable heroine is Sir Anthony.

She could be cruel on occasion, as became one into whose hands the poetic justice of the comedy was entrusted. She could blackmail the Abbé for his immorality, rob Sir Gentle initially, and in revenge marry him at last only that she might wrench from him £500 a year. But Sir Gentle is a fool and the Abbé a rogue, and as such both are her legitimate prey. Valentine points the current moral:

> Thus all things are provided for by fate:
> The witty man enjoys the fool's estate.[15]

Through the Pilgrim and the Abbé Southerne shoots his satire on religion, or on the abuse of religion. Palmer, even before he is discovered to be a fraud, is made disgusting by his sanctimonious airs and his miraculous accounts of the conversion of the wicked. Subsequently he reveals himself as an impostor who has "travell'd through ever[y] profession, and cheated in all; so having by my industry gather'd a hand-

[13] I, 1.   [14] I, 1.   [15] IV, 2.

some fortune, I converted that into jewels, and myself into a Pilgrim."[16] The Abbé is a worldly old reprobate eager to help Valentine, Sir Anthony, and Ilford capture his nieces, and believing thoroughly in the English institution of cuckoldry. Sir Anthony describes him as "a most considerable pillar [of the church] . . . to his own profit, and our pleasurable living in this town."[17] The church to which these two scalawags belonged was of course the Catholic, and so Southerne could satirize religion and at the same time receive the plaudits of all good English Protestants!

The women of the comedy, other than Sir Anthony, have parts of minor importance. Floriante and Charlotte belong to an easily-recognized type of Restoration ingénue. Both sisters have been suffering from parental restraint, and are waiting only for the chance to leap into a world of carnality. They are innocent through lack of opportunity to be otherwise. Southerne gives them the benediction of marriage before the final curtain falls, although the best that Charlotte can do in the lottery is to draw Count Verole. These girls come from the same stock as Prue in Congreve's *Love for Love* (1695), Hoyden in Vanbrugh's *Relapse* (1696), and Corinna in his *Confederacy* (1705), who long for love-adventures that a too-close guardianship has prevented them from realizing.

There is nothing in the characters of Valentine and Ilford that one may not find by placing his finger on almost any page of Restoration comedy. But they too are enclosed, before the play ends, within the haven of marriage, from which, in an act unwritten but clearly suggested, they might well sail forth to other and more conventional conquests. The men and women in *Sir Anthony Love,* then, emerge as natives of the thickly-populated country of Restoration superficiality and audacious brilliance. We shall see how aptly they fit into the panorama of contemporary comedy.

[16] III, 1. [17] I, 1.

Southerne's Comic Method

THE comic world of *Sir Anthony Love* is not essentially different from the wider area of comedy of which it was a part. The comic treatment of sex lies at its base and forms the motif of its numerous intrigues. There is no cuckolding here, but the absence of this, we feel, is entirely fortuitous: there are no husbands to be cuckolded. That the love pursuits are before marriage instead of after, and that the play ends with wedding bells for well-nigh all the characters does not rob the situations of their licentiousness, nor the speeches of their prurience. With what seems like strange generosity, Sir Anthony, who had followed Valentine into France in order to win him, urges her beloved to marry Floriante. This Valentine somewhat reluctantly consents to do. Sir Anthony's purpose, however, is not to lose Valentine, but to secure him by a psychology typically Restoration. Floriante would be a dangerous rival as a mistress, she argues,[18] but once married to Valentine her attractions for him would fade, and Sir Anthony could hold sole place in his heart. The supposition is that a sixth act would reveal Sir Anthony and Valentine more in love than ever!

Southerne's comic philosophy in this play is entirely within the artificial convention of the comedy of manners, and could be cited in support of Lamb's argument that after all, this world of comedy was another universe, and therefore could not be judged by the moral standards that we apply to our own. The treatment of sex here is intellectual rather than emotional. Passion is treated with a dryness altogether passionless. The characters are liable to no moral code, for the play gives no indication that a moral code exists. Southerne does not scoff at virtue, for virtue never enters the field of action! There is no evidence here of the luscious treatment of sex that later broke the lightly-poised equilibrium of the comedy of manners and touched wit with feeling. Southerne

[18] IV, 2.

does not, as did Farquhar later, admit the existence of a set of values that had only to breathe on artificial comedy to make the old situations bitterly immoral. In his next play, as we shall see, Southerne did exactly this, but in *Sir Anthony Love* morality could not operate because it was not known.

Many of Southerne's situations were the common currency of Restoration drama. As in other comedies, the joyous sense of the chase is everywhere. Waitwell asks what possible pleasure Sir Anthony can have in following the women when she can't enjoy them. Sir Anthony replies that she can make them ready for those who can; there are many such sportsmen, she says, "who beat about more for company, than the pleasure of the sport; and if they do start any thing, are better pleas'd with the accidents of the chase, the hedges and ditches, than the close pursuit of the game."[19] The same philosophy is expressed by Millimant in *The Way of the World:* "I'll fly, and be follow'd to the last Moment . . . I'll be solicited to the very last, nay and afterwards";[20] and by Angelica in *Love for Love:* "Uncertainty and expectation are the joys of life. Security is an insipid thing, and the overtaking and possessing of a wish discovers the folly of the chase."[21]

There are other stock characters and motives in *Sir Anthony Love*. The rakes, the lascivious cleric, the false pilgrim, the hoydenish girls, the foolish Count, the duped keeper —all are conventional types. The situation in which a girl assumes male attire in order to be near the man she loves had been used by Wycherley and was taken over later by Farquhar.[22] In *The Plain Dealer* (1676) Fidelia, lovesick for

---

[19] I, 1.   [20] IV, 1.

[21] IV, 2. Nicoll mentions this comparison between *Sir Anthony Love* and *Love for Love*. See *Restoration Drama*, p. 228.

[22] Also found in D'Urfey's *Virtuous Wife, or Good Luck at Last* (1679), where the Wife, Olivia, disguises herself as a gallant and courts her husband's mistress. See Kathleen M. Lynch, "Thomas D'Urfey's Contribution to Sentimental Comedy," *Philological Quarterly*, IX, 251 (1930).

Manly, follows him disguised as a man. And thinking her a man, Olivia falls in love with her. Silvia, in *The Recruiting Officer* (1706), disguised as Jack Wilful, follows Capt. Plume in order to keep him in her sight. As she says, she "only laid by the woman to make sure of my man."

The trick of arranging a marriage in which one of the contracting parties is deceived as to the identity either of the one he marries or of the person with whom he later consummates the marriage had been employed in one of the earliest comedies played on the Restoration stage, Cowley's *Cutter of Coleman Street* (printed 1663). There a double deception takes place; Aurelia, in a marriage in the dark, takes Lucia's place and marries Puny; Truman, Jr., seizes Lucia, thinking her Amelia, and takes her to the altar. In 1664, Thomas Killigrew, in *The Parson's Wedding,* created a similar scene. Mrs. Wanton, mistress to the Captain, is married to the unsuspecting Parson, "a Wit also." But they put Baud, Wanton's old and ugly maid, to bed with the Parson, in which predicament he is surprised and arrested for adultery. In Congreve's *Love for Love* (1695), Tattle, believing that he is wedding Angelica in nun's disguise, is tricked into marriage with Mrs. Frail. Southerne himself used much the same complication as that of the Ilford-Volante Sir Anthony imbroglio when he wrote the sub-plot to *Oroonoko* (1695). But nowhere else in Restoration comedy, as far as I know, does the fundamental situation of a play depend upon the assumption of male disguise by the leading female character.

It should be noted that there is an eighteenth century play the central idea of which seems to be taken from *Sir Anthony Love*.[23] In Leonard Welsted's *The Dissembled Wanton; or, My Son Get Money* (L.I.F., Dec., 1726) Lord Severne postpones his son's marriage to Emilia because he suspects her of loose relations with one Sir Harry Truelove, who is Emilia's close friend. The situation is cleared up when it is realized

---

[23] Nicoll points this out in *Early Eighteenth Century Drama,* p. 173 n.

that Sir Harry is really Lord Severne's daughter Charlotte in disguise. It had been supposed that she was in France, whither her father had sent her. Charlotte fools not only her family but her lover, Beaufort. The sentimental tone of the play, however, is as little as possible reminiscent of Southerne's comedy.

As we have seen, the town acclaimed *Sir Anthony Love*—partly, perhaps, as the Epilogue explains, because it would be willing to

> . . . hear with patience a dull scene, to see
> The female *Montford* bare above the knee.

But the play stands on its own legs as well as on Mrs. Montford's; "dull" is a word that does not apply to it. Southerne was a dramatist wise in his own generation, and although his wit was not of Congreve's mint, it stands as a fair specimen of that on the second order of excellence. More than on his wit, Southerne in *Sir Anthony Love* depended upon a genius for evolving situations rich in comic power. This, together with a great deal of bustle and confusion and a sufficient amount of good old English humor got him over the shoals of character and plot. *Sir Anthony Love* was a success in its own right.

CHAPTER V

THE WIVES' EXCUSE, or CUCKOLDS MAKE THEMSELVES

> Mrs. Teazall. . . . *why, your music-meetings, dancing-meetings, masking-meetings, all are but pretences to bring you together: and when you meet, we know what you meet for well enough.*
> Act V, sc. 2.

WITH *Sir Anthony Love* Southerne believed that he had found the key to a successful dramatic career, for the acclaim that had greeted his first comedy was no uncertain one. If comedy was what the town wanted, comedy he would give it according to its taste. We are not surprised, therefore, to find that within a year he had completed another play and that Drury Lane was engaged in giving it the best possible production. *The Wives' Excuse, or Cuckolds Make Themselves* was first acted in December, 1691,[1] but all the efforts of Betterton, Williams, Bowman, Montford, Mrs. Barry, Mrs. Bracegirdle, and Mrs. Montford were insufficient to prevent its almost immediate death. Its failure was as flat as the success of *Sir Anthony Love* had been great. Southerne's hopes had been high and his disappointment was keen enough to make him bitter against those who had damned the new play for what seemed to him inadequate reasons. "It is only the capacity and commendation of the common mistresses to please every body," he declared.[2]

From the Dedication we learn why the comedy was rejected. In the first place, the character of Mrs. Friendall, a wife true to her husband, displeased some. Southerne berates such critics roundly, asserting that "those sparks, who were most offended with her virtue in public, are the men that lose

[1] See *Gentleman's Journal* for Jan., 1691/2, pp. 51–2.
[2] Dedication.

little by it, in private; and if all the wives in town were of her mind, those mettled gentlemen would be found to have the least to do, in making them otherwise. . . ." The looser morals of Witwoud, another female character, should have pleased them, he goes on to say, but "she was no more understood to the advantage of the men, than the Wife was received in favour of the women." The Restoration theatre was likely to be sensitive to general social satire,[3] and some critics took exception to the scene in the first act satirizing a music-meeting, which the men and women of the play attended because they could there the more easily establish their intrigues. Southerne disclaims any purpose of attacking music-meetings as an institution: "As to the music-meeting, I always thought it an entertainment reasonably grown up into the liking of the town: I introduced it, as a fashionable scene of bringing good company together, without a design of abusing what every body likes; being in my temper so far from disturbing a public pleasure, that I would establish twenty more of them, if I could: and for the billet-doux, that was put into Mrs. *Sightly's* hand, upon leading her out, I have heard of such a thing in a church before now, and never thought the worse of the place."

Southerne did not yet despair "of pleasing the more reasonable part of mankind." Dryden, he says, had publicly declared that the town had been kind to *Sir Anthony Love* and needed only to be just to this. The master had even gone so far as to address to Southerne some lines on the failure of his comedy, lines which Southerne printed in the first edition of the play:

> Sure there's a Fate in Plays; and 'tis in vain
> To write, while these malignant Planets Reign:
> Some very foolish Influence rules the Pit,
> Not always kind to Sence, or just to Wit.

[3] Such a play as Dryden's *Limberham, or The Kind Keeper* (1678) seems to have failed partly for this reason. *Cf.* Ward, III, 373 n. See also Nicoll's *Restoration Drama*, p. 81.

And whilst it lasts, let Buffoonry succeed,
To make us laugh; for never was more need.
Farce, in it self, is of a nasty scent;
But the gain smells not of the Excrement.
The SPANISH Nymph, a Wit and Beauty too,
With all her Charms bore but a single show:
But, let a Monster MUSCOVITE appear,
He draws a crowded Audience round the Year.
May be thou hast not pleas'd the Box and Pit; ⎫
Yet those who blame thy Tale, commend thy Wit; ⎬
So TERENCE Plotted; but so TERENCE Writ. ⎭
Like his thy Thoughts are true, thy Language clean,
Ev'n Lewdness is made Moral, in thy Scene.
The Hearers may for want of NOKES repine,
But rest secure, the Readers will be thine.[4]
Nor was thy Labour'd DRAMA, damn'd or hiss'd,
But with a kind Civility, dismiss'd:
With such good manners as the Wife did use,
Who, not accepting, did but just refuse.
There was a glance at parting; such a look
As bids thee not give o're, for one rebuke.
But if thou wou'dst be seen, as well as read;
Copy one living Author, and one dead;
The Standard of thy Style, let ETHEREGE be:
For Wit, th' immortal Spring of WYCHERLY.
Learn after both, to draw some just Design,
And the next Age will learn to Copy thine.

---

[4] Motteux (*Gentleman's Journal,* Jan., 1691/2, p. 51) pays the play this tribute: "I do not doubt but you will own that it will bear a Reading; which some that meet with a better Fate too often do not." Another edition was printed in 1726 by W. Mears (12mo.). The first edition was dedicated to Thomas Wharton, later first Marquis of Wharton (1648–1715), who had been named Privy Counseller as soon as William was crowned. Swift attacked him as being wholly occupied by "vice and politics, so that bawdy, prophaneness, and business fill up his whole conversation." (*Short Character of T―― E―― of W――,* 1710/11. See *D.N.B.,* XX, 1333.) Southerne was so undiscriminating in his flattery that he could address this admitted rake as being "the very man I would chuse to be, if I could . . . Your wit and conversation, your person and address, would best recommend me to the women."

Dryden here implies another reason for the play's failure—its lack of bustling humor which a famous low-comedian like Nokes might act. Whatever the reason, the author had to take such consolation as he might from the "kind civility" with which the piece was dismissed.

It is hard to understand how anyone could have expected *The Wives' Excuse* to succeed, even in 1691. A drearier round of cuckolding and wenching would be hard to find in any writer approaching Southerne in talent. Here is all the mechanism of the typical comedy of manners, with little of the comic spirit essential if the old comic skeletons were to be renewed in a successful dance. The wit is not intolerable, but it is insufficient to animate a dull series of stereotyped intrigues; one or two good scenes, strong in *vis comica,* will not hold together a framework as weak and confused as this. The quantity of vigorous action that gave life to *Sir Anthony Love* is missing here. Original plotting, strong characterization, brilliant wit—any of these might have saved the play, but none is present in sufficient proportion. Our study of the comedy, therefore, must be a study in mediocrity, from which it will yet be possible to glean something of value to those interested in the continuity of English drama.

The story beats monotonously on the theme that Restoration comedy knew best. The names of the characters are themselves an index to the plot: Lovemore, Wilding, Courtall, Witwoud, Teazall. The manners are of a piece. In the very first scene, the conversation of the footmen shows how the philosophy of their masters had penetrated below-stairs. "Every man has hopes of a new marry'd woman," one asserts. "She has discover'd some of my master's intrigues of late," says another of his mistress, "that may help to fill the sails; but I say nothing, I will take fees on both sides, and betray neither." In the same scene the footmen characterize the genial people who are to make the play:

> I look upon Mr. *Wilding,* my master . . . to be the cleverest cuckold-maker in *Covent-Garden.*

The Wives' Excuse 81

. . . .

    Your master *Courtall* . . . will be as fond of the appearances of an intrigue, as she can be; to see him in the chase, you would think he had pleasure in the sport; for he will be as sure always to follow her, as never to press her . . .

. . . .

    She [Mrs. Witwoud] . . . has no business of her own, but a great deal of other people's. All the men in town follow her, but 'tis for other women.

Such persons have but one course of action open to them; to tell of their intrigues is to relate the story of the play.

    Friendall, accurately characterized as "an impertinent, nonsensical, silly, intriguing, cowardly, good-for-nothing coxcomb"[5] who counts that day lost in which he does not deliver half a dozen *billets-doux,* has been married three months, and has already tired of his wife. He tells us himself that the only reason he married her, aside from that of the inheritance, was that he might carry on his amours more swimmingly. He makes his wife invite people to their house so that he can pick his women with greater ease. Of these visitors Lovemore is chief, and he presses his suit to Mrs. Friendall with her husband's approbation—anything to keep her out of the way. Lovemore conspires against Friendall. Knowing that his hopes of the wife depend upon the husband's senseless behavior, he contrives a plot to show Friendall up as a coward in a fight. But Mrs. Friendall's ingenuity is too much for this trick. She pretends to hold her husband back and warns him (needlessly, as she knows) not to draw his sword before women. Mrs. Friendall is thoroughly tired of her match, yet she will not cuckold her husband with Lovemore.

    Mrs. Sightly is the center of the other intrigue. She is honorably loved by Wellvile and dishonorably sought by Wilding. Wilding's pursuit is aided by the efforts of a highly efficient amateur bawd, Mrs. Witwoud. Sightly learns that Witwoud is conspiring with Wilding against what virtue may

[5] III, 2.

be hers, and solely because Wilding is one who never spends a night with a woman without telling the town of it, she reviles Witwoud as an untrue friend. In revenge, Witwoud tells Wilding that she will arrange for him to get Sightly at Friendall's masquerade that night. She really is planning to impersonate Sightly and grant Wilding "the Favor," in order that he may spread abroad that he received it from Sightly. The masquerade is the big scene of the play. Witwoud succeeds in making Wilding believe that she is Sightly. She goes into an inner room, and he is about to follow her, when Wellvile convinces him that the woman within is not Sightly. Together they collar Friendall and send him in to Sightly, telling him that she is a mysterious stranger. Then someone bursts into the inner room, "the scene draws," and Witwoud and Friendall are seen on a couch, to their mutual confusion. Thus is Sightly revenged. Such a disclosure as this proves too much for Mrs. Friendall's fortitude, and she and Friendall agree to a separation. Friendall is quite pleased at recovering his liberty, while Mrs. Friendall regrets that "I must still be your wife, and still unhappy."

The rather fetid atmosphere in which these people carry on, with remarkable singleness of mind, their love-episodes, is of course that of London—the fashionable London of the fops and wits, where a *double-entendre* is of more value than a maid's virginity or a wife's integrity. The levées and masked balls and assignations that bring them together are those of the impeccable *beau monde*. Rosamond's Pond in St. James's Park is a favorite meeting place.[6] References are made to the Mall, the chocolate-house in St. Albanstreet, Banstead Downs, and Will's Coffee-house. Friendall is accustomed to refer familiarly to "Jock Dryden and Will Wycherly."[7] The women meet, Teazall tells Witwoud, "to hear you prate by the hour, flatter every body in the company, speak ill of every one that's absent, and scatter about the

---

[6] *Cf.* also *The Way of the World*, I, 1.
[7] III, 2.

scandal of the day." " 'Tis one of the most fashionable innocent diversions of the town," replies Witwoud.[8] The glass of fashion on whose surface shimmered the reflection of Lovewell and Wilding was that in which the court of the Merry Monarch had seen itself. And if times were changing, and if William had brought new manners as well as new morals to Hampton Court, comedy at least still continued the old tradition.

In such a society as that of *The Wives' Excuse,* wit is the gold of exchange, and satire the test of wit. Such *bons mots* as these are tossed lightly about:

Love. He that won't lie to his mistress, will hardly lye with her.[9]

. . . .

Wit. Conscience at cards, cousin! you are a better bred lady than to expect it.[10]

. . . .

Wild. A maidenhead's a jewel of no value in marriage—
Wit. 'Tis never set down indeed, in the particular of a woman's estate.[11]

. . . .

Wit. Indeed the woman should cheat the man, as much as she can, before marriage, because, after it, he has a title of cheating her as long as he lives.[11]

. . . .

Friend. [to Mrs. Friend.] I'll go home with you . . . but no man of fashion, you know, walks with his wife.[12]

From any point of view, it would be hard to support Dryden's exaggerated claim that Southerne's

> Thoughts are true, thy Language clean,
> Ev'n Lewdness is made Moral in thy Scene.

The fact is that in this play there is a well-defined advance into indecency over *Sir Anthony Love.* Coarseness of expression is more frequent, and the Prologue is an open invi-

[8] II, 1.   [9] IV, 1.   [10] IV, 1.
[11] II, 3.   [12] III, 2.

tation to the gallants to carry away the vizard-masks present. Few conversations could be franker than that between Wilding and his servant[13] after Fanny has left his lodgings neatly seduced (if that girl's eager capitulation could be called seduction), or than that between Witwoud and Wilding when the former has come masked into the latter's room.[13] The major climax of the play is the sudden exposure of Witwoud and Friendall in each other's arms on a couch. If lewdness is touched here with morality it is a strange morality indeed. Nor is the play open to the defense that might possibly be made for *Sir Anthony Love:* that any moral standards are unknown in this inverted world of comedy. As we shall see, the divergences from the standards of ordinary decency are made inescapably apparent by the introduction of at least one character whose virtue was as consciously moral as that of any sentimental heroine.

Characterizations—Traditional and Otherwise

FEW of the characterizations of this play extend beyond the artificial limits of the stock-types of the comedy of manners. Wilding and Lovemore live up to their names. Wilding declares his purpose in life with "my practice lies among the women,"[14] while Lovemore proceeds systematically about the business of trying to win Mrs. Friendall. He outlines his plans and at the same time explains the title of the play in the rhymed tag that closes the first act:

> Thus, who a married woman's love would win,
> Should with the husband's failings first begin;
> Make him but in the fault, and you shall find
> A good excuse will make most women kind.

Courtall is one to whom the chase means everything and the consummation nothing. Witwoud is aptly characterized by Courtall as being "never the worse bawd . . . for being a

[13] II, 3.   [14] II, 3.

gentlewoman."[15] Her delight comes in arranging intrigues for the men, and her base purpose is to bring "a general ruin upon all her friends."[16] The men make use of her skill in plotting against the virtue of others, but fear her biting wit. Thus Wilding makes love to her as long as she is masked, only to cool immediately when she reveals her identity. Witwoud soliloquizes on this, regretting her "setting up for a wit, to the ruin of other people's pleasure, and the loss of my own," and finding " 'tis not enough for a woman to be handsome, there must be a probability of making that handsome woman kind, to make a man in love with her. . . ." "If I had dy'd a maid," she continues, " 'tis but what I deserv'd for laughing so many honest gentlemen off their charitable design of making me otherwise."[17] That Witwoud, in attempting to revenge herself on Sightly, is herself exposed to the laughter of the assembled wits, is a satisfying display of poetic justice.

The character most alive is undoubtedly old Mrs. Teazall, aunt to Witwoud and the erring Fanny. She had been, in her time, "in at most of the pleasures of this town,"[18] and increasing age left undiminished the vigor of her spirits, at least. She is the defender of the old order against the new, and can hurl a vociferous epithet against the debased morality of modern times. When she is not inveighing against the "depravity in matrimony, on both sides now-a days,"[19] she is attempting, with small success, to keep her young niece Fanny from running into the arms of Wilding. In the last act she breaks in on the masquerade in search of Fanny. "God's my life!" she exclaims, "can't you keep up your masquerades, in the primitive institution of making cuckolds, as it us'd to be, without bringing the young wenches into the mystery of matrimony before their time?"[20] Wherever Mrs. Teazall goes, she carries with her an air of robust, if coarse vitality which smacks of a freshness strange to the mannered

[15] III, 2. [16] III, 2. [17] II, 3.
[18] III, 2. [19] III, 2. [20] V, 3.

vices of the wits and witlings whom she could wither in a breath.

The husband and wife whose marital difficulties give the comedy its name must enter importantly into any discussion of the play. Of the two, Friendall is the less interesting. He is a selfish blockhead, avowedly a libertine, absurdly proud of his poetic endeavors (which are so wretched that no one can set music to them) and of his tastes in women and wine. He is also a physical coward, and a fawner at the heels of persons of rank. It is fitting that he should be scorned by his acquaintances and exposed at last in an awkward intrigue. Certainly justice and all dramatic tradition call aloud for horns to be planted on his head. The opportunity is waiting ready. But at this point Southerne, who in other respects has been following faithfully the grooves of mannerized comedy, steps aside to create in Mrs. Friendall a character strangely un-Restoration.

A virtuous wife had been something of an anomaly so far in contemporary comedy. Five years later, Cibber in *Love's Last Shift* (1696) would present Amanda, wife to Loveless, as "a woman of strict virtue," who retained that virtue somewhat precariously in Vanbrugh's sequel, *The Relapse* (1696). Lucia, in Richard Estcourt's *The Fair Example* (1703) remains true to her cruel husband in spite of Springlove's vehement attentions. Lady Brute in Vanbrugh's *Provoked Wife* (1697) and Mrs. Sullen in Farquhar's *Beaux Stratagem* (1707) suffer the fires of temptation and come through only slightly singed, with chastity intact. Lady Brute, however, is saved from being ruined by Constant only through a chance intervention, and it takes the sudden surprise of a robbery to save Mrs. Sullen from capitulating to the charms of Archer. With the later flood of sentimental comedy, wifely virtue was to be the rule rather than the exception; in 1691 it is sufficiently rare to call for special comment.

Mrs. Friendall is true to her faithless spouse through no chance, but by reason of a strong morality. She knows that she has made a bad bargain. "Every woman carries her cross in this world," she says, "a husband happens to be mine, and I must bear it, as well as I can."[21] Lovemore woos her ardently but she dismisses him with a "kind civility": "Mr. *Lovemore,* you might have known me better, than to imagine your sly flattery could softly sing me into a consent to any thing my virtue had abhorr'd."[22] At first she is unwilling to admit that Friendall is a coward. But when he is insulted by Ruffle, she hastens to take the quarrel on herself, lest her husband should prove to be that which she fears in her heart he is. She defends her action to herself with ostrich-like reasoning: "I don't know that he is a coward; but having these reasons to suspect him, I thought this was the best way to hinder him from discovering himself: for if he had betray'd that baseness to me, I shou'd despise him; and can I love the man I must despise?"[23]

Her situation is the harder because her heart naturally inclines to Lovewell, whom she repulses half-tenderly: "therefore I entreat you, don't make it impossible to me for the future, to receive you as a friend: for I must own, I would secure you always for my friend: nay more, I will confess my heart to you: if I could make you mine . . ."[21] At last, the public revelation of Friendall's lechery makes it impossible for this suffering wife to continue further; so she effects a separation, though not a divorce. "I must still be your wife, and still unhappy," she mourns.[24] Lovemore pricks up his ears at the news of the separation. "What alteration this may make in my fortune with her, I don't know," he rejoices, "but I'm glad I have parted them."[24] Whether Mrs. Friendall's citadel of virtue remained intact beyond the fifth act must remain forever conjectural!

From this relatively insignificant comedy there thus emerges an element of some historical importance. Southerne twists into the fabric of Restoration comedy one character that links the play directly with later sentimental drama. Mrs.

[21] V, 3.   [22] IV, 1.   [23] II, 2.   [24] V, 2.

Friendall, the wronged wife, courageously patient and unwaveringly pure, is a moral type strangely incongruous in her setting, and blood sister to the sentimental heroines who were to follow her.[25] That Southerne realized the clash of antagonistic elements in his play is shown by his denial, in the Epilogue spoken by Mrs. Barry, of any moral purpose:

> Whether I've done my husband right, or no;
> Most women may be in the right, that do:
> Our author does not set up for reforming,
> Or giving hints to fools who won't take warning.

Nevertheless, the incongruity remains, and it is by all odds the most noteworthy thing in an undistinguished play.

[25] She speaks in their very cadences: "Nay, Mr. *Friendall*, I know what you will object to me; but you must hear me out. The concern and care of your reputation is as dear to me, as it can be tender to you; since I must appear to the world, only in that rank of honour which you are pleas'd to maintain." (II, 2.)

CHAPTER VI

THE MAID'S LAST PRAYER, or ANY RATHER THAN FAIL

> Dauphine: *They'll believe themselves to be just such men as we make them, neither more nor less. They have nothing, not the use of their senses, but by tradition.*
> Jonson's *Silent Woman*, Act III, sc. 1.

IN January, 1692/3, Motteux's *Gentleman's Journal* appeared with the following piece of theatrical news: "Mr. *Southerne's* New Comedy, call'd, *The Maid's last Prayers* [*sic*], *or Any rather than fail*, was acted the 3^d time this evening, and is to be acted again to morrow. It discovers much knowledge of the Town in its Author; and its Wit and purity of Diction, are particularly commended. You have here two of the Songs in it. Mr. *Congreve,* who made the words of the first,[1] hath written a Comedy, which will be acted in a little time, and is to be call'd, *The Old Batchelor.*"[2] Southerne had taken to heart Dryden's admonition that he should "not give o'er, for one rebuke."[3] Indeed, as he says in his dedication to Charles Boyle,[4] he fears that "a play once a year, looks very like turning into the profession." But "I am a little better acquainted with the town, than to impose myself this way upon them; and let it be the defence of my writing, that I have nothing else to do."

Once again Drury Lane gave its best actors to the play. The names of most of those who had supported the failing *Wives' Excuse* appear again in the cast of *The Maid's Last Prayer*. Betterton, however, was replaced by Powell and Un-

---

[1] Malone cites this as Congreve's first acknowledged work. See his *Life of Dryden,* in *Crit. and Misc. Prose Works,* I, pt. 1, pp. 227–8.
[2] p. 28.
[3] *To Mr. Southerne; on . . . The Wives Excuse.* See above, p. 79.
[4] See above, pp. 15–16, for Boyle.

derhill was introduced in the part of Captain Drydrubb. The mesdames Barry, Bracegirdle, Montford, and Betterton brought to the women's rôles a profusion of talent. Motteux's comment would indicate that the play was not unfavorably received, but whatever success it had must have been considerably under Southerne's expectations. In the Dedication he hints that it was not too warmly welcomed: "I have had my ends of this play, and should have been glad if it had answered every bodies: I think it has its beauties, though they did not appear upon the stage. . . ."

The Maid's Last Prayer exhibits the same defects and the same thin virtues that had belonged to *The Wives' Excuse*. All that might be said in summary of the one would apply with equal force to the other. Of plot there is almost none. Southerne balances three or four separate stories through a succession of scenes loosely constructed and throws them together at the end in a perfunctory conclusion. There are four actions that may be briefly outlined:

1. The least of these is that which gives the play its title. The maid whose last prayer was answered is the old maid Lady Susan Malepert, described as "youthful virgin of five and forty, with a swelling rump, bow legs, a shining face, and colly'd eye-brows . . . she'd no more miss a ball, than the curling her little finger when she eats, tho' she hobbles worse than *Abigail* in the *Scornful Lady* when she has broke her crupper."[5] This engaging creature is paid satiric compliments by one Granger until she is sure that at last she has captured a man. When she is disillusioned on this score she makes a hurried plea to Sir Symphony, musician and simpleton, and is accepted as the last curtain comes down. "Any rather than fail." The scenes in which Lady Susan's romance is developed form but a slim part of the whole.

2. Another minor plot develops the connubial bickerings of Mrs. Siam and her husband, Captain Drydrubb. The Captain is a blustery, vociferous, boasting fellow, who lives in con-

[5] I, 1.

stant fear of cuckoldry. His wife makes a business of raffling off Indian goods and doles out guineas to Drydrubb to keep him in the tavern and out from under foot. She finally decides that he has plagued her long enough and gives him a separate maintenance to be rid of him. The Captain agrees to this heartily. "I know your grievance," he says, "you would have me begin to propagate, like a patriarch, at threescore, and try to do good in my generation: but who the devil can do good upon you? you are past it as well as I; and so faith let's have a dance, and agree upon parting in the morning."[6]

3. The main intrigue revolves about the pursuit of young Lady Malepert by Gayman. The elderly Wishwell serves as bawd to Lady Malepert, selling her friend's honor where it will bring the highest financial returns. Lord Lofty (who does not appear in the play) has grown tired of paying and is withdrawing from the picture. Wishwell favors the silly Sir Ruff Rancounter, who would be good for £1,000, and frowns on the aspirations of Gayman, whom Lady Malepert likes. Wishwell fears that her charge will fall in love with Gayman and get so far out of her clutches that she can no longer sell her to such customers as Lofty and Sir Ruff. An appointment is made by Wishwell for Sir Ruff to come to Lady Malepert's room. Gayman, overhearing this, embroils Sir Ruff in a proposed duel with Sir Symphony and takes Sir Ruff's place with Lady Malepert, who does not discover the deception until well towards morning. Even then she is not highly chagrined, for she had been trying to imagine that the man in the darkness with her was Gayman instead of Sir Ruff. Wishwell also discovers the deceit, is angered at what she considers Malepert's trick, and shuts the doors of escape on the couple just as Lord Malepert ascends the stairs. Gayman succeeds in tricking the angered Malepert into the belief that his wife is innocent of offense. Then, despising Lady Malepert because she will sell herself to anyone for money, he proposes to Maria, a girl for whom he has shown a liking,

[6] V, 1.

and announces to the company their engagement. Lady Malepert is much distressed, and Gayman is revenged.

4. Still another intrigue is that between Granger, Gayman's friend, and Lady Trickett. Granger despises Trickett but finds her suitable for his amorous purposes. Trickett, for her part, is enraged at Granger because he is unwilling to pay as handsomely as she thinks he ought to for her kindnesses. She therefore forwards to old Lady Susan a note of Granger's asking for a rendezvous at Rosamond's Pond. When Granger, expecting to find Trickett, discovers instead the hopeful Lady Susan, Trickett is in the bushes nearby to laugh at his discomfiture.

Interwoven with the story of these intrigues are episodes of a farcical nature that have nothing whatever to do with the plot. The story as a whole is disjointed and aimless; for the first two acts there is no action at all—just an amount of witty talk. In a few scenes Southerne writes in terms of true comedy, but for the most part he sinks to a level of dulness below even that of *The Wives' Excuse*.

Knaves and Fools

HERE Southerne assembles within the limits of one play as graceless a lot of rogues and simpletons as comedy could well contain. Granger and Gayman are the usual witty pair of Restoration philanderers, heartlessly bent on the eternal chase. Lady Trickett is a distinctly unpleasant person, odiously affected. She attempts to cheat Maria out of £150 at cards. Her person is for sale only to those who will bid well for it. Granger describes her vividly: "There's not a rogue so nauseous, but is welcome to her for his money: all that will be losers, lenders, or givers, have an equal claim to her good graces: from the grinning stinking lord, to the fat booby 'squire . . ."[7] No less mercenary is Wishwell, who, for a sum, handles Lady Malepert's intrigues. Over fifty, and unable to attract men herself, she accepts willingly the position

[7] I, 1.

of bawd. Her chief fear is that her mistress will fall in love with Gayman and so cut off her trade. The microcosm of Restoration comic philosophy is wrapped up in her line: "For love is nature's appetite diseas'd."[8] Lady Malepert herself is a spineless creature who is yet shrewd enough to fool her husband. Her affection for Gayman appears to be the one honest thing in her life. Granger despairs of her: "That a woman at eighteen, an age when love and pleasure us'd to rule, shou'd in the midst of plenty, value herself upon the reputation of a publican, and always sit at the receipt of custom! rot her, she has less mercy than a mountebank's bill."[7] This, then, is Southerne's gallery of knaves, and ugly enough it is.

In Lord Malepert Southerne has created one of the most amenable cuckolds in Restoration comedy. He is proud of what he calls his wit, proud of his ability in state affairs, and so conceited that he would not join the army because they told him that riding would teach him to turn in his toes and thus spoil his dancing. He even plumes himself on his wife's friendship with Lord Lofty, and on Lofty's desire to consult with her on political matters. ". . . my lord and she," he boasts, "went into the little room, with the crimson couch, to talk of state affairs."[9] Such a husband of course pays the price of his stupidity. The others frequently make fun of him to his face, hinting broadly at his wife's defection, but all such wit passes over his head. He lives in an enchanted Utopia of his own creation, and the play ends with his simple trustfulness unconfounded.

It is strange that such a dolt as this should appeal to one's sympathies, yet in an intangible way that is exactly what he does. Drydrubb calls him "beardless, shambling, wheyfac'd,"[10] and doubtless he is all of that, but there hangs over him too something of the wide-eyed, wistful eagerness for experience and the delight in his own accomplishments that was known by another aspiring person of quality, Sir An-

[8] II, 1.   [9] I, 1.   [10] II, 2.

drew Ague-cheek. His naïve enthusiasms keep pace with his almost unbelievable credulity. The pleasures of the town, that were to the others almost a business, had for him a constant charm. The prospect of a masquerade stirs his enthusiasm: "I love disguise," he chortles, "when every body knows one mightily."[11] He likes to dumbfound a country cousin.[12] "I love sweet things mightily," he says,[13] and again, "I love serenading mightily."[14] When Lady Malepert, in order to keep him from suspecting her, pretends to want to leave for the country, he waxes eloquent over the pleasures of the town: "O law! what shou'd I do in the country? There's no levées, no mall, no plays, no opera, no tea at *Siam's,* no *Hyde-Park,* no music-meeting, no basset, no drawing-room, no masquerades, nor no hackney-coaches to run about in; and you know I love running about mightily."[15] All there is to do in the country is to read, and "if I read three minutes together, I fall asleep." Then comes the revelation of the fear that must haunt all such empty minds: "and then if I shou'd chance to be alone, what wou'd become of me? I never think, but it puts me into the spleen . . ." Lord Malepert's gullibility passes understanding; still, with all his affectations, there is about the man an elusive something—a relish for living, perhaps—that gives him reality.

The most colorful person in the play is Captain Drydrubb, who had been only a corporal in the civil wars, and who, his wife tells us, had assumed the title of Captain that he might the more easily run into debt. He is jealous enough, Siam declares, to be a man of honor.[16] He blusters his way along, cursing with a vitriolic wealth of allusion and epithet. His favorite oath is "by Pompey." His breeziness is refreshing in the midst of the stuffy atmosphere of intrigue that surrounds him. A "humour" character, to be sure, but one likes him too well to class him either as rascal or fool.

As a whole, this is not a very pretty set of people. In

[11] V, 1.   [12] IV, 1.   [13] III, 3.
[14] V, 1.   [15] IV, 1.   [16] II, 1.

several instances they are debased beyond most of their brethren in Restoration comedy, whose intrigues had at least the verve and excitement of the chase. In this play, the battle of the sexes disappears before a coldly commercialized corruption. Witwoud, in *The Wives' Excuse,* found a certain inverted pleasure in playing bawd, whereas Wishwell trades on Lady Malepert's chastity for sheer love of gain. Trickett despises Granger only because he will not give enough cash for her favors. Lady Malepert is content to be hired out to the paramour whose lust brings with it the most guineas. In her case, depravity is deepened by the intrusion of emotion into a situation that was bad enough when it remained on an intellectual plane. Having just spent the night with a man whom she believed to be Sir Ruff, she languishes after Gayman: "O love! what can'st thou not do in a woman's heart! that brutal thing, whom, as I thought, I loath'd, thy gentle fires hath soften'd by degrees, and melted into *Gayman:* night be still my friend, let me not see him, and I will think it was my *Gayman* still."[17] The treatment of sex needs only a touch of such lusciousness to make it smell to heaven. It is interesting to conjecture what Wycherley might have done with such a group of characters; how he would have presented them in their iniquity only to whip them mercilessly with his satire. Southerne's method shows how far the tone of *The Maid's Last Prayer* was from that of *The Plain Dealer.* He finds in the ungenial vices of his characters no material with which to lash his age, but only the stuff of an unbarbed laughter that is critical merely in a superficial way.

The only honest person in the play is Maria, of whom we see almost nothing. Two things we learn about her: that she likes to gamble at cards, and that as a reward for her virtue she receives in marriage the libertine Gayman, who takes her as much to spite Lady Malepert as for any love he bears her. This match, it is to be feared, would prove for Maria the biggest gamble of all.

[17] V, 1.

These are the puppets who dance on our author's wires of sensuality or silliness. A comparison of this play with *The Wives' Excuse* makes clear the paucity of Southerne's inventive fertility. The characters in both are drawn from the same bag. Gayman and Granger, Lovemore and Wilding, are the same witty rakes under different names. Wishwell is another bawd like Witwoud, Malepert an affected fool as ripe for antlers as was Friendall. In each play there is a rendezvous at Rosamond's Pond, and in each an assignation in which the people are deceived as to each other's identity, and in which the erring one is discovered by his spouse. Such a situation of mistaken identity is one without which Southerne seemed unable to complete a comedy. *Sir Anthony Love, The Wives' Excuse, The Maid's Last Prayer,* and *Oroonoko,* all, with slight variations, make use of the same formula.[18] Once he had tried a character or a situation and found it good, Southerne was not likely to cast it aside merely because it was worn. It must be remembered, of course, that the whole pattern of Restoration comedy was closely circumscribed. The current conception of character did not allow a wide range of freedom to one who, like Southerne, was content to write within conventional limits.

There is, however, one character whose motives are directly the opposite of her prototype's in *The Wives' Excuse.* Southerne had learned through unfortunate experience that a faithful wife was a dangerous burden to any comedy. So in place of the virtuous Mrs. Friendall he sets Lady Malepert, of whose corruptibility there could be no doubt. The contrast

[18] Nicoll (*Restoration Drama,* p. 229) calls attention to the fact that a comedy by "J.D." called *The Mall, or The Modish Lovers* (D.L., 1674) had employed a situation similar to that in which Lady Malepert discovers that she has had an assignation with Gayman instead of with Sir Ruff. In *The Mall,* Mrs. Woodbee mistakes Courtwell in the dark for her neglectful husband, Lovemore, and in that belief yields to him. The two are not surprised by anyone, as were Lady Malepert and Gayman.

furnishes an illuminating commentary on Southerne's eagerness to trim his plays to fit the public's demand.

As would appear from what has already been said, the plot, dialogue, and characterizations of *The Maid's Last Prayer* are of about the same calibre as those of *The Wives' Excuse*. Now and then, to be sure, one comes as it were by chance on a scene of which a greater than Southerne might well have been proud. Such a one is that in which Granger baits Lady Susan by the shores of the Pond, or the last climactic episode where Gayman and Lady Malepert are caught together by the latter's husband, whom suspicion has finally overtaken. Oases like these are few in a desert of scenes the most of which are congenitally dull. One even becomes grateful for such interludes of obvious farce as that of Sir Symphony's concert, where, as that maestro tunes his bass viol, two "bullies" unwind the pegs over his head and draw his bow through a candle. When they finally enrage him so that he breaks his bass viol over their heads slapstick becomes a relief. With all the good-will in the world, it is impossible to grant Southerne in this play any high degree of comic success. His failure is the more irritating because of those occasional stretches of truly meritorious achievement which he was unable to maintain with any consistency.

CHAPTER VII

THE FATAL MARRIAGE, or THE INNOCENT
ADULTERY

> *Each Bosom heav'd, all Eyes were seen to flow,*
> *And sympathize with Isabella's Woe.*
> —Fenton's Prologue to *The Spartan Dame*.

THREE comedies in as many years had run from Southerne's pen before he turned at last for his dramatic medium to tears instead of laughter. In February, 1694, *The Fatal Marriage, or The Innocent Adultery* appeared at Drury Lane, and overnight its author became the most popular tragic dramatist of the day. To be sure, there were few to dispute his reign. Lee had followed Otway to whatever Elysium awaits popular but starving playwrights. Rowe would not venture the stage for six years yet; Congreve had still to make his single excursion into tragedy. Dryden's career was closing, and with the possible exception of John Banks, who was still turning English history to dramatic use, Southerne was the only playwright in London who could be looked to for solid achievement in tragedy. There were many who could turn the comedy of manners as neatly as he, but none for whom fair tears would flow as freely.

The Fatal Marriage was an immediate success. To some degree the honor went to the distinguished cast which first acted it. Mrs. Barry, the most famous tragic actress of her day, brought to the part of Isabella the same sympathetic power that she had shown as Monimia and Belvidera in Otway's tragedies. Southerne acknowledges his debt to her in the Dedication: "I could not, if [I] would, conceal what I owe Mrs. Barry; and I should despair of ever being able to pay her, if I did not imagine that I have been a little accessary to the great applause that every body gives her, in saying she out-plays herself . . . I made the play for her part, and her part has made the play for me; it was a helpless infant in the arms of the father, but has grown under her care; I gave it just motion enough to crawl into the world, but by her power and spirit of playing, she has breathed a soul into it, that may keep it alive."

Mrs. Bracegirdle appeared as the vivacious Victoria, Betterton himself played Villeroy, and Powell took the part of Carlos. Underhill, the great comedian, played Sampson, the porter.

Motteux reports the play's success in his *Gentleman's Journal* for March, 1694. "Mr. *Southern's* new Play call'd, *The Fatal Marriage:* or, *The Innocent Adultery,* has been so kindly receiv'd, that you are by this time no stranger to its merit. As the world has done it justice, and it is above my praise, I need not expatiate on that subject. . . . [The play is] one that has deservedly ingross'd all the Applause which the Town can well bestow in some time on new Dramatic Entertainments."[1]

Malone prints a letter by an unknown correspondent dated "London, March the 22, 1693-4," which includes *The Fatal Marriage* in its discussion of the new plays.[2] Of Congreve's *Double-Dealer* the writer says: "It has fared with that play as it generally does with beauties officiously cried up; the mighty expectation which was raised of it made it sink, even beneath its own merit." Dryden's *Love Triumphant* is "in my opinion one of the worst he ever writt, if not the very worst. . . . It was damn'd by the universal cry of the town, *nemine contradicente,* but the conceited poet." Of Settle's *Ambitious Slave:* "I never saw a piece so wretched, nor worse contrived." Certainly this playgoer cannot be accused of easy liking. But *The Fatal Marriage* he praises unreservedly: "It is not only the best that author ever writt, but is generally admired for one of the greatest ornaments of the stage, and the most entertaining play has appeared on it these 7 years.

[1] p. 63.
[2] *Historical Account of the English Stage,* 1800, pp. 179-80 n.

... I never saw Mrs. Barry act with so much passion as she does in it; I could not forbear being moved even to tears to see her act."

Old Downes bears further witness to the continued popularity of the play to 1706. "These 3 plays," he says [*The Orphan, Venice Preserved,* and *The Fatal Marriage*], "by their Excellent performances, took above all the Modern Plays that succeeded."[3] The legend runs that Dryden, being asked on the first night of the play his opinion of Southerne's genius, declared that he thought him another such genius as Otway.[4] Beyond all question Southerne's first tragedy had established his reputation in the form.

In his dedication to "Ant: Hammond, Esq. of Somersham-Place" Southerne confessed himself "indebted to the goodnature of the town in general," and more particularly to "the indulgence and patronage of particular men of quality, who were all most industrious and contriving for the fortune of this play; to make it considerable to the world in its reputation, and to me in the profit of the third day." Anthony Hammond (1668-1738) was a wit, poet, and pamphleteer who became an M.P. in 1695 and obtained in Parliament a reputation as an eminent speaker. He edited a *Miscellany of Original Poems* (1720) of which no small share was his own. Evidently he fancied himself as a writer, for there is an entry in his manuscript diary, under date of August 14, 1694, of somewhat amusing interest here. "I was married at Tunbridge, and went from there to Northiam. About the latter end of Feb: Mr. Tho. Southerne dedicated the play called the Fatal Marriage, or Innocent Adultery to me. I perus'd it

---

[3] *Roscius Anglicanus*, facsimile reprint of the original of 1708. Ed. Joseph Knight, 1886, p. 38.

[4] See Cibber's *Lives*, V, 329. "When this reply was communicated to Mr. Southern," the story goes on, "he considered it as a very great compliment, having no ambition to be thought a more considerable poet than Otway was." And indeed *The Fatal Marriage* owes much in tone and treatment to *Venice Preserved* and *The Orphan*.

The Fatal Marriage

as it was writ and alter'd, or added as I thought fit."[5] It may be assumed that his share in the writing was slight.

Southerne's elation over the success of his tragedy may be imagined. His modesty did not prevent him from prefixing to the first edition (though to no other) some very honied lines by one "W.S.," who was in all probability William Smith (d. 1696), the famous actor, barrister of Gray's Inn, and man of social position. First in the Duke of York's Company under Sir William Davenant, and later at Lincoln's-Inn-Fields and the new Theatre Royal he created many important parts, among which was that of Lorenzo in Southerne's *Disappointment*. He retired from the stage after the accession of James II, but returned to play Scandal in *Love for Love* in 1695.[6] Here, in involved metaphor, he mourns his inability to praise Southerne sufficiently, going on to say

> Should I attempt to say what Praise is due,
> 'Twere to tell all, what they already knew.
> So fine your Passions; so sublime your Thought;
> All, ev'ry part, so exquisitely wrote;
> So short your Repartees and yet so plain,
> That Criticks lose their old accustom'd Aim.
> . . . .
> Whilst through the Theatres, the Court, and Town
> Fame speaks aloud, and makes the Author known.

Ever-sensitive to the public dramatic-pulse, Southerne could be counted upon to capitalize to its fullest extent this his first major triumph. He might not appear to speak for himself, but he would make sure that Fame's speech was not altogether unheard.

The Story and its Sources

THE main plot of *The Fatal Marriage*, like those of all Southerne's tragic actions, is very simple in outline. Biron,

---

[5] *Diary* of Anthony Hammond, Rawlinson Mss. A245, Bodleian. [R.G.H.]

[6] See *D.N.B.*, XVIII, 552.

reported dead after his capture by pirates at the "siege of Candy," returns to Brussels after a forced seven years' absence to find that his wife, though still grieving for him, has bestowed her hand if not her heart upon the honorable and generous Villeroy, who has been pleading for her love for seven years. Isabella agrees to marry him only after she has been spurned by her father-in-law, Count Baldwin, and after Villeroy has satisfied, unknown to her at the time, the creditors who were forcing her to financial ruin. The fatal marriage has been promoted by Carlos, the scheming brother of the supposedly dead Biron, in his eagerness to clear his own title to the inheritance. Carlos has been intercepting his brother's letters and answering them himself, warning Biron against returning home. Unlike Enoch Arden, the returned husband, ignorant of the second marriage, reveals himself to his wife. The main characters are innocent of crime, yet are unable to resolve a seemingly hopeless situation. The adultery, though innocent, proves fatal, and the play ends with the treacherous killing of Biron by Carlos and the madness and ultimate suicide of Isabella. Before the end, the villainy of Carlos is exposed through the forced confession of one of his accomplices in the murder.

The sub-plot, which is very loosely connected with the main plot, concerns the courtship and elopement of Frederick and Victoria under the very eyes of old Fernando, Victoria's jealous and suspicious father. Fabian, brother to Victoria, abets the marriage in order that he, at present in disgrace with his father, might upon Victoria's defection be reinstated and assured of the whole family fortune. Julia, Fernando's young wife, aids a plan by which her husband is given a sleeping potion. When he awakes, he is made to believe that he has been dead and in purgatory and is revived only by a miracle—whereupon he renounces his jealous ways forever, and receives again to his arms his wife and his estranged children.

An extremely simple source-problem was for some time

complicated by a curious set of circumstances. Southerne himself, with an habitual disarming frankness that makes source-hunting frequently an unnecessary sport, says in his Preface to the play that he got a "hint" for his story, but little more, from a novel of Mrs. Aphra Behn's called *The Fair Vow-Breaker*. In his life of Southerne in the 1774 collected edition of the plays, Thomas Evans amplifies this title to *The Nun, or Fair Vow-Breaker*. No novel under this title had been printed in any of the collected editions of Mrs. Behn's works, but Mr. P. Hamelius of Liége, attacking in 1909 the problem of Southerne's source,[7] declared that Mr. Edmund Gosse had informed him that the plot was the same as that of Behn's *The Nun, or the Perjured Beauty,* which in turn has only a very slight resemblance to the play. This set Hamelius off on a hunt for Spanish parallels. The difficulty of finding a suitable source drove him to the conclusion that Southerne was perhaps drawing from some lost version of the story by Mrs. Behn herself. That his inference was correct was proved when Gosse lent Mr. Montague Summers his copy of *The Nun, or the Fair Vow-Breaker* (pub. 1689) and it was found to have the same plot as Southerne's play. Mr. Summers printed the text of this novel in his collected edition of Mrs. Behn's works, in 1915.[8]

Southerne surcharges with tragic pathos what with Mrs. Behn is a rather ordinary tale of blood, working, as we shall see, with the sure instinct of a trained craftsman in the theatre. But even a cursory examination of novel and play shows that Southerne took far more than a "hint" from his source; in many details the plots are the same. Thus the names are

---

[7] *Mod. Lang. Rev.,* April, 1909. IV, 352 ff.

[8] V, 262–324. It might be mentioned here that the conjecture of Ward (III, 421 n.) and others that Southerne's *Innocent Adultery* is the book mentioned in Sheridan's *Rivals* (I, 2) is shown by Professor G. H. Nettleton (*Major Dramas of Sheridan,* N.Y., 1906, lxxiv) to have been wrong. It was Scarron's novel of that title that Lydia Languish perused.

similar. The heroine in both pieces is Isabella; her second husband is in the novel Villenoy, in the play, Villeroy. Beroone, the name assumed by Isabella's first husband, Henault, becomes Biron with Southerne. In both versions Isabella renounces her vows as a nun to marry, and as a result is looked on with disfavor by her father-in-law, though she is forgiven by the church. The lost husband's seven-year period of slavery is the same in novel and play. Southerne follows his source very closely in the scene of return and recognition: the changed appearance of the husband, his ring conveyed to Isabella by the servant, Isabella's terror, her renewed hope when she sees an apparent stranger, and finally the horrible revelation. Many minor details are the same. Both Isabellas are concerned about their reputations:

(The novel, p. 312, Summers' ed.)	(The play, IV, 3.)
She finds by his Return, she is not only expos'd to all the Shame imaginable; to all the Upbraiding, on his part, when he shall know she is marry'd to another; but all the Fury and Rage of Villenoys, and the Scorn of the Town, who will look on her as an Adulteress.	Isa. My reputation! O, 'twas all was left me;/The virtuous pride of an uncensur'd life;/Which the dividing tongues of *Biron's* wrongs,/And *Villeroy's* resentments tear asunder,/To gorge the throats of the blaspheming rabble.

Each Isabella, too, leaves her returned husband to go to her prayers, and with the same result:

(The novel, p. 315.)	(The play, IV, 3.)
'Tis true, *Isabella* essay'd to Pray, but alas! it was in vain, she was distracted with a thousand Thoughts what to do, which the more she thought, the more it distracted her; she was a thousand times about to end her life . . .	Isa. I'll but say my prayers, and follow you—/My prayers! no, I must ne'er pray again. * * * * * * * And what's to come, is a long line of woe;/Yet I may shorten it—

The changes that Southerne makes in his material are, however, much more significant than his borrowings. Here we can watch his mind at work in an attempt to throw the story into a new pattern, with an entirely different emphasis. His conception of tragic character was not that of Mrs. Behn's, nor did the novel's rather stark account of the fatal consequences attending the violation of sacred vows strike the springs of pity that it was his purpose to tap. "Punishment follows broken vows" is the declared moral of the novel. Southerne ignores such a conception of guilt and disaster; the only hostile reflections on Isabella's desertion of the nunnery are placed in the mouth of Count Baldwin, and it is made clear that his anger is based on his son's failure to marry a dowry. In denying *The Fatal Marriage* the status of true domestic tragedy, Professor Bernbaum bases his contention on the supposition that "the miseries of Isabella are at times thought of as justly incurred."[9] But a moral stigma is placed on Isabella's conduct only by Count Baldwin, and is on his part entirely hypocritical.

Up to the crisis of the husband's return, Southerne's divergences from his source are not striking. But thence to the conclusion he deserts the novel to hew out his own conception of tragic fate and character. The Isabella of the novel, with two husbands on her hands, strangles the one she had thought dead. Villenoy, her second husband, helps her dump the body into a sack to be taken to the river. Isabella, determined to destroy all possibly accusing evidence, sews the sack to Villenoy's coat, so that when he swings the corpse over the bridge he follows it to the bottom. In spite of her ingenuity, Isabella is discovered as the double murderess, and at last ascends the scaffold, breathing a warning to all vow-breakers.

Southerne's heroine is of different stuff. True, she approaches Biron to stab him as he sleeps, but she is temporarily mad, and is saved the deed by a sudden return of her senses. Solution by murder is not within the conception of her character. Her part is to suffer, and to die ultimately on the horns of a dilemma beyond her power of escape, rather

[9] *Drama of Sensibility*, pp. 56–7.

than to show assertiveness either of crime or of innocence. It is passive endurance on the part of stricken purity and beauty to which Southerne directs our attention. Pity rather than terror is the chief element of his tragic method. Since both husbands are as incapable of solving the tangle as is Isabella herself, that responsibility falls on the shoulders of the accommodating villain, Carlos. His creation is entirely Southerne's, for Mrs. Behn had no need of such a catalytic agent when Isabella herself had more than the necessary determination.

There are other minor changes. In the novel, Villenoy preceded Henault to the siege of Candia, saw, as he thought, his friend fall there, and returned to woo Isabella. In the play there is no indication that Villeroy had ever been at Candia or had ever known Biron. Thus Southerne neglected to use the hint offered him by Mrs. Behn, and make the two men friends. Villenoy and Henault, in the source, never meet after Henault's return; Villenoy sees his rival only after he has been killed by Isabella. The dramatic conflict is here increased in the play by placing in opposition the distress of Biron and Villeroy over the impossible situation. Again, the Isabella of the novel remarries within three years of the reported death of her husband, while in the play she waits seven years. In the former, five years elapse after Isabella's second marriage before Henault returns from the dead; in the latter he re-appears, much more dramatically, on the wedding night. Southerne also introduces with good pathetic effect Isabella's child, only mentioned in the novel.

The general trend of Southerne's alterations and additions is clear; he has softened the character of Isabella and given it that pathos and tenderness which it lacked in the novel. Beyond this, he has by skilful changes in emphasis and by more subtle development of characterization enriched the situation with a depth of humanity that it originally lacked. A study of his use of Mrs. Behn's story, while revealing clearly his limitations in tragic power, helps us to understand with what precision he fashioned his elements to give the effect intended.

There remains to be indicated the source of the comic portion of *The Fatal Marriage,* and it may be well to include here all that is to be said about the sub-plot in its artistic relation to the play. The relative slightness of the tragic action is emphasized by the prominence that Southerne gives his comic scenes—without which, as became evident in Garrick's adaptation, the play was so shortened that an afterpiece was necessary to pad out an evening's entertainment. Although the last act is entirely concerned with the tragic catastrophe, a full half of the first four acts is given over to the bustling intrigue of the comic action. It is significant that in including such a plot in his two major tragedies, Southerne ran contrary not only to the accepted critical dicta of the time, but to the practice of those dramatists most temperamentally akin to him: Otway[10] and Rowe. Instead of tragedy he gives us definite tragi-comedy. Nothing indicates better the temper of Southerne's artistic sensitiveness and at the same time his frankly professional attitude toward the theatre than the slight uneasiness under which he labored as he presented his tragi-comedy to the world. "I have given you a little taste of comedy with it," he says in his Dedication, "not from my own opinion, but the present humour of the town: I never contend that because I think every reasonable man will, and ought to govern in the pleasures he pays for." The drama's laws the drama's patrons give![11]

---

[10] *Venice Preserved* has, of course, some comic admixture, but *The Orphan* is straight tragedy. And even in the former play, the comic elements are relatively slight.

[11] Without discussing the effectiveness of tragi-comedy as an artistic form, I think it worth noting that the two plots here do contain a motive that is the same, although one plot develops its comic implications, the other its tragic: in each plot a scheming brother tries to marry his sister (or sister-in-law) out of the family in order to secure for himself the estate.

The comedy is neither organic to the play nor strikingly original in conception. Main plot and sub-plot are joined only perfunctorily; Carlos, villain of the chief action, and Frederick, the young lover of the minor action, are friends. Frederick understands something of Carlos' motives in marrying Isabella to Villeroy, and Carlos takes part in Frederick's plot against old Fernando. Villeroy is a kinsman of Fernando's, and as a result Fernando, Victoria, Fabian, and Frederick—all members of the underplot—attend Isabella's wedding; more, we feel, to fill the stage with wedding-guests than to assume an integral part in the tragedy. The comic characters are types cut from the well-worn pattern of Restoration humor. We see again a woman in man's clothes, an old husband who has married a young wife and who reeks with the not altogether unjustifiable suspicion that he is a cuckold; we hear the bickering scenes between husband and wife, and the asides of the witty man-servant. *Double-entendre* pokes up its head at frequent intervals, and over all is thrown the glitter of that which would pass for comic gold.

To say, however, that Southerne here succeeds only in rearranging the stock formulae of Restoration comedy is to do him less than justice. He invests these scenes with a hearty and a true humor. Their effectiveness lies not so much in the sallies of wit, which are not particularly brilliant, as in the genuine humor of situation, for which Southerne had always an instinctive tact. Strangely enough, some of his best comic writing lies here in the midst of his best tragedy, and is inserted to give body to an otherwise too-short play. There are at least three episodes of high comic merit. In the first, while Fernando is grumbling at Frederick and daring him to try to communicate with his daughter Victoria, Frederick's servant manages to tie a letter to the old man's coat-tails, from which precarious position it is later rescued by Victoria herself, even as her father is telling her sardonically that *he* would be happy to be their messenger; just let them give *him* their letters! Later, Frederick advances with ladder and lantern to elope with Victoria. The girl is about to descend, when her father surprises her, takes her place, and descends the ladder to confront Frederick with a blunderbuss. Just as he is triumphing, Victoria walks out of the house in man's clothes, and while her father cries "thief!" she escapes with Frederick. Frederick does not recognize her either, nor does she reveal her identity until she has baited him for a time with stories of how she (he) was Victoria's paramour. The climax of the sub-plot is reached in the strange cure for jealousy inflicted on Fernando by his wife and family. He is drugged and laid in a tomb. Upon awakening he is made to believe that he has been dead and in purgatory. So glad is he to be restored even to a world of cuckoldry, and so pleased to hear of his wife's sorrow for his death, that he swears to reform.

Southerne develops these situations with a good sense of comic values. The gusto which animates them bespeaks an almost Elizabethan vitality. There is one touch, however, that foreshadows the new morality that was descending upon the drama that had been Wycherley's and Vanbrugh's. Her husband drugged, Julia is pursued by Carlos for the customary purpose. With strange resolution, she who had so often threatened to plant horns on her husband's head, now refuses to do so. "But for the future, sir," she addresses her would-be seducer, "you may believe there are women, who won't be provok'd to injure their husbands."[12] Carlos nevertheless replies in the ancient tradition: "O virtue! virtue! what an enemy art thou to a woman's good inclinations!"

Gildon first pointed out that "the Hint of *Fernando* being persuaded to believe that he had been dead, buried, and in Purgatory, seems to be owing to *The Little Thief* of *Fletcher.*"[13] *The Night Walker, or The Little Thief* (pub. 1640) written by Fletcher and revised by Rowley, was a popular play in the Restoration theatre. Part of the plot concerns a greedy justice, Algripe, who is given a sleeping po-

---
[12] IV, 1.
[13] Gildon's Langbaine's *Lives,* p. 135.

tion. When he awakes he is threatened by two persons, as Furies, intent on carrying him to hell. He repents and forswears usury and lechery for the rest of his life. It is more probable, however, that Southerne got the machinery of his trick from a story of Boccaccio's in the *Decameron,* the eighth story of the third day. There Ferondo (whose name is more reminiscent of Fernando's) is drugged and entombed for dead by an abbot bent on enjoying his victim's wife. After he is aroused, Ferondo is made by the monks to believe that he is in purgatory. He is finally set free to rear as his own "a child begotten of the abbot on his wife." Southerne borrows only the outline of the deception; the story he makes his own.

Since Southerne's venture twelve years before with *The Loyal Brother* into the realms of heroic drama, he had written only the comedies discussed above. *The Loyal Brother* he had called a "Tragedy" but it was in fact less than that. On the other hand, *The Fatal Marriage* he terms simply a "play," when it is tragedy in the true sense. There is indeed little in his previous writing to prepare us for this success; attempting a new form, he bursts full-blown upon the world of tragedy with what is beyond reasonable question his best play. He deals here with love that is domestic rather than heroic, trusting for his appeal to the sympathies of the human heart and not to any gigantic conception of princely love or honor. Southerne of course was no pioneer in the field of sentimental tragedy. Otway had already made familiar to Restoration playgoers the spectacle of innocence in distress, and Banks with his she-tragedies had pushed a little further the feminine tendency in drama. Otway in particular had substituted pity for fear in the formula of tragedy, and in *The Fatal Marriage* Southerne only perpetuates the tradition of *The Orphan.* Although he was no originator, he was intensely sensitive to the trend of the times. The shoals of bourgeois drama lay beyond the turn of the century, yet it is possible to trace thus early the encroaching softening and domestication of tragedy which was to find logical issue in *The London Merchant.*

Southerne's Tragic Method

ANY discussion of *The Fatal Marriage* must center on the character of Isabella, for in every sense the tragedy is hers. If not the first, she is certainly the most famous of Southerne's suffering heroines. We never see her really happy. Our first glimpse of her is as she is being driven from the doors of her cruel father-in-law. Soon her creditors descend like vultures to seize her few remaining household goods, and she is saved from financial ruin only by the intervention of Villeroy, whom she then marries more out of kindness and gratitude than love. Rapidly a darker fate settles down upon her: Biron returns, she discovers that she is a bigamist, and before long madness and death are her portion. Here is purity engulfed by a storm not of its own brewing, whose lot is not to act but to be acted upon by a destiny from which there is no escape. Something of the inevitability of Greek tragedy hovers over the play. Isabella accepts her fate as something written in the stars. Thus she exclaims:

> Do I deserve to be this outcast wretch?
> Abandon'd thus, and lost? But 'tis my lot,
> The will of heav'n, and I must not complain.[14]

Again, in response to the nurse's question "what will you do, madam?" she replies "Do! nothing, no, for I am born to suffer." And when Biron returns and she realizes her fatal dilemma, her resignation is still complete:

> The baleful planet rises on my fate,
> And what's to come, is a long line of woe.[15]

Yet the tone of the play is far from Greek, for Southerne's emphasis is on the pathos of the situation and his tears are

[14] II, 2.   [15] IV, 3.

those of sensibility. Moreover, the feeling of fate which is an element of great tragedy and is seemingly persistent here is weakened for us by the realization that had the protagonists contemplated their situation sanely, it would not have proved unresolvable. The acquisition of two husbands need not in itself argue any moral guilt on the part of the unfortunate wife, but such a degree of intellectual analysis is wholly beyond the minds of Southerne's characters, to whom it is given to feel rather than to think. With the exception of the energetic Carlos, the main characters accept the situation as given. Southerne would lead us into a dramatic impasse where we can only exclaim "the pity of it!" His pathos, then, is not that of Shakespeare's which lies in the spectacle of a noble soul in conflict with itself. There is little internal conflict in *The Fatal Marriage;* the characters are exceptionally simple in motive. It is their part to suffer rather than to do. It may be said that Desdemona herself had no chance to fight the chain of circumstances that sent her to her death, but then Desdemona is not the chief object of our interest in *Othello,* while Isabella *is* the play for Southerne. But for the attack on our tenderer sensibilities there would be no play. As a heroine, then, Isabella lacks the necessary tragic flaw, unless, indeed, it be that of an inability to come to grips with a distressing situation. Southerne would have us believe her in the vise of a circumstance not of human making and beyond her power to modify. Nothing is left but to die.

This brings us to the heart of Southerne's failure as a great tragic dramatist: his poverty of intellectual incisiveness. The play is sicklied o'er with the pale cast of thought, but too frequently that which seems like thought is only emotion. Again and again the characters seem to think when they only feel. A brooding sententiousness is substituted for the warm glow of living idea. Isabella warns all women never to "think they can be safe Within the reach and tongues of tempting men."[16] Again,

[16] I, 3.

The Fatal Marriage

> Hope is a lying, fawning flatterer,
> That shews the fair side only of our fortunes.[17]
>
> . . . .
>
> Sooner or later all things pass away,
> And are no more: the beggar and the king,
> With equal steps, tread forward to their end.[18]
>
> . . . .
>
> The load grows light, when we resolve to bear.[19]

Such examples could be multiplied endlessly. Indeed, the play ends with an aphoristic moral:

> Hence learn, offending children to forgive:
> Leave punishment to heav'n, 'tis heav'n's prerogative.[20]

Plot and Pathos

IT would be unfair to dwell longer on what Southerne fails to give us, and to ignore the positive values of his tragedy. He has been justly compared with Otway; to say only that he falls short of Shakespeare is to obscure the importance of his relation not only to the drama of his time but to the whole development of English tragedy. He had to a greater degree than most a power over the affections of the human heart. With a simple directness remarkably free from bombast he could wring the last degree of pathos from such a spectacle of unmerited suffering as Isabella's. Here is found at once his true worth and the secret of his popularity for nearly a century and a half.

Southerne's dramatic technique contributes much to the unity of effect in *The Fatal Marriage*. Isabella remains the center of storm throughout the play. The characters of the others involved are clearly indicated—the nobility of Villeroy, the baffled helplessness of Biron, Count Baldwin's coldness and Carlos' iniquity—but all are of interest only as they concern Isabella. The play's tragic action proceeds firmly and economically to its climax. Isabella's fortunes, low at the be-

[17] IV, 3.   [18] II, 2.   [19] II, 3.   [20] V, 5.

ginning, take on a glow of false hope when she marries Villeroy, but sink again still lower when Biron returns and precipitates the catastrophe. Simplicity and directness mark the plot development, which moves in steady crescendo through a series of dramatic scenes. The first of these—Isabella's encounter with Count Baldwin—is effectively charged with pathos through the introduction of Isabella's child, and the intensity of the mother's determination not to give him to the Count, even though she might have to beg from door to door "to feed his daily wants."[21] "Then have your child, and feed him with your prayer," is Baldwin's reply. Melancholy smiles hopefully in the next important scene, in which Villeroy pays off Isabella's creditors and wins her reluctant consent to marry him. The first major climax appears with the return of Biron and Isabella's consequent wild distraction. From this the play proceeds rapidly through the violence of her grief to her maddened attempt to kill Biron, and then her later attempt, upon coming to her senses, to stab herself. Villeroy prevents her, but before long her tortured mind cracks altogether, and driving a knife to her heart, she dies beside the body of Biron, who has himself been murdered by Carlos.

There is a constant heightening of dramatic potential throughout this succession of episodes. Southerne rises each time to a little higher climax, until finally humanity can bear the load no longer, and death closes what would soon become intolerable anguish. The sentiments do not always ring true, to be sure, notably in the last act when Isabella "throws herself upon the floor; after a short pause . . . raises herself upon her elbow" and in a soliloquy as long as it is unconvincing, traces the growth of madness in her own brain. But such false notes are few. Usually, the intensity of the passion burns the dross from the dramatic ore.

[21] This use of a child for pathetic effect is common in the tragedy of the time. Addison ridicules the abuse of the device in the *Spectator*, No. 44.

Southerne's skill in plotting appears again in the introduction of the porter and the nurse. They are not only useful to convey necessary exposition at the first of the play, but with their garrulous comments they offer in the midst of the tragic action a certain degree of natural comic relief. They serve still another and more important function. They are the only participants in the tragic story who are not immediately concerned in the series of disastrous events. Hence amid a group of people flushed with their own emotions, they constitute a norm, or point of rest, to which all divergences may be referred. Addison's attention was caught by this homely clearheadedness of Sampson, the porter. He writes in the *Spectator*:[22] "It is something pleasant enough to consider the different notions, which different persons have of the same thing. . . . Common people are, in particular, very much astonished, when they hear of those solemn contests and debates, which are made among the great upon the punctilios of a public ceremony. . . . I am mightily pleased with a porter's decision, in one of Mr. Southerne's plays. . . . [When Biron returns] honest Sampson thinks the matter may be easily decided, and solves it very judiciously, by the old proverb, that if his master be still living, 'The man must have his mare again.'"

Throughout the play Southerne reveals in the tragic plot a direct simplicity that strengthens the prevailing impression of pathos.

Elizabethan Elements

By the side of the pathetic strain that forms the most distinctive quality of Southerne's tragedy there runs a note that can only be called Elizabethan and that calls our attention to the continuity to be traced in English tragedy. This is found here in Shakespearian reminiscences, but even more in a cer-

[22] No. 481. Thursday, Sept. 11, 1712. See G. A. Aitken's edition, 8 vols., 1898. VII, 37 f.

tain intensity of emotion which gives occasional passages kinship with the passionate ejaculations of the late Elizabethans. Thus the scenes in the last act in which Isabella goes mad have a violent power beyond that of mere pity. Torn between her two allegiances, she cries out

> *Villeroy* and *Biron* come: O! hide me from 'em—
> They rack, they tear; let 'em carve out my limbs,
> Divide my body to their equal claims:
> My soul is only *Biron's;* that is free,
> And thus I strike for him, and liberty.[23]
> (*Going to stab herself,* Villeroy *runs in, and prevents her.*)

A little later, Biron has died upon her kiss, and Isabella for a moment comes to herself:

> Where have I been! methinks I stand upon
> The brink of life, ready to shoot the gulph
> That lies between me and the realms of rest;
> But still detain'd, I cannot pass the streight.
> Deny'd to live, and yet I must not die.
> Doom'd to come back like a complaining ghost,
> To my unbury'd body—Here it lies
> (*Throws herself by* Biron's *body.*)
> My body, soul, and life. A little dust
> To cover our cold limbs in the dark grave,
> There, there we shall sleep safe and sound together.[24]

When they attempt to take her away from Biron, "she drags the body after her, they get her into their arms, and carry her off."

> O, they tear me! cut off my hands,
> Let me leave something with him,
> They'll clasp him fast—
> O cruel, cruel men.[24]

Webster or Ford might have written that. The very frenzy of maddened despair is in it, as it is also in the same scene

[23] V, 4.   [24] V, 4.

when Isabella, with her mind at last totally incoherent, enters distracted, "held by her women, her hair dishevel'd, her little son running in before, being afraid of her."[24] The fright of the child adds the last touch of gruesome terror to a use of madness which is itself another link with the Elizabethan playwrights.

In the use of physical horror as well Southerne's method echoes the old tragedy of blood. At one point in the last act the scene is suddenly thrown open and there, stretched upon a rack on the inner stage, is Pedro, one of Carlos' accomplices in the murder of Biron. He is tortured until he confesses the crime. This use of the Elizabethan inner stage is also typical of Southerne's structural technique. Frequently there are directions within the act such as this: "Scene opens, and shows Carlos and Villeroy with the officers." Or, "Scene drawn, shows Biron asleep on a couch."

Shakespeare's influence is thrown in a diffused light over the whole play. Carlos, for instance, is much like Edmund in *King Lear*. The one, because he is a younger brother, the other, because he is illegitimate, is deprived of his inheritance. Each revolts against his fate, and lays a plot against his brother. Neither plans murder at first, but is led deeper into crime as the play advances. Carlos, when he enters into the comic plot against Fernando, shows also something of Edmund's sense of humor. Much of the verbal coloring is Shakespearian. Isabella, when Biron sends her his ring, describes such spells and portents as Gloucester might have spoken of to Edmund:[25]

> I've heard of witches, magic spells, and charms,
> That have made nature start from her old course:
> The sun has been eclips'd, the moon drawn down
> From her career, still paler, and subdu'd
> To the abuses of this under world:
> Now I believe all possible.[26]

[25] *King Lear*, I, 2.   [26] *Fatal Marriage*, IV, 3.

In the same scene, Biron, still ignorant of the true situation, but disturbed by Isabella's obvious distress, tries to quiet her:

> The fit is past; all may be well again,
> Let us to bed.

Here is the same unconscious irony as that in the speech of Claudius, in *Hamlet,* who in the face of impending catastrophe murmurs just before he prays, "All may be well."[27] One more Shakespearian coloring is discernible in Isabella's speech as she commits suicide—a speech which rises to a climax identical with Othello's:

> Will nothing do! I did not hope to find
> Justice on earth; 'tis not in heav'n neither.
> *Biron* hath watch'd his opportunity.
> Softly; he steals it from the sleeping gods,
> And sends it thus.
> (*Stabs herself.*)[28]

The Poetry

SOUTHERNE was celebrated in his own day and throughout the eighteenth century for the simplicity and naturalness of his poetry. Motteux commends one of his plays for "the Purity of its Language."[29] George Colman the Elder speaks of him as one possessed of the "antient Simplicity," and calls him "the last of our Dramatick Writers, who was, in any Degree, possest of that magnificent Plainness, which is the genuine Dress of Nature."[30] Francis Gentleman praises him as "remarkably free in his versification."[31] It is true that his blank verse in this play lacks the heroic ranting, the artificial and inflated diction that had come to be associated with Restoration tragedy. It can be effectively simple at times and

---

[27] III, 3.   [28] V, 5.
[29] *Gentleman's Journal,* Jan., 1691/2, p. 52.
[30] In *Critical Reflections on the Old English Dramatick Writers,* prefaced to Coxeter's ed. of Massinger (4 vols., 1761), I, 20-21.
[31] *Dramatic Censor, or Critical Companion,* 2 vols., 1770. II, 470.

The Fatal Marriage 119

bitingly intense at others. But in spite of this the total effect of the verse is not that of great poetry. He gains a good degree of variety from a relatively small vocabulary, yet does not possess that fine sensitiveness to words which can bend them to its will. All comes gracefully but too easily, and there are many long stretches where smoothness becomes simply lack of color. Occasionally the poetry slips into the trap that waits for too-barren simplicity, and becomes just iambic prose; again, in the more elevated portions, where the aphoristic thought is not sufficient to fertilize the emotion, it takes on the sponginess of ill-health.

Yet if there is not much that is distinguished, there is little that is ignoble. Such a passage as the following illustrates the level excellence of much of Southerne's verse, tightening at the end into a simple poignancy of which it was frequently capable.

> *Isa.* When thou shalt hear how much thou hast been wrong'd,
> How wilt thou curse thy fond believing heart,
> Tear me from the warm bosom of thy love,
> And throw me like a pois'nous weed away.
> Can I bear that? bear to be curs'd and torn,
> And thrown out from thy family and name,
> Like a disease? can I bear this from thee?
> I never can: no, all things have their end.
> When I am dead, forgive and pity me.[32]

Technically, the verse is more regular than varied. The iambic rhythm pounds ahead without much use of interpolated trochaics or spondees. There are few enclitics or proclitics, and not many feminine endings. He is perhaps too sparing in his use of enjambement, although the frequent change of the place of pause within the line adds somewhat to the variety. The pauses occur often, but they are spaced without much reference to the demands of poetry, tending to fall rather on the close of a sentence or a clause. Southerne catches from Dryden the use of the short line and employs it

[32] IV, 3.

often, driving it down to three or even to two feet. Thus he gains often the broken, colloquial effect of real dialogue:

> *Biron.* Thy words are wild; my eyes, my ears, my heart
> Were all so full of thee, so much employ'd
> In wonder of thy charms, I could not find it:
> Now I perceive it plain—
> *Isa.* You'll tell nobody— (*Distractedly.*)
> *Bir.* Thou art not well.
> *Isa.* Indeed I am not; I knew that before,
> But where's the remedy?
> *Bir.* Rest will relieve my cares; come, come, no more,
> I'll banish sorrow from thee.
> *Isa.* Banish first the cause.
> *Bir.* Heav'n knows how willingly.
> *Isa.* You are the only cause.
> *Bir.* Am I the cause? the cause of thy misfortunes?
> *Isa.* The fatal innocent cause of all my woes.[33]

Such a passage does not leave us on the highest peaks of poetry, but it does have the tang of reality. Southerne spoke more truly than he knew when he declared in the Dedication to *The Fatal Marriage,* "My poetry will never run away with me." Yet without being exciting, it is eminently respectable, and is well-suited to bear the weight of pathos with which it is loaded.

Garrick's Adaptation

ALTHOUGH *The Fatal Marriage* remained a popular stock play even beyond the eighteenth century, after 1757 it was no longer known in Southerne's original version. That year Garrick made his adaptation, and henceforth it was *Isabella, or The Fatal Marriage* that was acted and read. Times had changed, a new delicacy had crept upon the theatre, and audiences who were quite willing to weep with Isabella preferred not to laugh at Fernando. So Garrick performed the necessary operation, extracting wholesale the comic sub-plot. The process was not difficult, for the connection between the two

[33] IV, 3.

plots was slight. Yet we must be grateful to him for the tenderness with which he treated the tragic portion of the play. His excisions from it were almost negligible, and his additions relatively slight. The play was still Southerne's, purged for a generation that knew not Sodom.

Garrick makes clear in his "Advertisement" that he has no objection to tragi-comedy as a dramatic form. The elision of the comic scenes, he explains, was made necessary by their immorality. Some of the speeches of the porter and the nurse were all that he could salvage for representation. And indeed it would be hard to do away altogether with those two genial gossips. He defends his additions to the play on the obvious ground that something had to be supplied to take the place of the omitted scenes; as it is, the play is well-nigh a third shorter. *Isabella,* therefore, is no perversion of *The Fatal Marriage.*

The most notable addition is a new motive for Carlos' intrigue against Villeroy. With Southerne, Carlos urges the marriage in order to get Isabella and Biron's son out of the family. In the new version, Carlos also hates Villeroy because he had been refused the hand of Villeroy's sister, who "lives in my heart, and fires me to revenge."[34] Southerne gives no hint of such a sister. Since Carlos obviously hopes that Biron will never return to discover the bigamous marriage, he can hope for this revenge only through Villeroy's association with a mysterious "evil fate" that seems to hover about Isabella. Carlos had originally expressed himself in dialogue to the persons of the sub-plot; here he lays bare his motives in a rather poor soliloquy that is entirely Garrick's.

The only scene that Garrick adds to the play is one of some fifty lines in the third act between Count Baldwin and Carlos, in which Carlos reports the wedding of Villeroy and Isabella, and in which Baldwin calls down curses on the alliance, urging Carlos to take warning from Biron's disobedience and be firm in his filial duty.

[34] I, 1.

The few remaining lines that are new are an attempt on Garrick's part to deepen the pathos still more. Thus he has Biron exclaim:

> Horrors come fast around me;
> My mind is overcast—the gath'ring clouds
> Darken the prospect—I approach the brink,
> And soon must leap the precipice! O, heav'n!
> While yet my senses are my own, thus kneeling
> Let me implore thy mercies on my wife,
> Release her from her pangs; and if my reason,
> O'erwhelm'd with miseries, sink before the tempest
> Pardon those crimes despair may bring upon me.[35]

With the exception of such inconsiderable changes as the omission of the rather suggestive epithalamiums and the insertion of more graceful lyrics, and the softening of such phrases as Sampson's "this going to bed together" to "this matrimony," Garrick takes Southerne's lines word-for-word. He makes almost no attempts at "literary improvement." All that he removes is that which was objectionable to contemporary taste.

The adaptation was first produced Dec. 2, 1757, at Drury Lane, with Garrick as Biron and Mrs. Cibber as Isabella. It was repeated the next night to "a crowded Audience," said the *London Chronicle*[36] the next day, and it was presented fourteen times that season.[37]

Translations of The Fatal Marriage

IN 1749, *The Fatal Marriage* was published in volume eight of *Le Théâtre Anglais* as "*L'Adultère Innocent,* comi-tragédie de M. Southerne."[38] This translation includes the subplot, but shortens it considerably, and summarizes large por-

---

[35] V, 2. [36] Dec. 3, 1757, p. 543.
[37] Joseph Knight: *David Garrick,* 1894, p. 165.
[38] *Le Théâtre Anglais* (1746–49) of Pierre-Antoine de la Place had in its 8 vols. synopses and partial translations of 23 plays.

tions of it. Except for these shortenings it is almost speech-for-speech a prose rendering of the original, and a more or less perfunctory performance.

There exists also a German translation of the tragedy, published in 1792 in *Deutsche Schaubühne, Neunter Band,* made by Friedrich Ludewig Schröder (1743–1816) under the title *Die unglückliche Heurath.* Schröder follows Garrick's version, for there is no comic plot. He reduces the play to a compass of three acts. Several of the names are changed: Count Baldwin becomes Graf Antonio; Biron, Pedro (Southerne's Pedro is servant to Carlos); Carlos, Claudio; Sampson, Bernardo; and Pedro, Paulino. Even Biron's son, nameless with Southerne, is given his father's name, Pedro, and a definite age of seven years.

This is really an adaptation rather than a translation. Although no new characters are introduced and the general sequence of the story remains about the same, scenes are freely transposed and merged. The play opens with an entirely new scene between Claudio (Carlos) and his servant, in which the fact of Pedro's (Biron's) absence is made clear, as is the fact that no letters have been received from him. Claudio fears his near return, which would deprive Claudio altogether of his hopes for his father's fortune. If he could only marry Villeroy to Isabella, the chance of the estate's being settled on Isabella's child would be blocked. Then, if Pedro did come back, he would probably die from the shock of seeing his wife in another man's arms. All this is adumbrated by Southerne in scattered bits throughout the play, but here it is brought together in workmanlike fashion and presented as a first scene. One difference between the translation and its original is to be noted: Claudio had *not* been receiving letters from Pedro, and is astounded to learn from Paulino that Pedro lives. Isabella does not die on the stage at the end; she is only in process of dying. The nurse says: "Weh, ihre Ende ist nich mehr ferne."

The Humours of Purgatory

SOUTHERNE'S comic plot, shunned by Garrick, had yet received the somewhat doubtful honor of being taken for the basis of a roaring farce by Benjamin Griffin called *The Humours of Purgatory*. It was produced at Lincoln's-Inn-Fields in 1716 and published the same year. Beyond the bare situation, it has no likeness to Southerne's action. There are no verbal resemblances, and the development is entirely different. In this two-act after-piece a grouchy old father suffers from the hallucination that he is dead, and will give his family no peace until they have buried him. After they have convinced him that he is in purgatory, he falls asleep, to waken later and agree to his daughter's marriage, which he had stubbornly opposed before. The temper of the piece may be gathered from the scene of the funeral procession, in which the old man rises from his coffin to denounce as liars several citizens whom he has overheard branding him as thief and villain.

Stage History

ON June 16, 1830, Sir Walter Scott saw and heartily applauded Fanny Kemble's performance in *Isabella* on the Edinburgh stage.[39] And in all probability not a year had elapsed since 1694 that had not seen Isabella's woes displayed in some theatre. I have collected distinct dates for 203 performances on the London stage alone, and my list is only partially complete. At least as late as 1843 it was produced in America. To name those who have played the part of Isabella is to call the roll of the great English tragic actresses: Barry, Porter, Yates, Cibber, Crawford, Siddons, O'Neill, Young, Kemble. Critics and public alike acclaimed the play, and crowded the theatres to see their favorite actress as the pathetic heroine. It has been printed at least fifty-three times.[40] Such an enduring popularity needs to be explained.

[39] J. C. Dibdin, *Annals of the Edinburgh Stage*, p. 331.
[40] See Bibliography, in Appendix.

Doubtless part of the answer lies in the increasingly sentimental nature of the eighteenth-century world of letters and the theatre. Feminine appreciation had been Southerne's since the first, and those possessed of "sensibility" who had suffered in their closets with Pamela and Clarissa were eager to stir their emotions gently in the theatre with Isabella's distresses. *Isabella* was just the sort of tragedy to please an age of unbuttoned sentimentalism. Again, the eighteenth century was a period of great players rather than great plays. In *Isabella* the powerful emotional actresses found a rôle admirably fitted to their talents.

Mrs. Siddons was perhaps the most popular Isabella in the history of the theatre. On the 10th of October, 1782, she chose the play for her first appearance at Drury Lane, with her own eight-year-old boy, Henry, playing the part of Isabella's child. The character had been recommended to her by the father of Richard Brinsley Sheridan, who had seen her in it at Bath.[41] The next day, the *London Chronicle* testified to her success: "The different scenes of distress, in which the Poet has placed Isabella, were accurately attended to, and finely preserved . . . but the best panegyric we can make upon this Lady's performance of the pathetic scenes, is to remark, there was scarce a dry eye in the whole house, and that two Ladies in the boxes actually fainted." J. F. Molloy sketches in the picture: "Everything she did had the look and tone of truth, her laugh as she plunged the dagger into her heart so electrified her audience that they forgot to applaud, and the curtain went down in a profound silence that a couple of seconds later was rent with a fury of voices struggling to express admiration. The town rang with her name; her impersonation of Isabella was repeated eight times; . . . there was something idolatrous in the enthusiasm she excited."[42]

There exists another anecdote told by Dibdin which is worth repeating: "On the evening that *The Fatal Marriage*

[41] Thomas Campbell, *Life of Mrs. Siddons*, 2 vols., 1834. I, 155.
[42] *Romance of the Irish Stage*, II, 216.

was performed,[43] Mrs. Siddons was so carried away by the emotions incidental to the part, that when the curtain fell she had to be assisted off the stage. Such acting had a wonderful effect upon the audience. A young heiress—Miss Gordon of Gight, in Aberdeenshire—was carried out of her box in hysterics, screaming loudly the words caught from the great actress—'Oh my Biron! my Biron!' Chambers says that several people who were in the theatre that night declared they never forgot the ominous sounds, 'Oh my Biron!' A year afterwards this Miss Gordon met, for the first time, the Hon. John Biron, who paid his addresses to and eventually married her. It was for her a fatal marriage in several respects, although it gave to the world the poet Lord Byron."[44]

The play as Mrs. Siddons and Mrs. Cibber before her had acted it, was over three hundred lines shorter than Garrick's published version, in which he had placed inverted commas about the lines omitted in the actual stage representation.

I have made no attempt to trace the stage history of the play in the provinces, but undoubtedly it was as popular there as in London. In Edinburgh, it was presented in the original version at the Canongate Playhouse, April 24, 1756.[45] Mrs. Siddons in 1784 thrilled Edinburgh audiences as Isabella,[46] and she was playing it at Bath in 1808. As we have seen, Sir Walter Scott in 1830 saw Fanny Kemble repeat her aunt's success in the same part.

The popularity of Garrick's adaptation of *The Fatal Marriage* as a stock play is clearly seen in its history on the American stage. The United States was first introduced to the play when Dennis Ryan's company acted it in Annapolis late in April, 1783.[47] Thence it was taken to Baltimore and presented there May 27 and June 9, 1783.[47] New York saw *Isabella* for the first time when the same company played it

---

[43] On the Edinburgh stage, June 3, 1784.
[44] *Op. cit.*, p. 188.   [45] *Ibid.*, p. 83.
[46] *Ibid.*, p. 188. (On June 3.)   [47] Seilhamer, II, 86, 93.

there July 23, 1783.[48] Seilhamer and Odell together record thirty more New York performances, the last on April 20, 1840, with Mrs. John Sloman as Isabella.[49] Philadelphia, Boston, and even Hartford and Providence saw the play, acted at various times by Mrs. Whitlock, Mrs. Sloman, and Fanny Kemble. Indeed the great theatrical event in Providence for the year 1799 was the appearance on the 4th of July of Mrs. Whitlock as Isabella.[50] The last performance on the American stage of which I can find any record was in New York, Sept. 28, 1843, when Mrs. Shaw made her first appearance as Isabella.[51]

[48] Odell, I, 227-8.   [49] *Ibid.,* IV, 87.
[50] Chas. Blake, *Hist. of the Providence Stage,* Providence, 1868, p. 60.
[51] Odell, V, 20.

CHAPTER VIII

OROONOKO

> Oroonoko. *Let the fools*
> *Who follow fortune, live upon her smiles.*
> *All our prosperity is plac'd in love.*
>
> Act II, sc. 4.

WITH the praises of the town for *The Fatal Marriage* still ringing in his ears, Southerne set himself to repeat, if possible, his former success, holding shrewdly to the tragi-comic formula that had hit so well the public taste. As before, the popularity of his feminine appeal to pity was tremendous. "Oh! the Favourite of the Ladies," was a 1702 comment on *Oroonoko*,[1] and such it was to remain for many generations of play-goers.

The first production of *Oroonoko* has always been dated 1696; Nicoll places it about January of that year.[2] As a matter of fact it was first performed not later than the early part of December, 1695. An advertisement in the *London Gazette* for December 12–16, 1695, runs as follows: "This day is Published Oroonoko, a Tragedy, as it is Acted at the Theatre Royal by His Majesties Servants. Writted by Tho. Southerne," etc. The play's immediate success was a matter of no small moment to the Drury Lane theatre, the fortunes of which had declined sharply since the secession, the previous season, of Betterton and others to the theatre at Lincoln's-Inn-Fields. A good play was a matter for managerial rejoicing. Together with *Aesop* and *The Relapse, Oroonoko* "subsisted *Drury-lane* House, the first two or three Years."[3]

---

[1] *A Comparison Between the Two Stages*, p. 30.

[2] *Restoration Drama*, p. 145. Nicoll infers his date from an advertisement for the play in Dilke's *Lover's Luck*, which is entered in the *Term Catalogues* for Feb. 1695/6.

[3] *A Comparison Between the Two Stages*, p. 33.

Again, "It had indeed uncommon Success, and the Quality of both Sexes were very kind to the Play, and to the Poet."⁴

In spite of the fact that Betterton was no longer available, the play was presented by a strong cast. As Oroonoko, Jack Verbruggen achieved a personal triumph. "By doing the Author Right, [he] got himself the Reputation of one of the best Actors of his time," testifies Gildon.⁵ In his dedication, Southerne thanks the Duke of Devonshire for suggesting Verbruggen for the part: "it was your opinion, my lord, that directed me to Mr. *Verbruggen;* and it was his care to maintain your opinion, that directed the town to me."⁶ Anthony Aston describes the actor's success in the rôle: "And you may best conceive his manly, wild Starts, by these Words in *Oroonoko,—Ha! thou hast rous'd the Lyon* [*in*] *his Den; he stalks abroad, and the wild Forest trembles at his Roar:—* Which was spoke, like a Lyon, by *Oroonoko,* and *Jack Verbruggen:* for Nature was so predominant, that his second Thoughts never alter'd his prime Performance."⁷ The beautiful Mrs. Rogers created the part of Imoinda, and Mrs. Verbruggen, the company's star comedienne, played Charlott Welldon. In describing Mrs. Verbruggen's success, Aston reveals quite frankly her reluctance to play the part. She "was very loath to accept the Part of *Weldon* in *Oroonoko,*" he tells us, "and that with just Reason, as being obliged to put on Men's Cloaths—having thick Legs and Thighs, corpulent and large Posteriours;—but yet the town (that respected her) compounded, and receiv'd her with Applause; for she

---

⁴ *Ibid.,* p. 30.

⁵ Gildon's Langbaine's *Lives,* p. 136.

⁶ Aston, with more detail, gives a different story in *A Brief Supplement to Colley Cibber, Esq; His Lives of the late Famous Actors and Actresses,* (n.d. [1747–8]) printed by Lowe in his edition of Cibber's *Apology,* II, 311. "The late Marquess of *Halifax* order'd *Oroonoko* to be taken from *George Powel,* saying to Mr. *Southern,* the Author,—that *Jack* was the unpolish'd Hero, and wou'd do it best." Powell played the part of Aboan.

⁷ *Ibid.,* p. 311.

was the most pleasant Creature that ever appear'd."[8] It is hard for dramatic criticism to be at once so bald and so gracious as this.

Congreve contributed a witty epilogue in which he makes an ironical contrast between the steadfast affections of Imoinda and the more cultivated wisdom of London wives.

> Then bless your stars, you happy *London* wives,
> Who love at large, each day, yet keep your lives:
> Nor envy poor *Imoinda's* doting blindness
> Who thought her husband kill'd her out of kindness.
>
> . . . .
>
> Her error was from ignorance proceeding:
> Poor soul! she wanted some of our town-breeding.
> Forgive this *Indian's* fondness of her spouse;
> Their law no christian liberty allows:
> Alas! they make a conscience of their vows!
> If virtue in a heathen be a fault;
> Then damn the heathen school, where she was taught.
> She might have learn'd to cuckold, jilt, and sham,
> Had *Covent-Garden* been in *Surinam*.

In the Dedication Southerne mentions with some pride the favors shown him by people of quality. Chief of these was William Cavendish, Duke of Devonshire (1640–1707), to whom the Dedication was addressed. Cavendish was a strong Tory, who had vigorously promoted the exclusion bill against York. Under William he became privy counsellor and Knight of the Garter. In many ways his life typified the virtues and vices of the Restoration courtier: profligate in his private life, he was yet an excellent judge of architecture and fine art, a good critic of music, and no inconsiderable Latin scholar. Above all, he was munificent in his donations, and here again Southerne gave proof of his adeptness in attaching himself to patrons who were able and willing to add gold to a poet's pocketbook as well as stature to his reputation.

[8] Cibber, *Apology*, II, 313.

The Story of the Play

OROONOKO is an African prince sold into slavery in the English colony of Surinam in South America. He is proud, not only of his noble lineage, but of his moral superiority to his brutal slave-masters. Moreover, he is heart-broken at having been separated, before he had been taken from Africa, from his young wife, Imoinda. The King of Angola, Oroonoko's own father, had wanted to add Imoinda to his harem, and when he found that she was married to Oroonoko, in his rage he either killed her or sent her away—Oroonoko is uncertain of her fate. During the course of the play he discovers that Imoinda is a slave in the same colony and is being pursued by the Lieutenant-Governor with no honorable intentions. This touches Oroonoko with noble anger in a way that his own slavery had not, and he leads his fellow slaves in a revolt which results in defeat and makes him, from fear of a worse fate, kill first his wife and then himself. The treachery of the Governor is successful over the efforts of certain sympathetic Englishmen to save them.

Aphra Behn and Oroonoko

NEVER supremely inventive, Southerne took his tragic plots pretty much where he found them. Two years before, he had gone to Mrs. Behn for the main action of *The Fatal Marriage,* and had been rewarded with a popular success. Once more he turned to Aphra for inspiration, and from the midst of one of her most vivid novels took the framework for his next play. Mrs. Behn's *Oroonoko, or The Royal Slave* (published about 1688) is one of her strongest, as it has been her most popular prose tale. The vivid realism of its best portions is shot through with a pathos that shines clear amid the embroidery of artificiality that surrounds it. And here, in the love-distress that lies at the heart of the novel, Southerne found ready at his hand a story waiting only to be thrown into dramatic form. "I have often wondered," he says, "that she [Mrs. Behn] would bury her favorite hero in a *novel,* when she might have revived him in the *scene."*⁹

As in the case of *The Fatal Marriage,* Southerne hastens to forestall criticism by owning freely his source. This acknowledgment moves Gildon, no mean source-hunter himself, to spontaneous admiration. "I have quoted this," he says, "because 'tis very uncommon with Authors to speak well of those they borrow from in their Writings, for I have known a great Man perpetually rail at the French Authors, and yet contradict his Reflections on them, by filling his Writings with their Wit and Designs; and I have so often experienc'd this Particular, among the Writers of our Age, that when I hear any of them condemn, either our Ancient or Modern Authors, I conclude, he has been robbing there, and would deter us from finding out his Theft."¹⁰

A comparison of play and novel reveals a deft hand translating into dramatic terms a rather rambling story—foreshortening and compressing here, amplifying there, building the whole into a well-knit structure with major and minor climaxes, and humanizing with a warmth of characterization events which in the novel oscillate between stark realism and patent artificiality.¹¹ The first part of Mrs. Behn's novel is taken up with the story of Oroonoko's life in Africa in the country of Coramatien¹²—of his courtly accomplishments and valor in battle, his courtship of Imoinda, the old king's attempt to secure Imoinda for himself in spite of her love for Oroonoko, the lovers' defeat of the scheme, the king's baffled rage which results in Imoinda's sale into slavery, and the final

---

⁹ Dedication to *Oroonoko.*   ¹⁰ Gildon's Langbaine, p. 136.

¹¹ Mrs. Behn insisted that her story was a true one. When still a child, she had been taken by her family to Surinam, and there, she declares, she met Oroonoko and heard his story. "I was myself an Eye-witness to a great Part of what you will find here set down." (*Oroonoko, or The Royal Slave,* in Behn's *Works,* ed. Summers, V, 129.)

¹² With Southerne, this becomes Angola, and the king, instead of being Oroonoko's grandfather, is his father.

capture of Oroonoko by the English slave-merchant and his deportation to Surinam.[13] All this becomes antecedent action with Southerne, and is only briefly summarized in the play.

Southerne follows his source in many details. The tragic situation leading to the deaths of Oroonoko and Imoinda is the same. In the romance, Oroonoko is sold to one Trefy, "a Man of great Wit, and fine Learning," who conceives a vast liking for Oroonoko, and promises him future release. Really but a slave in name, he stays in his house and receives visitors. In the play, Blandford, under whose charge Oroonoko comes, is just such a kind master. Oroonoko's slave name is Caesar, and Imoinda's Clemene in both versions. With Mrs. Behn and Southerne alike Oroonoko is roused to revolt by the thought that his child, which Imoinda is now carrying, will be a slave too. Tuscan, Oroonoko's fellow slave and attendant in the novel, becomes Aboan in the play, but shows the same fidelity to his lord, staying by his side when all the other slaves desert the revolt through the blandishments of the lying Governor. In the drama, Oroonoko is not tortured, but only chained, and is finally released for a time. Aboan bears all the tortures that both Tuscan and Oroonoko suffer in the novel.

There are some verbal parallels, of which a few typical ones will suffice as illustrations:

Novel	Play
Come, my Fellow-Slaves, let us descend, and see if we can meet with more Honour and Honesty in the next World we shall touch upon.	Now we are fellow slaves! . . . . Whatever world we next are thrown upon Cannot be worse than this.
Summers' ed., V, 166–7.	I, 2.

[13] On the coast of South America between 2° and 6° n. lat. and 53° 50′ and 58° 20′ e. long. Now Dutch Guiana, ceded to Holland by England in 1667. Bernbaum (*Kittredge Anniversary Papers*, 1913) attempts to show that Mrs. Behn's story had no basis in reality.

Novel	Play
My Lord, we have listened with Joy and Attention to what you have said; and, were we only Men, would follow so great a Leader through the World: But O! Consider we are Husbands and Parents too, and have Things more dear to us than Life; our Wives and Children, unfit for Travel in those unpassable Woods, Mountains and Bogs. p. 191.	Great sir, we have attended all you said, With silent joy and admiration: And, were we only men, would follow such, So great a leader, thro' the untry'd world. But, oh! consider we have other names, Husbands and fathers, and have things more dear To us than life, our children and our wives, Unfit for such an expedition.[14] III, 4.
. . . should a few Shrubs oppose them, which they could fire before 'em . . . and the rivers could be no Obstacle, since they swam by Nature . . . p. 192.	Woods we can set on fire; we swim by nature. III, 4.
[The Gov. said] It was not that he any longer fear'd him, or could believe that Force of two Men, and a young Heroine, could overthrow all of them . . . but it was the vast Esteem he had for his Person the Desire he had to serve so gallant a Man and to hinder himself from the Reproach hereafter, of having been the Occasion of the Death of a Prince,	Alas! we cannot fear, that your small force, The force of two, with a weak woman's arm, Should conquer us. I speak in the regard And honour of your worth, in my desire And forwardness to serve so great a man. I would not have it lie upon my thoughts, That I was the occasion of the fall Of such a prince, whose courage carried on

---

[14] The above parallels have been noted by Friedrich, p. 46.

Novel	Play
whose Valour and Magnanimity deserved the Empire of the World . . . this Flight of his should be look'd on as a Heat of Youth . . . p. 195.	In a more noble cause, would well deserve The empire of the world. . . . . Your undertaking . . . shall be Regarded only as the fire of youth. IV, 2.

The differences, however, are as important as the similarities. Southerne's hero is cut on grand proportions, but he rants less than Mrs. Behn's Oroonoko, is less proud and violent, and much more pathetic. In the romance, Oroonoko thirsts for English blood. "We were possess'd with extreme Fears . . . that he . . . would come down and cut all our Throats," said Mrs. Behn.[15] Again, she finds Oroonoko "pleasing his great Heart with the fancy'd Slaughter he should make over the whole Face of the Plantation."[16] The Oroonoko of the play is by nature as gentle as his prototype was fierce. "The means that lead us to our liberty Must not be bloody," he insists,[17] and "We'll not set out in blood."[18] Only as he is driven to extremity does he kill Capt. Driver, the brutal slave-trader who had shanghaied him, and the evil Governor. Southerne's Oroonoko is granted a noble melancholy that in the novel is only stoic defiance. He is poetic in a way that the other was not, and the play lacks, too, the stilted, flowery love-episodes of the novel. Compare, for instance, Oroonoko's moving recital in the play of his courtship of Imoinda, with Mrs. Behn's description of her hero's lovemaking.

When he came [says Mrs. Behn], attended by all the young Soldiers of any Merit, he was infinitely surpriz'd at the Beauty of this fair Queen of Night, whose Face and Person were so exceeding all he had ever beheld, that lovely Modesty with which she receiv'd him . . .

[15] Summers' edition, V, 198.
[17] III, 2.
[16] Summers' edition, V, 201.
[18] III, 4.

and the Sweetness of her Words and Behaviour while he stay'd, gain'd a perfect Conquest over his fierce Heart, and made him feel, the Victor could be subdu'd . . . while *Imoinda*, who wish'd for nothing more than so glorious a Conquest, was pleas'd to believe, she understood that silent Language of new-born Love; and, from that Moment, put on all her Additions to Beauty.[19]

Here Southerne's hero speaks. He has just returned from the battle in which Imoinda's father was killed defending him.

> When I came
> Back to the court, a happy conqueror;
> Humanity oblig'd me to condole
> With this sad virgin for a father's loss,
> Lost for my safety. I presented her
> With all the slaves of battle to atone
> Her father's ghost. But when I saw her face,
> And heard her speak, I offer'd up myself
> To be the sacrifice. She bow'd and blush'd;
> I wonder'd and ador'd. The sacred pow'r
> That had subdu'd me, then inspir'd my tongue,
> Inclin'd her heart; and all our talk was love.[20]

Various motives of the novel are in the play changed or amplified. Aboan plays a more important part than did Tuscan. He is the moving spirit of the revolt, and stirs Oroonoko to action. In the novel, Oroonoko does not need such incitement to escape, but arrives at the decision speedily himself. The Governor, whose only interest with Mrs. Behn is in keeping the slaves from escaping, is given in the play an added incentive to perfidy. In the latter, he is in love with Imoinda and is determined to secure her at all costs. It is this determination of the Governor's that makes it plausible, later in the play, for Oroonoko to decide that only by death from their own hands can he and Imoinda be released from a hopeless fate. Also, Hottman, the slave who talks loudly of rebellion but who, when the test comes, betrays the others to the English, is a new character with Southerne.

[19] Summers' edition, V, 137–8.   [20] II, 2.

As in *The Fatal Marriage,* Southerne rejects Mrs. Behn's catastrophe for one more dramatically effective. The novel ends with a gruesome realism impossible on the stage; Oroonoko takes Imoinda out into the woods and kills her to save her from the English. But he cannot bring himself to leave the body, lingers there for eight days, and at the end of that time is too weak to execute his revenge. When he is found by a party of English, he attempts to commit suicide. After cutting off a piece of his own neck and hurling it at his enemies as a gesture of defiance, he tries to disembowel himself, without complete success. He is later tied to his old whipping post and gradually dismembered by some English ruffians. His fortitude is shown by his smoking steadily at a pipe while they cut off his ears and nose and one of his arms. It is not until they hack off the second arm that he succumbs, the pipe drops, and he dies.

Such violence was no part of Southerne's plan, which called for the pathos as well as the horror of death. The lovers gradually arrive at the conclusion that death is the only means of escape. Oroonoko helps Imoinda stab herself. Just then the Governor and his party come in, opposed by Blandford and his party, who are ready to fight the Governor on Oroonoko's behalf. (There is no such effort expended for Oroonoko in the novel.) But Oroonoko resolves the situation by killing the Governor and then himself.

One minor but significant change is in Imoinda's color. Both Oroonokos are black, but Southerne makes Imoinda the white daughter of a European who had taken up residence in Angola and had become commander of the army there.[21] Southerne no doubt realized the implausibility of making white planters sigh after Mrs. Behn's "Black *Venus* to our young *Mars.*" As that lady puts it in the novel, "I have seen

---

[21] This sounds like an extension of the office of Mrs. Behn's "Frenchman of Wit and Learning," who had been "banished out of his own Country for some Heretical Notions he held" (p. 160), and had become Oroonoko's teacher in Angola.

a hundred White Men sighing after her, and making a thousand Vows at her Feet, all in vain and unsuccessful."[22]

Southerne's method in adapting his source is evident. It was his purpose first to clear the story of irrelevancies and extravagances and to give it a more compact dramatic organization, in which cause and effect would be more subtly united. Beyond this it was necessary to purge the piece of the physical horror which might have titillated the senses, but which would have destroyed altogether the intended dramatic effect—that of tender, frustrated love, driven to the last extremity, descending nobly and pathetically to an inevitable tragic end. The play is a distinct advance over the novel in its hold on reality. Southerne's emphasis is not on the exotic or the horrible, but, as in *The Fatal Marriage*, on the essential humanity of his tragic characters. The pathos is largely Southerne's, as the poetry is all his; none of his better passages is borrowed. The plot is the plot of Behn, but the voice is indisputably that of Southerne.

Southerne's Noble Savage

ONE who expects to find in Oroonoko the prototype of Rousseau's primitive man will be disappointed, yet he may discover by the way certain sentiments glorifying the state of savage innocence. For instance, Oroonoko brings the Christian civilization that he has met into unfavorable contrast with his own. He refers scornfully to

> Your christian gods, who suffer you to be
> Unjust, dishonest, cowardly, and base.[23]

[22] Summers' edition, V, 137. There is an interesting contemporary comment on the discrepancy in color between the Oroonoko and Imoinda of the play in the satiric poem *The Tryal of Skill: or, a New Session of the Poets*, 1704, p. 20:

> Were his Heroine but like his Heroe, not Fair,
> Since their Breath in one Country they drew,
> And She that was Born in an *Indian* Air,
> Set forth in an *Indian* Hue.

[23] IV, 2.

Again, he meditates:

> If I should turn his christian arts on him,
> Promise him, speak him fair, flatter, and creep
> With fawning steps, to get within his faith—[24]

He refers to "our native innocence," but we cannot help thinking of his own lecherous father, who sold Imoinda as a slave and maintained, according to Oroonoko's own statement, a rule

> where, cursed court!
> No woman comes, but for his amorous use.[25]

After that, it would be hard to make out a case for Angola as a haven of purity and rest.

No, Oroonoko was not any more the glorified Indian of the eighteenth century than he was a representation of the real flesh and blood savage. In general, the savage of Restoration drama was a sorry excuse for the real thing. Dryden's Aztecs and Davenant's Incas were highly conventionalized types used, as H. N. Fairchild puts it in his admirable study *The Noble Savage,* "to satisfy a demand for more violent action, more ranting, more elaborate scenic effects and richer costumes than would be decorous in plays with Greek or Roman characters."[26] Oroonoko was no rough, untutored African, but a polished gentleman and courtier. As Mrs. Behn describes him and as Southerne takes him over,

the most illustrious Courts could not have produced a braver Man, both for Greatness of Courage and Mind, a Judgement more solid, a Wit more quick, and a Conversation more sweet and diverting. He knew almost as much as if he had read much . . . He had heard of the late Civil Wars in *England,* and the deplorable Death of our great Monarch, and would discourse of it with all the Sense and Abhorrence of the Injustice imaginable . . . He had nothing of Barbarity in his Nature, but in all Points address'd himself, as if his Education had been in some *European Court.*[27]

Surely this is not Nature's simple plan!

[24] V, 3.
[25] II, 2.
[26] New York, 1928, p. 33.
[27] Summers' edition, V, 135.

The sense of reality in the play is somewhat weakened by several incongruities. Oroonoko had never been on a ship before his capture, yet he plans to seize the vessel in which he had been brought to Surinam, and escape in it! He is a sun-worshipper, but makes glib references to the blindness of the god of Love.[28] And the slaves, when they sing songs to relieve their worries, render two typically Restoration pieces about nymphs and swains, Cynthia's power and Cupid's darts![29]

Oroonoko represents no child of Nature, nor is it any more correct to call it the first emancipation play. The spectator's sympathy was drawn to the oppressed blacks without any general humanitarian feelings being aroused. Slavery is accepted as a legitimate business out of which has grown an unfortunate situation. Capt. Driver is a brute and a villain, but the horror of Blandford and Stanmore at his capture of Oroonoko is all because of Oroonoko's rank, not because slavery itself is conceived of as wrong. "Most of 'em know no better," says Blandford. "They were born so, and only change their masters. But a prince born only to command, betray'd and sold! my heart drops blood for him."[30] Oroonoko himself had bartered his fellow-countrymen to Driver before his capture. He acknowledges as much:

> If we are slaves, they did not make us slaves;
> But bought us in an honest way of trade:
> As we have done before 'em bought and sold
> Many a wretch, and never thought it wrong.[31]

Capt. Driver and the Governor are made abhorrent because

---

[28] V, 5.   [29] II, 4.

[30] I, 2. There is a record of an interesting performance at Covent Garden in 1749, which was witnessed by an African prince and his companion, both of whom had been kidnapped, and redeemed by the British government. They were powerfully affected by a story so like their own, and their distress moved the audience more than the play. See *The Gentleman's Magazine*, XIX, 90 (1749).

[31] III, 2.

they are fundamentally cruel and deceitful, not because they trade in slaves.

Southerne's delineation of his royal slave's character is a curious and artistic mingling of the heroic and the pathetic. In the novel Oroonoko was rampantly heroic, and some of this quality is carried over into the play, where the old Almanzor tradition spits fire again. Oroonoko moves in an aura of princely dignity, with only the haughtiest kind of scorn for the barbarous English. To him it is frequently granted to speak blank verse in the midst of the others' prose. In battle he is invincible; his "single arm" drives off the attacking Indians, to the open-mouthed amazement of the others and the Governor's eulogy:

> Thou glorious man! thou something greater sure
> Than *Caesar* ever was![32]

He can rave at times in the best heroic vein:

> Dig up this earth, tear, tear her bowels out,
> To make a grave, deep as the center down,
> To swallow wide, and bury us together.[33]

Again, in referring to his own wrath:

> Ha! thou hast rouz'd
> The lion in his den; he stalks abroad,
> And the wide forest trembles at his roar.[34]

Perhaps the most typical heroic reminiscence is the conflict that arises in Oroonoko's mind between love and honor. "A lover cannot fall more glorious Than in the cause of love," he reflects.[35] Still, his honor demands that he be revenged on the Governor. It is the familiar dilemma, on which he soliloquizes at length:

> To honour bound! and yet a slave to love!
> I am distracted by their rival powers,
> And both will be obey'd. O great revenge!

[32] II, 4.   [33] V, 5.   [34] III, 2.   [35] II, 4.

> Thou raiser, and restorer of fall'n fame!
> Let me not be unworthy of thy aid,
> For stopping in thy course: I still am thine:
> But can't forget I am *Imoinda's* too.[36]

His final decision rests on good tradition:

> Love, love will be
> My first ambition, and my fame the next.

In like manner, it was the thought of Imoinda that made him surrender to the Governor when the other slaves had deserted the cause, whereas honor would have girded up his loins for battle. Love rules throughout the play.

Yet it is love of quite another stamp than that which had swelled the hearts of the super-men who swept triumphantly through heroic tragedy. Its hall-mark is warm humanity, even sentimental softness, rather than extravagant assertion. We have seen what it could be at its best, at its worst it could descend to depths of bathos. Oroonoko is considering whether to fight the Governor or to give himself up and thus save Imoinda and her unborn child:

> Methinks I see the babe, with infant hands,
> Pleading for life, and begging to be born:
> Shall I forbid his birth; deny him light?
> The heav'nly comforts of all-cheering light?
> And make the womb the dungeon of his death?
> His bleeding mother his sad monument?
> . . . .
> No, my *Imoinda!* I will venture all
> To save thee, and that little innocent.[37]

Oroonoko's more sententious speeches are infused with a spirit of high-minded nobility. He reflects that he might trick the Governor, but no. "Lying's a certain mark of cowardice," and "Honour shou'd be concern'd in honour's cause."[38] "Being just myself," he says elsewhere, "I am inclining to think

[36] V, 5.   [37] IV, 2.   [38] V, 3.

others so."³⁹ As noted above, unlike the Oroonoko of the novel, he will not at first shed blood to gain his freedom. He refuses to murder the "innocent" men against whom Aboan is urging him to rebel. Here Oroonoko cannot be excused from more than a trace of smugness:

> but we find
> The load so light, so little to be felt.
> . . . .
> We ought not to complain.⁴⁰

Well might he say this, who had been shown every consideration by Blandford,—with chains removed, Imoinda restored to him, and promise of future release given! Aboan goes on to paint the horrors that the others have been suffering, and to plead for his master to relieve them. Oroonoko says piously

> I pity 'em,
> And wish I could with honesty do more.⁴⁰

When he is shown, however, that all his *children* will be slaves too, he forgets his generous treatment by his captors, and leads the slaves into the unsuccessful rebellion.

Method and Effect

IN spite of the novelty of its background and its savage protagonists, *Oroonoko* does not extend much the frontiers of Southerne's tragic power. It moves in a far-off world of romantic vagueness without sacrificing a single motive that *The Fatal Marriage* had made familiar to the patrons of Drury Lane. Imoinda and Isabella opened identical floodgates of pathos, and Oroonoko's woes, stripped of external circumstance, tapped the same regions of the heart as did Biron's. Hence it is inevitable that the fundamental qualities of *Oroonoko* must be discussed in much the same terms as those of *The Fatal Marriage,* for reduced to the least common multi-

[39] II, 2.   [40] III, 2.

ple, their appeal is similar. Love is again the supreme moving force—love distressed and torn, not by inner dubieties but by an external fate, and marked by a doom as cruel as it is unmerited. Once more, too, that love is on a domestic level.

Character and situation are bent to achieve the maximum of pathos. The plot advances with a cumulative power built up by firm economy of structure, each climax rising on the heels of one slighter than itself, until major climax, catastrophe and dénouement come at once in a last tremendous scene. Hope for the hero increases through the first part of the play, then turns suddenly downward to emerge in settled despair and death. To trace the fluctuations of fortune: Oroonoko's original resignation and scorn give way slightly before the generous treatment of Blandford, whose kindness almost makes the captured prince believe that a Christian can be honest. And Oroonoko's valorous fight against the Indians attacking the plantation brings him new respect on the part of his captors. His reunion with Imoinda lifts his fortunes to their peak. From there, with the attempt at escape, they start to decline. Hope springs up for a moment when Oroonoko is persuaded to surrender, ironically enough, through the pleas of his friend Blandford, who trusted the promises of the Governor. Soon, however, the Governor's perfidy becomes apparent, and the end closes in on the star-crossed lovers. There is no wavering in the simple directness of the narrative.

Southerne's control of his medium appears in the skill with which he builds up scenes instinct with all that makes for theatrical effectiveness. The fight with the Indians, the recognition scene between Oroonoko and Imoinda, the scene in which Aboan moves Oroonoko to rise against the English, the rescue of Imoinda from the Governor's arms by Blandford, and the final touching death of hero and heroine—these scenes offer great actors' opportunities and must have been thrilling to contemporary audiences. In the death scene of Oroonoko and Imoinda Southerne opens all his stops of pity;

indeed, in an effort to wring the last ounce of sympathy from the spectator, the parting kisses, the irresolutions, the pain and terror are extended almost beyond the limits of dramatic propriety. Yet real passion and tragedy are here. Occasionally there are passages of white simplicity that strike with undeniable power. So, as Oroonoko helps his wife strike home the dagger to her heart, she says:

> Thus, thus 'tis finish'd, and I bless my fate,
> That where I liv'd, I die, in these lov'd arms. (*Dies.*)
> Oroo. She's gone. And now all's at an end with me,
> Soft, lay her down. O we will part no more.[41]

The whole scene is impregnated with an infinite tenderness that makes the comparison of Southerne and Otway not altogether unjust.

Southerne's method in tragedy, with all its theatrical effectiveness, is not one that is concerned with subtleties of characterization. He gives us strong lights and deep shades, without penetrating into the elusive half-lights and shadows by means of which a dramatic portrait takes on the very texture of reality. Men are good, or men are bad, but seldom do good and evil struggle for possession of one man's soul. Oroonoko, Imoinda, Blandford—such are beyond reproof; the Governor, Capt. Driver, and Hottman are villains unrelieved. So it is that there can be little deterioration or strengthening of character, and the motivation remains largely external. There is discernible in *Oroonoko,* however, a slightly different conception of tragic fate from that in *The Fatal Marriage,* where a relentless destiny allowed little space for human initiative.

Imoinda is, to be sure, entirely passive—an exotic flower crushed by an unworthy civilization—but Oroonoko determines somewhat the progress of his own career. His pride of lineage and his hatred of the thought that his children would be born in servitude allow him to be stirred to participation

[41] V, 5.

in a plot against which his instincts had at first revolted. The humanitarianism that made him forbid Aboan to murder the cowardly Hottman led to the betrayal and defeat of his plans for escape. At the very end, the tragedy of his self-inflicted death might have been averted had he trusted to the energetic efforts of Blandford to save him and Imoinda. In a certain sense, then, the conduct of the action is determined by the protagonist's character.

Thought and Poetry

THE plains of intellectual flatness, as well as the swamps of sentimentalism, lurk for those poets who cannot offer ideas to correspond to the emotions displayed. Here was Southerne's deeper lack. Eager to seem profound, he grappled with thought, but always it just eluded him. Out of a mountain of effort there came too often only the mole of aphorism. Such sententious expressions as these are scattered thick throughout the play:

>Lying's a certain mark of cowardice.[42]
>. . . . . . .
>Honour shou'd be concern'd in honour's cause.[43]
>. . . . . . .
>Live still in fear, it is the villain's curse.[44]
>. . . . . . .
>Men live and prosper but in mutual trust.[45]
>. . . . . . .
>An oath is a recognizance to heav'n[46]
>. . . . . . .
>It is not always granted to the great,
>To be most happy.[47]
>. . . . . . .

[42] V, 3.   [43] V, 3.   [44] I, 2.
[45] I, 2.   [46] V, 2.   [47] V, 5.

>   But christians guided by the heav'nly ray,
>   Have no excuse if we mistake our way.[48]
>
>   .   .   .   .
>
>   We know our strength only by being try'd.[49]
>
>   .   .   .   .
>
>   Pity's a kin to love.[50]

The last of these has passed into proverb. Perhaps part of Southerne's popularity in a later sentimental theatre can be laid to his ability to create the illusion of thought without the reality, and to state obvious truths oracularly. Thus he could encourage his audiences in thinking that they were following him into deep speculation, when as a matter of fact they were only paddling in philosophical shallows.

The quality of Southerne's poetry is extremely uneven. We have seen how, at times, under the influence of the Elizabethans, particularly of Shakespeare, it could become luminous with intensity or with pathos. The greater part of his blank verse is neither good nor bad, except that as a whole it does deserve the contemporary acclaim that it received for its simplicity and its easy-flowing smoothness. At other times it has the false inflation of pulpy heroics or labored metaphor. Thus Oroonoko to Imoinda:

>   Thou art my only guide, my light of life,
>   And thou art leaving me: send out thy beams
>   Upon the wing; let them fly all around,
>   Discover every way . . .[51]

There is also to be remembered the passage in which he declaims, "Between us lies the gaping gulph of death."[52] Worst of all is Oroonoko's epitaph for the Governor, whom he has just killed:

>   I have sent his ghost
>   To be a witness of that happiness
>   In the next world, which he deny'd us here.[53]

[48] V, 5.   [49] IV, 1.   [50] II, 2.
[51] V, 5.   [52] IV, 2.   [53] V, 5.

Oroonoko admits more of this sort of thing than did *The Fatal Marriage,* because here the hero is poured into the mold of the heroic giant, whose very breath was drawn in hyperbole. Mrs. Behn's original was still more extravagant. Southerne was at his worst in heroics, and here they clashed incongruously with his totally different aptitude for unadorned, simple emotion.

The Comic Sub-plot

IT would be idle to dwell long on the comic action of *Oroonoko,* for it is as dull and uninspired as that of *The Fatal Marriage* was humorous.[54] The situation is an old one, used by Southerne before in *Sir Anthony Love,* in which a young woman disguised as a man woos and marries another woman, putting to bed with her a friend of whose manhood there is no question.[55] Very briefly: the story concerns two sisters, Charlott and Lucy Welldon, lately come to Surinam because they found that when they had reached the advanced age of twenty-one, they were no longer sought by the London beaux! Charlott, in man's clothes, makes love to the rich and lascivious old Mrs. Lackitt, a six months' widow. With no difficulty at all she marries the widow, securing first for her sister Lucy the hand and inheritance of Mrs. Lackitt's booby son, Daniel. To consummate her marriage with Lackitt, Charlott sends in her friend Jack Stanmore. Charlott herself is really in love with Jack's brother, whom she finally succeeds in capturing. Much of the fun revolves about the ignorant lovemaking of the half-wit boy, Daniel, his later inability to sat-

---

[54] Mr. Montague Summers seems to me uncritical when he refers to this as "an excellent comic underplot, full of humour and the truest *vis comica*." (Mrs. Behn's *Works,* V, 128.) I should prefer to say with Gildon, "The Comick Part is below that Author's usual Genius." (*Comparison Between the Two Stages,* p. 30.)

[55] Southerne's widow plot is exactly that of Middleton's *No Wit, No Help, Like a Woman's,* altered in 1677 as *The Counterfeit Bridegroom, or The Defeated Widow.* The same situation appears again in William Taverner's *Artful Husband* (L.I.F. 1717).

isfy the too-insistent nuptial demands of Lucy, and Lucy's abuse of him in public. There are a few good touches[56] in the character of the widow, but the whole thing is inept and forced. In *The Fatal Marriage,* Southerne had with his comic plot made of tragedy a strange but not unpleasing monster; here again he caters successfully to the public taste, but with notable poverty of comic force.

A full two-fifths of the play is taken up with this prose sub-plot, which runs well into the last act. Congreve, in his Epilogue to *Oroonoko,* gives a sidelong glance at this action, making for it a somewhat perfunctory defense:

> We weep, and laugh, join mirth and grief together,
> Like rain and sun-shine mixt, in *April* weather.
> Your different tastes divide our poet's cares:
> One foot the sock, t'other the buskin wears:
> Thus while he strives to please, he's forc'd to do't,
> Like *Volscius,* hip-hop, in a single boot.
> Critics, he knows, for this may damn his books:
> But he makes feasts for friends, and not for cooks.

There is little attempt to join the two plots; they are essentially two plays, carried on side by side. Sub-plot touches main plot once when the Widow and Capt. Driver quarrel over the apportionment of slaves, and once when the widow, Charlott, Lucy, and Stanmore petition the Governor for Oroonoko's release.

This comic plot compressed, but taken almost word for word from Southerne, was combined with several scenes from Fletcher's *Monsieur Thomas* to make a lusty two-act farce called *The Sexes Mis-match'd; or a New Way to get a Husband.* (Published in the volume *The Strollers Pacquet Open'd,* 1741.) The names are changed, and Surinam becomes Gibraltar; that is the only difference.

[56] There is a speech, possibly a personal reminiscence of Southerne's, worth quoting; Welldon refers to "the young inns-of-court beaux, of but one term's standing in the fashion, who knew nobody, but as they were shewn 'em by the orange-women." I, 1.

Oroonoko *in the Eighteenth Century*

Oroonoko was first adapted for the more refined sensibilities of the eighteenth century in 1759 by John Hawkesworth, editor of the *Adventurer* and of Swift's *Works,* and friend of Dr. Johnson. His first move, of course, was to delete as "loose and contemptible" all the comic scenes. He explains his attitude in the prologue:

> This Night your tributary Tears we claim,
> For Scenes that *Southern* drew; a fav'rite Name!
> He touch'd your Fathers' Hearts with gen'rous Woe,
> And taught your Mothers' youthful Eyes to flow;
> For this he claims hereditary Praise,
> From Wits and Beauties of our modern Days;
> Yet, Slave to Custom in a laughing Age,
> With ribbald Mirth he stain'd the sacred Page;
> While Virtue's Shrine he rear'd, taught Vice to mock,
> And join'd, in Sport, the Buskin and the Sock;
> O! haste to part them!—burst th' opprobious Band!

Beyond this, he "bows with Rev'rence to the hoary Sire," and Southerne emerges little damaged by the altering process. The excisions are generally commendable. "Some Passages are left out," says Hawkesworth in the preface to the printed copy, "merely because the Speeches in which they occurred, were too long both for the Audience and the Actor." In the last act, he cuts out the last half of Oroonoko's first soliloquy, with its poetic, but undramatic similes. He splits up Aboan's long speech beginning "spare my shame,"[57] giving part to Oroonoko and part to Aboan, and obtains a better effect of broken dialogue. He trims, elsewhere, parts of Oroonoko's more philosophical passages, and cuts out altogether the long speech beginning "It is not always granted to the great To be most happy"[57]—an eloquent discourse, but one that clogs the action at a critical moment. All in all, he takes from the last scene of the play some sixty lines, speeding up the action to an appreciable extent.

[57] V, 5.

The most significant addition is a brief one, and concerns the relations of Aboan, Hottman, and Oroonoko. It seemed to Hawkesworth, accurately enough, that if Oroonoko and Aboan had suspected Hottman's disloyalty, as Southerne makes clear, then they were extremely foolish in divulging to him so much of the plan for the uprising. Therefore the adaptor makes Aboan convinced, at first, of Hottman's loyalty. Later, distracted because his credulity had enabled Hottman to betray them, he tries to stab himself, and is only prevented by Oroonoko's quickness. This latter scene is Hawkesworth's only sizable addition to the play. He refers to it modestly in his preface as "a new Incident of that Kind which has generally been thought affecting in a great Degree." Into the first scene between the Governor and Imoinda[58] he inserts "Some tender Expostulations of *Imoinda* against the Governor's Importunity . . . expressing that refined Sensibility which always increases Pity."[59] The "Expostulations" are meant to add appreciably to the specific gravity of the distress.

Hawkesworth does Southerne a service in removing the absurd lyrics sung by the slaves. In their place he sets a chorus less artificial, if too consciously philosophical.

> Come, let us be gay, to repine is in vain,
> When our Loss we forget, what we lose we regain;
> Our Toils with the Day are all ended at last;
> Let us drown in the present all thoughts of the past,
> All the future commit to the Powers above;
> Come, give me a Smile as an earnest of Love.

This optimism is hard to live up to, however, for pleasures disappear when one is a slave—love and joy

> Must both be free, for both disdain
> The sounding Scourge and galling Chain.
> . . . .

---

[58] II, 3 (Southerne's version).   [59] Preface, p. vi.

But gentle Evening comes in vain
To soothe the Slave from Sense of Pain.[60]

There exists a review of the play attributed by the *Biographica Dramatica* to Dr. Johnson, which seems to have been overlooked by Johnson scholars.[61] It is therefore of sufficient interest to be quoted in part:

> The original play, as it came out of the hands of Southern, is well known; and the public will only expect from us an account of the alterations. That it was necessary to alter it, cannot be denied: the tragic action was interrupted, not only by comic scenes, but by scenes of the lowest buffoonery, and the grossest indecency. Of this unnatural and disgraceful association, the writer of the adventitious part, speaks with great spirit and propriety in the prologue . . .
> If these particulars be distinctly considered, it will be found . . . that the law prescribed by the alterer to himself, of sparing the tragic part, has been rather too carefully observed: many lines are retained which severe criticism would have expunged; but he that errs on the side of modesty, will be easily forgiven:
> That he has very little indulged declamation, a mode of writing, to which modern tragedies owe much of their excellence, and much of their tediousness; but has broken his insertions into short speeches, and lengthened the action by a very rapid dialogue, animated with frequent changes of gesture, and expressions of emotion:
> And that the plan of the play proceeds with sufficient regularity, from the first act to the last, so well interwoven with the several insertions, that there is no loss of any thing omitted.
> As the writer has not amused himself with picking flowers of language, or of sentiment, and the beauty of his scenes consists principally in vigour of dialogue, and tendency to the main design, few passages can be selected as specimens, since that grace, which is derived from connection, is destroyed by separation . . .
> If there be any who looks into this performance, with a desire of finding faults, let him first consider how few opportunities of excellence the reformation of a play affords. The characters are already settled: so that no great knowledge can be discovered of human na-

---

[60] II, 3.
[61] In the *Critical Review* for Dec., 1759, VIII, 480 f. It is most likely that the Doctor might have reviewed his friend's alteration of Southerne's play. Professor C. B. Tinker assures me, on the basis of style, that the review is undoubtedly Johnson's.

ture, or of human life. The events of the play are fixed; for a play that wants amendment in the great events, is scarcely worthy to be reformed: even sentiments are very little in the reformer's power; for the necessary connection of the new scenes with the old, confines the writer to a certain line of transition, from which he cannot pass aside, whatever treasures of sentiment might reward his deviations. There is, likewise, a necessity of yet greater constraint, by conforming the diction and thoughts to those of the first author, that no apparent dissimilitude may discover what is original, and what is additional. These are obstructions, by which the strongest genius must be shackled and retarded, and the writer who can equal Southern under such difficulties, may be expected to excel greater authors, when he shall exert his natural powers without impediment, by adapting his own sentiments to his own plan.

The adaptation was first produced at Drury Lane, Dec. 1, 1759, with Garrick as Oroonoko and Mrs. Cibber as Imoinda. It was played at least eight times during the remainder of the season. Davies tells us that "Garrick seldom failed; but he was not equally successful in Oroonoko; the lustre of his eye was lost in the shade of the black colour; nor was his voice so finely adapted to the melting and passionate addresses and feelings of the lover as to the more violent emotions of the heart."[62]

Two more alterations of *Oroonoko* appeared in 1760. The one was by an unknown editor who added, to replace the omitted comic scenes, six hundred lines of dialogue and two new characters of his own. He declares in an address "to the Reader" that he "has not carried that Presumption to an Alteration of a single Line, or Circumstance, in the Original Tragic Scenes: But, he has attempted only, to interweave an under Plot, to lengthen them into Five Acts; and rescue so meritorious a Work, from appearing with coarse, and indelicate Ribaldry." This editor admits no prose at all; even Southerne's few prose passages are chopped up into a kind of bastard blank verse. The two new characters are *"Heartwell,* President of the Council," and *"Maria,* Sister to the

[62] *Dramatic Miscellanies,* III, 450.

Lieut. Governor, and contracted to Blandford," two dripping sentimentalists who pad out the play with pompous, flowery utterances, of which one sample is more than sufficient:

> Love is the Leveller of all Degrees—
> The Pride of Birth, and Indolence of Wealth,
> Without Distinction fall its Victims—
> The wanton, heedless God, in Laughter scorns,
> The haughty Limits would direct *his* Sway:
> Pointing his Shafts, with smiling Chastisement,
> At purpl'd Princes—

Imoinda, in her scene with the Governor, is given some added laments that are unbelievably bad. The author in his preface hints darkly at the enmity of the managers who refused his play a production, for it was never acted. But a reading of the play clearly vindicates the managers.

The other 1760 version was that of Francis Gentleman, and it was acted with some success at Edinburgh. The *Advertisement* says that the alteration "was first hinted to the Author by a Noble Personage, who has eminently distinguished himself in the literary world;[63] and who recollected to have heard Mr. SOUTHERNE declare, in his latter days, that he most heartily regretted his complying with licentious taste, by writing any thing so offensive to modesty, as the comic part of his works; especially that which was so unnaturally joined to the tragedy of the play." The editor further acknowledges the kind reception that Edinburgh had given the piece, especially since it "laboured under some lamentable deficiencies in the representation."

James Boswell was the recipient of the rhymed dedication, which, after some elevated thoughts dealing with the power of Reason to invoke Content, asks and answers the question

> Shall I for some exalted title seek,
> And cringe to fortune, not to merit speak?
> No—she disdains a task so meanly low,

[63] In all probability, as the *Biog. Dram.* suggests, this was "Lord Corke" [John Boyle].

In ev'ry shape to flattery a foe:
But where with honest pleasure she can find,
Sense, taste, politeness with good-nature join'd;
There, gladly, will she raise her humble voice,
Nor fears to tell that BOSWELL is her choice.

Beyond removing the characters of the comedy, Gentleman makes few changes in the conduct of the play.

There is one other alteration of *Oroonoko,* called *The Prince of Angola, a Tragedy; altered from the play of Oroonoko, and adapted to the Circumstances of the present Time,* by J. Ferriar, acted at Manchester, and printed there in 1788. "The Circumstances of the present Time" were the efforts that had been begun in Manchester to abolish the African slave trade, and the play was turned into a tirade against slavery. I have not been able to see a copy of the piece, but there is a review of it in the *Gentleman's Magazine* that summarizes its purpose and indicates its weakness. "The author . . . has chiefly employed Dr. Hawkesworth's altered edition, 1775 [*sic*], and given the whole a turn more favorable to the negroes, and more adverse to the slave-holders. He sets out with abusing Southerne's original play, as not containing *one respectable character.* . . . He proceeds to tell us, that he has thrown out Hawkesworth's alterations as in general *injudicious* and *proving him no poet.* But Mr. Ferriar's principal design is 'to communicate and extend those impressions of the African slave trade which are already received by so large a proportion of the people of England.' "[64]

[64] April, 1788, LVIII, pt. 1, 342. There is also a review of the book in the *Monthly Review,* LXXVIII (June, 1788, p. 522). There the reviewer makes the following ingenious defense of slavery: "It should also be fully known, whether, by abandoning the traffic, we should not abandon the cause of humanity, and leave the wretches, who are exported from Africa, to a worse lot in their own country." For a description of the horrors of the slave trade see *The Liverpool Privateers, with an account of the Liverpool Slave Trade,* by Gomer Williams, London and Liverpool, 1897. (Chap. V, 582 f.) Also Ramsay Muir's *History of Liverpool,* Liverpool, 1907. (Chap. XII, 190 f.)

It is worthy of note that *Oroonoko* was never permitted to be played in Liverpool, the great center of the slave trade.[65]

Other Slave Plays in English

OBVIOUSLY influenced by *Oroonoko,* while departing from it in treatment and style, is *Victorious Love,* a heroic "tragedy" by an eighteen-year-old youth, William Walker. The play was acted at Drury Lane in 1698. It is a poor thing, which is like *Oroonoko* only superficially. In each play a captive king or prince is held prisoner, with his wife, by an enemy. In each the heroine is white, her husband African. (Barnogasso, the hero of *Victorious Love* is not, however, a slave, as was Oroonoko.) In each the capturing ruler desires the girl and plots to kill the husband. In each, the two captives have a friend among the enemies (Blandford and Gen. Barsiloa), who works for their release. Here the likeness ends. At no place is Walker's play reminiscent in tone of *Oroonoko.* It is not pathetic, but heroic, in the worst bombastic tradition. *Oroonoko* ends tragically with the death of the lovers; *Victorious Love* ends with the villain dead and the lovers triumphant. Some of the lines read almost like a burlesque of heroics:

> Dafila.   Who will not weep, that knows Zaraida's dead?
> Barnogasso. Dead! 'tis impossible; by Heav'ns! 'tis false,
>   Her Father Sun would be obscur'd by grief,
>   But why should he? Oh no, he'll shine for joy
>   That she his Emanation is return'd.[66]

Tom Thumb cannot outdo that.

There are three eighteenth-century plays reminiscent of Southerne only in that they are concerned with slaves: *The Noble Slave,* a tragedy by Thomas Harwood (apparently never acted; printed at Bury St. Edmund's, 1788); *The Negro Slaves,* an anonymous English translation made in

[65] Inchbald's *British Theatre,* 1808, VII, 4.
[66] I, 2.

1796 of Kotzebue's play, and called "a Dramatic-Historical Piece, in Three Acts"—a highly sensational piece written to reveal the horrors of the slave trade and provided with two endings presented for the choice of the reader, one happy, the other tragic; and a one-act bit called *Negro Slaves,* by one Maclaren, brought out in Scotland in 1799. The scene lies in America, where a slave-master uses cruelly a worthy slave and his wife, who are finally released by the generous Firmlove.

A three-act musical drama that was played at Covent Garden in 1816 shows somewhat the influence of *Oroonoko.* It is *The Slave,* written in prose by Thomas Morton. The scene is Surinam. Gambia, the slave-hero (played by Macready) is a more or less stilted prig. He, as had Oroonoko, sold slaves to the English in Africa before being captured himself. One or two of the scenes are reminiscent of *Oroonoko;* when the slaves revolt, Gambia is given a sword, and he is the chief instrument in helping suppress the rebellion—just as Oroonoko had helped the English against the Indians. Also, Zelinda, who is Lindenberg's slave (as she puts it: "the slave of him, who is himself the slave of passion"), is attacked by her master, but saved by Gambia.[67]

Obviously, Southerne was no Harriet Beecher Stowe nor *Oroonoko* an *Uncle Tom's Cabin,* and his influence on later drama is not to be found primarily in the humanitarian plays of the later eighteenth century. It lies rather, as we shall see, in more general though none the less powerful tendencies.

There are two translations of *Oroonoko;* one in German by Wolfgang Herbert von Dalberg (1750-1806) : *Oronoko, Trauerspiel nach dem Englischen,* 1786. The other is a French version (1751) by P. Jos. Fiquet Dubocage, published with his translations of Pope, Mrs. Centlivre, and others. I have been able to see neither of these translations.

[67] There is in the Yale Library a play-bill advertising this piece for the Theatre-Royal in Birmingham, on Aug. 25, 1828—twelve years after its first presentation, with Macready again as Gambia.

Stage History

IF nothing else about Southerne were worthy of attention, the long endurance on the stage of his two best tragedies would demand recognition. It is somewhat surprising, even to the theatrical historian, to realize that *Oroonoko* was played at Drury Lane as late as 1829, and that in the hundred and thirty-odd years intervening since its first night seldom a season passed in which it was not performed at least once. A very recent revival of the play has given the present generation an opportunity to test its qualities. *Oroonoko* was played with striking success at the Malvern Festival in the summer of 1932. Bonamy Dobrée, reviewing the production in *The Spectator* for August 13, says of it:

> It is not a first-rate heroic tragedy, and there is little mind behind the comedy portions, but it was probably the best play that could have been chosen for popular presentation of heroic tragedy; a modern audience would not appreciate the recondite beauty of a full-blown example, and would find it unthinkable and absurd, unless the poetry should win them over. As it was, neither was the play silly, nor the interest merely academic. The whole was acceptable, much of it even moving, and it says a great deal for Mr. Ralph Richardson's power and dignity as the noble savage that no one was for a moment tempted to laugh at the part of Oroonoko.

Genest has printed the record of 127 performances; I have found definite dates for 101 more, making a total of 228 times that London alone saw the play. And still the list is far from complete. Since 1696 *Oroonoko* has been printed 57 times in English of which I am aware;[68] beyond this there have doubtless been other editions. Such a record bespeaks an unusual vitality for the play. Here again, as with *The Fatal Marriage,* part of the explanation must lie in the prevailingly sentimental tone of the eighteenth-century theatre, which liked its pathos in large doses; but the explanation can-

[68] See Bibliography.

not obscure the importance of Southerne's place in dramatic history.

Verbruggen's success as Oroonoko has already been mentioned. There were few great tragedians subsequent to him who did not at one time or another essay the same rôle. It must have been considered a good part in which to test a young actor, for in a surprising number of instances we find listed as Oroonoko one "who never appeared on any stage before." Barton Booth's first part in the theatre was that of Oroonoko at the Smock Alley Theatre in Dublin in 1698.[69] Elrington was introduced most successfully upon the stage in the same rôle at Drury Lane in 1711,[70] as was Dexter a generation later (D.L. Oct. 22, 1751).[71]

Robert Wilks played Southerne's royal slave at Drury Lane in 1703. It is amusing to note in connection with these performances the handicaps under which tragedy labored at the turn of the century. The newspaper announcements state that there will be presented

a Play call'd *Oroonoko*, with several surprizing Entertainments . . . Particularly the famous Mr. *Evans,* lately come into *England,* Vaulter

---

[69] W. R. Chetwood: *General History of the Stage,* 1749, p. 91. ". . . therefore he [Booth] resolv'd for *Ireland,* and safely arrived in *June* 1698. His first Rudiments Mr. *Ashbury* taught him, and his first Appearance was in the Part of *Oroonoko,* where he acquitted himself so well to a crouded Audience, that Mr. *Ashbury* rewarded him with a Present of Five Guineas, which was the more acceptable as his last Shilling was reduced to Brass (as he inform'd me)."

[70] Robert Hitchcock: *An Historical View of the Irish Stage,* 2 vols., Dublin, 1788. I, 65.

[71] Genest, IV, 340. The *Daily Courant* for Oct. 20, 1715, advertises the part of Oroonoko "to be perform'd by Mr. Paul, who never appear'd on the Stage before." Other actors who played the part, not, however, as their first, are: Ryan (1720); Walker (1721); Boheme (1722); Marshall (1731); Delane (1731); Milward (1733); Holland (1754); Ross (1761); Jackson (1762); Powell (1764); Barry (1769); Lacy (1774); Peile (1778); Bannister, Jr. (1781); Pope (1785); Dimond (1785); Holman (1792); Eliston (1802); Warde (1815); Young (1829).

of the manag'd Horse, where he lyes with his Body extended on one Hand in which posture he drinks several Glasses of Wine with the other, and from that throws himself a Sommerset over the Horses head, to the Admiration of all that see him.[72]

Again, another performance of Wilks' was eked out by

> several Entertainments of Singing . . . With Danceing by the Famous Monsieur *Du Ruell* and others . . . And the Famous Mr. *Clynch* will once more perform his Imitation of an *Organ* with three Voices, the *Double Curtell,* the *Flute,* and the *Bells,* and the *Huntsman* with his *Horn* and *Pack of Dogs.*[73]

Well might it be, as Fenton put it later in the Prologue to Southerne's *Spartan Dame,* that

> The Muses blush'd, to see their friends exalting
> Those elegant delights of jigg, and vaulting.

Garrick first played Oroonoko on December 1, 1759, when Hawkesworth brought forth his adaptation of the play. Eighteen years before that, however, his first part on the stage was that of Aboan in *Oroonoko,* when under the assumed name of Lyddal he appeared at Ipswich in the summer of 1741. Says Davies, "The first effort of his theatrical talents was exerted in Aboan, in the play of Oroonoko, a part in which his features could not easily be discerned; under the disguise of a black countenance, he hoped to escape being known, should it be his misfortune not to please. . . . Our young player's applause was equal to his most sanguine desires."[74] When he came to London, the part of Aboan was added to his repertoire there on Jan. 23, 1742.

Master William Henry Betty, England's "young Roscius," having conquered London and the provinces alike with his impersonations of Romeo, Hamlet, and Macbeth, played Oroonoko at Covent Garden on March 22, 1806. The play was repeated only once.

---

[72] *Daily Courant,* April 23, 1703.
[73] *Ibid.,* June 19, 1703.
[74] *Memoirs of the Life of Garrick,* 2 vols., third ed., 1781. I, 17–18.

Kean, the last great actor to play the part, first attempted it Jan. 20, 1817, at Drury Lane. "We consider it as one of his best parts," wrote Hazlitt in the *Examiner,* going on to say:

> . . . Mr. Kean, when he fully gives up his mind to it, is as great in pure pathos as in energy of action or discrimination of character. In general, he inclines to the violent and muscular expression of passion, rather than to that of its deep, involuntary, heartfelt workings . . . His performance of *Oroonoko* was for the most part decidedly of a mild and sustained character . . . The strokes of passion which came unlooked for and seemed to take the actor by surprise, were those that took the audience by surprise, and only found relief in tears.[75]

In the Provinces and the United States

In Edinburgh, Francis Gentleman's alteration of *Oroonoko* was acted during the season of 1759–60. Another version[76] produced there in June, 1759, is of particular interest because it was the subject of a review attributed to James Boswell, in connection with a proposal for a series of criticisms of the contemporary theatre.[77] In this rather indifferent review Boswell does little more than apportion praise and blame among the actors; Dexter had played the part of Oroonoko. There is record also of two other tragedians appearing in *Oroonoko* in Edinburgh. Between January and April, 1762, John Jackson played the title rôle three times.[78] Henry Erskine Johnson appeared in the same part July 25, 1795.[79]

Barton Booth played *Oroonoko* in Dublin in 1698–99,[80] and the play was a favorite one with Elrington (1688–1732)

---

[75] *Works,* ed. A. R. Waller and Arnold Glover, 12 vols., 1902–04. XI, 301 f.
[76] Obviously another because it includes the comic characters, while Gentleman's does not.
[77] The review is reprinted from the *Edinburgh Chronicle* of June 21–23, 1759, in *A View of the Edinburgh Theatre During the Summer Season, 1759,* "by a Society of Gentlemen," Edin., 1760.
[78] John Jackson, *Hist. of the Scottish Stage,* Edinburgh, 1793.
[79] Dibdin, p. 227.   [80] Chetwood, *op. cit.,* p. 91.

who was "for near twenty years the ornament and delight of the Irish stage."[81] Barry appeared as Oroonoko at the Smock Alley Theatre on Feb. 3 and 19, 1755.[82] Previous to that, in May, 1753, Dexter had come from Drury Lane and had made his first appearance in *Oroonoko,* with Mrs. Woffington as Widow Lackitt. And on Monday, June 9, 1760, says Hitchcock, "the Crow-street theatre closed one of the most brilliant and successful seasons ever known in Ireland, with the tragedy of Oroonoko. Oroonoko, Mr. Barry, Imoinda, Mrs. Dancer. . . ."[83] John Henderson (1747–85), an actor considered only second to Garrick, appeared in the play in Dublin during the last quarter of the century. During the spring season of 1828, his first in Dublin, Charles Kean played Oroonoko.[84]

Dennis Ryan presented the play for the first time in America, as nearly as I can discover, in New York on Oct. 18, 1783. His company also acted the play in Baltimore on Dec. 9, 1783.[85] Junius Brutus Booth revived the piece in New York on Nov. 29 and Dec. 5, 1832. It was Booth who startled the States by his realism in playing Oroonoko with bare feet, insisting that it was absurd to put shoes on a slave.[86] Philadelphia, Charlestown, and Boston also saw the play during the last decade of the eighteenth century.

[81] Hitchcock, *op. cit.,* I, 69. [82] *Ibid.,* I, 256.
[83] *Ibid.,* II, 38.
[84] *History of the Theatre Royal, Dublin,* Dublin, 1870, p. 71.
[85] Seilhamer, *op. cit.,* II, 103, 105, 107.
[86] J. W. Cole, *Life and . . . Times of Charles Kean,* 2 vols., 1859. I, 92.

CHAPTER IX

THE FATE OF CAPUA

Magius. *But all my bravery is in my tongue,*
I can but talk, and that unminded now.

Act II, sc. 1.

BETWEEN 1682 and 1695 Southerne had written seven plays, an average of one every two years. Fifty years of life lay ahead of him, but his period of productive effort was well-nigh over. After 1700 only twice did he attempt the stage. Four years elapsed between *Oroonoko* and his next play—already, for reasons at which we can only guess, he was withdrawing from dramatic activity. Charles Boyle, in his prologue to the new play, comments on this:

> Our Bard resolv'd to quit this wicked town,
> And all poetic offices lay down.

Certainly the town's reception of *The Fate of Capua* was not one to stimulate Southerne to further effort. Produced at Lincoln's-Inn-Fields about the middle of April, 1700,[1] it failed dismally, in spite of the efforts of Betterton and Mrs. Barry as Virginius and Favonia and those of Verbruggen as Junius. There are no records of performance; Downes, however, gives the verdict: *"The Fate of Capua,* wrote by Mr. *Southern,* better to Read then Act; 'twas well Acted, but an-

[1] Nicoll (*Early Eighteenth Century Drama,* p. 355) on the basis of the advertisement of the printed copy in the *London Gazette* and *Post Man* for April 21, 1700, dates it *ca.* March, 1699/1700. But a letter of Dryden's under date of April 11, 1700, places it more closely: " 'The Revolt of Capua' will be play'd at Betterton's house within this fortnight. I am out with that Company, and therefore, if I can help it, will not read it before 'tis acted, though the authour much desires I shou'd." Scott-Saintsbury *Dryden,* XVIII, 179.

swer'd not the Companies Expectation."[2] The phrase "better to read than act" epitomizes the reasons for the failure of a play which is in parts as moving as anything Southerne wrote, but which sinks inevitably under its own load of dull, patriotic declamation.

For the first time, Southerne turned to a classical subject for tragedy. It is significant that he should do so, for the choice marks a distinct departure from the tragi-comic form that he had employed with such success. Probably he was growing restive under the criticism that must have been directed against *The Fatal Marriage* and *Oroonoko* by energetic advocates of French "rules" and decorum. And in spite of many contemporary protests against classical authority, the "rules" were gaining ground in England. Southerne's friends—Dryden, Congreve, Dennis—had either effected a compromise between Greek theory and English practice, or were out-and-out defenders of neo-classic regularity; now he himself joins their ranks. Each of his last two tragedies—*The Fate of Capua* and *The Spartan Dame*—was a dramatization of classical history and admitted no comic action whatever.

Another influence may have been operative in leading Southerne to exclude from his tragedy any semblance of comic sub-plot. The dispute precipitated by Jeremy Collier's *Short View of the English Stage* (1698) had recently immersed the stage in a bitter pamphlet warfare. The parson's blasts against Restoration indecency brought to a climax sentiment that was already beginning to be felt in favor of a purged stage. Even Vanbrugh's and Congreve's counterblasts against Collier's indictments, and their continued writing of comedy in which Restoration license still winked a bawdy eye, could not disguise the fact that a new morality was descending upon the stage. The times were such that he who would be safe must needs purge his drama of possible

[2] J. Knight's 1886 facsimile reprint of Downes' *Roscius Anglicanus*, p. 45.

The Fate of Capua 165

offense. It is improbable that, since 1695, Southerne had been won to sudden virtue. But he was eminently cautious, and in a crisis such as this he preferred to err with the angels. Hence he threw himself into tragedy which even a Collier might approve, and which, if it did not please, would at least not offend. Ironically enough, *The Fate of Capua* did neither.[3]

The Fate of Capua is classical only in a broad sense. To the "unities" of time and place Southerne gave scant attention; the action takes place entirely within the city of Capua, but its time, at the very least, must have extended over a fortnight. The more important unity of action is observed with some fidelity. Although the play lacks a hero, and owns a double action with the intermingling of elements familiar to contemporary "classical" tragedy (that is, a complication of distressed love played before a background of war and patriotism), still, both plots are phases of one tragic action. The persons in both are the same, and the downfall of the city and the love-catastrophe occur simultaneously. The restricted action, the long oratorical moralizing, and the few persons concerned, all smack of French influence. But through the warp of all this neo-classicism runs the woof of native English weaving more familiar to Southerne. So we have the comic epilogue, the inserted irrelevant songs, and the numerous deaths in full sight of the audience. Indeed, the play ends only when all of the five people most intimately concerned

---

[3] The play was printed without a dedication. However, Charles Boyle, Southerne's friend and patron, wrote a prologue which contains an interesting criticism of Southerne's muse:

> "This Poet has no sly inveigling arts,
> He'll try to gain, but he'll not steal your hearts.
> His muse is rustic, and perhaps too plain,
> The men of squeamish tastes to entertain:
> Who none but Dutchesses will deign to toast,
> And favours only from front boxes boast.
> That's all grimace: when appetites are good,
> Be the dress coarse, the air and manners rude,
> You can take up with wholesome flesh and blood."

meet violent deaths. How patly in the tradition of bloodshed come such stage directions as "Favonia *enters with a Dagger in one Hand, and a Bowl in t'other . . . She drinks, throws the bowl one way, and the dagger another"!*[4] Southerne could not so soon shed the Elizabethanism which was part of his dramatic baggage; consequently the play is as much English as it is an attempt to conform to the new criticism. For this juxtaposition of contrasting elements Southerne found ample support in contemporary practice.

The historical part of the plot deals with the alternating allegiance of Capua, first to Rome and then to Carthage, with the final capture of the city by Rome, and the death or dispersion of its inhabitants. The play begins, smoothly enough, with a scene in the Senate that gives the necessary exposition, presents the major historical characters, and leads up to the first crisis. Hannibal has defeated the Romans at Cannae, and the question arises whether Capua, which has been protected by Rome, is to throw herself into defense of Rome or to declare for Carthage. Pacuvius Calavius is Hannibal's chief advocate in the Senate; old Decius Magius holds out staunchly for Rome. Word comes that the populace has revolted in favor of Hannibal and, led by Virginius, is advancing on the senate-chambers clamoring for senatorial blood. The diplomacy of Pacuvius saves the senators when he gets the people to disagree among themselves as to whom they would elect for senators after they had killed the present ones. The mob decides, finally, that the evils they are best acquainted with are the ones most easily to be borne.

This mob of citizens appears frequently throughout the play, usually to give information about the course of political events. It is a typically Shakespearian mob, treacherous, fickle, easily swayed by florid senatorial oratory. As with Shakespeare, the aristocracy uses but despises it. Virginius expresses the others' contempt when he speaks of "the crazy constitution Of their weak, wavering minds."[5]

[4] V, 2. [5] I, 2.

The Senate, with the exception of Magius, swings to support of Hannibal. Speedily it regrets its decision, for no sooner have the Carthaginian soldiers entered than they begin to plunder. Soon Hannibal withdraws his forces from the region, and the Romans, eager for revenge on the traitorous city, encamp without the walls. They refuse to parley, and the play ends when they enter the gates, having sworn to kill all the senators and to scatter the inhabitants throughout Italy.

Only two men take any prominent part in the political part of the play—Magius and Pacuvius. Of these Magius is by far the more interesting. He not only expresses the political ideals of the opposition, but to a notable extent he *is* the opposition. Alone against the tide in favor of Hannibal, he calls down anathema on those who would desert Rome in her hour of need. Hannibal's occupation of the city makes him only more bitter in his denunciation of his fellow-senators, and he is jailed by Hannibal as a danger to the public peace. He emerges from there when the Romans attack, after Hannibal's withdrawal, to serve on a hopeless mission asking for clemency. The Romans offer Magius his life, although they refuse to save the city. He prefers death to the sight of the downfall of his beloved commonwealth, and joins the other senators in suicide. Magius is the true patriot grown old in service of the state, indomitable in the face of personal misfortune, suffering more for Capua than for himself. Drinking, at the last, the common cup of poison, he declares

> Let it be said of us, we would have dy'd
> To save our country; since we could not that,
> Nothing could tempt us to survive its fate.
> Now lay us gently down.[6]

Such a speech of Spartan courage as this is his:

> Distress is virtue's opportunity;
> We only live, to teach us how to die.[7]

[6] V, 3.   [7] II, 1.

Unfortunately, Southerne loads this noble character down with a burden of long, oratorical addresses taken from Livy. And this flood of patriotism, taken at its tide, leads only to dramatic misfortune and dulness.

Pacuvius is all that Magius is not. Though powerful in the Senate, he is no patriot, but a self-seeking politician. He betrays Rome, hoping to gain from the Carthaginian rule new access of power. When he fails in this, he soliloquizes:

> I cannot be surpriz'd, that *Hannibal*
> Should leave a garrison, should not trust me
> With full command, which I had just before
> Abus'd, betray'd, and given up to him:
> To him, I mean to my ambition:
>
> . . . .
>
> Had *Hannibal* marcht this way, I had design'd
> The senate's slaughter, to deliver up
> The city so.[8]

Southerne's characterization of this man is uneven and relatively unsuccessful. He is perfidious, but in spite of his cold-blooded ambition there is an attempt made to draw sympathy to him. He saves the senators from death at the hands of the populace; as many resounding declamations are given to him as to Magius; it is he who, rather than be on the losing side, takes poison at last and offers it to the others. The scene between Pacuvius and his son Perolla is meant to be warmly human. Perolla's sympathy is so much on the side of his father's enemy, Magius, that he proposes to assassinate Hannibal at a banquet-table. For no discernible reason, he tells his father of the plan, and there follows a highly emotional scene in which Pacuvius pleads with him as a father not to commit the rash deed, winning his point finally by declaring

> If you will stab him, stab him then through me.
> My breast oppos'd, first you must reach my heart,
> Before your dagger can arrive at him.[9]

[8] III, 3.   [9] III, 1.

Ignobility and courage, iniquity and tenderness are all Pacuvius's, but he is not a successful tragic blend of these qualities.

The big scene toward which the historical plot moves and with which the play ends is the final spectacular death of the senators. With the Romans clamoring outside the city, they meet at Pacuvius's house, on his invitation. There they feast, and afterwards form a circle, "lock'd in a strict embrace," to drink each the "cordial draught,"

> A noble and preventing remedy;
> To free our bodies from the punishment,
> Our minds from the reproach, and infamy . . .[10]

It is impossible to mete out any high degree of praise to the political parts of *The Fate of Capua*. There are in them far too much haranguing and too little action. The tragic fate of a whole city, as presented here, fails to move either the imagination or the feelings.

Love-Tragedy

WHEN we turn to the minor plot of the play—minor in the sense that its action is only a third of the whole—we find Southerne working more effectively in channels more familiar. In spite of obvious weaknesses, the story of the husband and wife, Virginius and Favonia, and of the friend and lover Junius, lives and moves on a high tragic plane. Here for once Southerne seizes on a situation of real tragic, as well as pathetic implication.

It is domestic tragedy again, motivated and resolved by character, and marked this time by internal conflict rather than by an impassive fatalism. Favonia, daughter to Pacuvius and wife to Virginius, has been in love with her husband's best friend, Junius, and he with her. Both, strictly honorable, have denied themselves any indulgence of their passion, al-

[10] V, 3.

though Favonia cannot help being cool to her husband. Junius had fled to the army to prevent being a traitor to his friendship, and as the play opens, Virginius brings sadly to Favonia the report of his death.

Favonia is torn between grief and a sense of relief that death has solved her problem for her. Love is a tyrant,

> But he's depos'd, and Death has set me free:
> A greater tyrant gives me liberty.[11]

Her respite is brief, for soon Junius turns up alive, a captive now—he had been in the Roman armies that are at present hostile to Capua. He is taken by Virginius to a friendly imprisonment in the house he had hoped never to see again, and is commended by his friend to Favonia's own care!

In a tensely emotional scene, Favonia and Junius waver between the call of love and the demands of honor and friendship. The tragedy here is real and penetrating. Junius's agony overcomes him:

> Since I am doom'd to be a sacrifice
> Of fatal friendship, and of hopeless love,
> Here let me fall, I would be offer'd here;
> Allow me dying to confess my love
> In my last sigh, and at your feet expire.
>   (*Falls at her feet; she breaks his fall,
>   and kneels by him to recover him.*)
>
> Fav. 'Tis I am bound, and torn upon the rack!
> I cannot bear it, *Junius, Junius:*
> Look up, and live, and I'll confess enough
> For you, and for my self, all that I know,
> All that I ever heard of wretchedness;
> What you have undergone, what I have felt;
> What I now feel from this tormenting love.[12]

Junius later slips into Favonia's bedroom to look at her asleep and to kiss her hand. He is surprised by Virginius and

[11] I, 3.   [12] II, 2.

Pacuvius, but makes his escape before they can discover his identity—not, however, before they see that a man has been in the room. Favonia, suddenly awakened, is unable to explain the situation, and there descends upon her all the wrath of an outraged husband and father. From here on, the story thus far so finely and intensely wrought, breaks down. Virginius degenerates into an implacable revenger, bent on killing his wife after a maximum of spiritual torture. Evidently remembering the success of his introduction of Isabella's child into *The Fatal Marriage,* Southerne attempts to add pathos to Favonia's dilemma by a similar appeal. Virginius, to consummate his revenge on his wife, brings in their child and taunts her with it, only to snatch it away and banish it forever from her sight. The scene does not ring true; it has a palpable air of having been introduced only for effect.

Virginius tells Favonia that she must remain imprisoned for life, but sets suggestively at her side the gifts her father has sent her—a dagger and a bowl of poison. She chooses the poison, and dies just as Virginius brings Junius into the room. Junius, enraged, forces Virginius to fight, and both are killed, though not before Junius has revealed the truth to his friend.

Southerne must have had Othello in mind when he drew in the scenes of Virginius's maddened jealousy. But the very virulence of his passion, unrelieved by any symptoms of humanity, makes us lose sympathy with him. Until Favonia's death we hear from Virginius only maledictions. We miss the supreme tragedy of Othello's tenderness and love breaking through his jealousy. This is only to say, of course, that Virginius is not an Othello, and that the Virginius-Favonia story, so strong at the beginning, weakens steadily toward the end, finishing with all the violence of the tragedy of blood. Virginius's repentance when he has learned the truth from Junius, just before both die, adds nothing to the total effect.

The best poetry of the play is found in the Favonia-Junius scenes. There, occasionally, against a setting of pity and terror, Southerne's simplicity pierces home with real poignancy. Thus the grief of the lovers:

> *Fav.* But Oh! the torment, and the rack of soul!
> To keep our thoughts forever on the bent
> Upon themselves, still labouring to forget,
> What, by the labour, we remember more,[13]

> *Jun.* . . . the accent of my voice is chang'd:
> You cannot know it now in misery.
> There was a time, in the gay spring of life,
> When every note was as the mounting lark's,
> Merry, and cheerful, to salute the morn;
> When all the day was made of melody.
> But it is past, that day is spent, and done,
> And it has long been night, long night with me.[14]

In general, the verse shows the same qualities that we have learned to expect; Southerne has shown little if any advance in poetic power since *The Fatal Marriage*. The lines are clear, smooth—if too frequently end-stopped—and of an undistinguished adequacy.

It is not surprising that the play failed in representation. There is in it altogether too much talk at the expense of the action. Even in the love-plot Favonia and Junius are given soliloquy after soliloquy that tend to run off into sententious moralizings of insufferable length. Then too, Southerne's usual well-articulated plot is absent. The play, in both plots, breaks down about the middle. All the conflict is over and there is nothing to wait for but the deaths of husband, lover, and wife on the one hand, and the spectacular wholesale suicide of the senators on the other.

Yet in the face of these patent weaknesses, the impartial critic must concede the play a certain respectable value, residing chiefly in a few scenes nobly conceived and firmly executed.

[13] I, 3. [14] II, 2.

Southerne's Debt to Livy

For the historical background of the Carthaginian wars as they concerned Capua, Southerne draws from Livy,[15] following his source closely. Book 23 of Livy contains the episode of Pacuvius's shutting the Senate in the Senate-house, and saving them from the mob that would annihilate them by the ruse of pretending to the people that he would be an accomplice in the meditated crime. There he says that he will order the senators to appear one by one, and will leave it with the mob whether each one will live or die, asking only that before sentence be executed on each culprit a fresh senator be elected to supply his place. As with Southerne, the mob disagrees amongst itself, and finally separates. Southerne takes this scene over in every detail.

As Livy records it in Book 23, and Southerne borrows it, the Capuans desert Rome, which has been defeated at Cannae, and join Hannibal over the remonstrances of Decius Magius, who pleads in vain for loyalty to Rome and is rewarded by being cast into chains by Hannibal. He is led off, in both versions, before a lictor, haranguing the multitude. With Livy, however, Magius is banished from Capua and never returns, while with Southerne he is released from imprisonment only to die, with the other senators, by his own hand just before the city falls. Southerne creates the incident in which Magius is sent to ask the Romans for mercy and returns unsuccessful.

Southerne uses, exactly as Livy relates it, the incident in Book 23, chapters eight and nine—even to verbal borrowing —in which Perolla reveals to his father Pacuvius Calavius his plan to assassinate Hannibal at the feast and is dissuaded by his father's pleas. Southerne does not amplify the scene, but incorporates it as it stands in Livy.

As with Southerne, the Romans besiege Capua (Bk. 25,

[15] His material comes from Bk. 23, chs. 2-10, year 216 B.C.; Bk. 25, ch. 22, yr. 212 B.C.; Bk. 26, chs. 12-14, yr. 211 B.C.

ch. 22), and the nobles shut themselves up in their houses, in daily expectation of the city's downfall. Seventy (with Southerne, fifty) messengers attempting to get through to Hannibal are caught by the Romans, scourged, and with their hands cut off are sent back to Capua. Vibius Virius (with Southerne, Pacuvius) tells the Senate how little mercy the town may expect from the Romans, and invites the senators to a feast at his house. There, joining hands, they take poison, and breathe their last as the gates are opened to the enemy.

The characterizations in the political plot of *The Fate of Capua* remain about the same as in the source. The part of Decius Magius is considerably lengthened and he is made to remain on the scene until the very last, to be given opportunity for his noble renunciation of pardon. Contrary to what Friedrich says in his monograph on Southerne,[16] Magius is the only true patriot in Southerne's play. Pacuvius remains in the play as Livy characterizes him: "nobilis idem ac popularis homo, ceterum malis artibus nanctus opes," who "trucidato senatu traderet Capuam Pœnis."[17] Southerne incorporates with the rôle of Pacuvius that of Vibius Marius, who, in Livy, suggests the final suicide-party.

The close of *The Fate of Capua* follows Livy, where "impletæ cibis vinoque venæ minus efficacem in maturanda morte vim veneni fecerunt: itaque noctem totam plerique eorum et diei insequentis partem cum animam egissent," etc.[18]

Southerne's love-plot, apparently original with him, does not appear in Livy.

As mentioned above, Southerne turns frequently to Livy for verbal inspiration. One instance out of many should serve to illustrate this:

[16] p. 51.   [17] XXIII, 2.   [18] XXVI, 14.

The Fate of Capua

Livy

Pœnus hostis ne Africæ quidem indigenam, ab ultimis terrarum oris, freto Oceani Herculisque columnis, expertem omnis juris et condicionis et linguæ prope humanæ militem trahit. Hunc natura et moribus immitem ferumque insuper dux ipse efferavit, pontibus ac molibus ex humanorum corporum strue faciendis, et quod proloqui etiam piget, vesci humanis corporibus docendo.

XXIII, 5.

Play

What are the forces that he brings along?
Not only *Africans,* but nations drawn
From the extreamest limits of the earth;
Hercules's Pillars, and the ocean's bounds:
Who have no knowledge of humanity;
And but in human speech differ from beasts;
Brutal and bloody: but their leader has
Advanc'd their natural barbarity;
Erecting monstrous bridges of the dead,
On human bodies urging his proud way—

. . . . . .

And, as an absolute master of the war,

. . . . . .

Has taught 'em to devour the flesh of men.

II, 1.

CHAPTER X

THE SPARTAN DAME

*Our vet'ran bard resumes his tragic rage:
He throws the gauntlet Otway us'd to wield.*

—Fenton's Prologue

Two decades passed over the head of the unsuccessful *Fate of Capua*, and Southerne's voice in the theatre was still silent. Already he was thought of as belonging to a past age. Those dramatists who had been his early friends were either dead or no longer productively active, and a new generation of theatre-goers was cheering a new race of playwrights. Otway had been gathered to his fathers over a quarter of a century before; Dryden's chair at Will's had been empty these twenty years; Wycherley's last play, *The Plain Dealer*, was forty-five years old, and his last bride a three-years' widow. Congreve had long since given up the title of dramatist for that of gentleman. Strange humours were being thrust upon comedy by Colley Cibber and Sir Richard Steele, while Rowe was now the accepted master of the tragic muse. In spite of the fact that *Oroonoko* and *The Fatal Marriage* were performed at more or less regular intervals, not much was expected of their fifty-nine-year-old author in the way of fresh dramatic activity.

But Southerne was not the man to be counted out at threescore. On Friday, Dec. 11, 1719, he brought out at Drury Lane *The Spartan Dame,* a tragedy which turned overnight into a booming popular triumph. "The success of *The Spartan Dame* has been . . . extraordinary," is the way Southerne puts it in his dedication to John Campbell, Duke of Argyle and Greenwich.[1] It was acted about nine times the

[1] 1678–1743. Distinguished soldier under William and later under Anne. Campaigned with Marlborough in 1706 as brigadier-general, and had a military reputation second only to that of Marlborough. Later he became concerned with Scottish politics, on the death of Anne was ap-

first season,[2] and went through three printings in three weeks.[3] We are told that it brought Southerne £500,[4] much of which amount must have come through his solicitation for tickets among the many "persons of quality" who were his friends.[5] Chetwood paid £120 for the copyright.[6] This unprecedentedly large purchase price was the subject of a caustic comment ascribed to John Dennis:

> . . . and the present Actors, who are the Managers of the Play House, have given all the World an irrefutable Proof, that they have still less Knowledge of Plays than had any of their Predecessors. For have not they turn'd Booksellers *mal 'a propos,* and given a Hundred and twenty Pound for the Copy of a Play, for which none of their Predecessors would have given Five Pound? Perhaps they may say, that they depend upon the Interest of the Author, and a numerous Cabal. A very foolish Dependance! and which sets in a full Light their want of Understanding. For tho' the Interest of an Author, and a numerous Cabal, may go a great way towards Theatrical Success; they be so far from availing a Bookseller, that on the contrary, the Publishing of a damn'd Play, which has had Success upon the stage, is very certain to put an End ev'n to that Success.[7]

pointed general and commander-in-chief of the king's forces in Scotland, and suppressed there the Jacobite uprising. See *D.N.B.* III, 821.

[2] See Nicoll's hand-list of plays, *Early Eighteenth Century Drama,* p. 356.

[3] There are three "editions" dated 1719. The second is only another issue of the first, with the words "The Second Edition" forced into the title-page. In like manner, what is called "The Third Edition" differs from the first only in having a different decoration at the head of the dedication and a differently embellished "T" to begin the preface.

[4] *Biog. Dramat.,* III, 294.

[5] Matthew Prior writes to Lord Harley, Dec. 15 [–26], 1719: "However careful I may seem of managing your purse, I have put you to the expense of a guinea; Southern, my old acquaintance, having asked my assistance in getting him off with some tickets for his *Spartan Dame,* I took one for you, though—as I told him—you were not in town, and he is to make his compliment to you for your favour when you come." *Hist. Mss. Comm. Report—Bath Mss.,* III, 476, 1908.

[6] See Southerne's Preface to *The Spartan Dame* in the 1721 collected edition of his plays, also in the 1774 edition.

[7] *The Characters and Conduct of Sir John Edgar,* 1720. The B.M.

The accuracy of this prophecy is considerably weakened by the fact that within two years of its first performance, *The Spartan Dame* had gone through five editions.[8]

The play received a brilliant production by the full strength of Drury Lane. Mills and Booth acted the parts of the rival kings, Leonidas and Cleombrotus, Wilks played Eurytion, and Colley Cibber the arch-villain Crites. Nance Oldfield and Mary Porter, each in the full height of her powers, appeared as Celona and Thelamia respectively. With such a cast even an inferior play might have succeeded.

Fenton wrote the Prologue, which was spoken by Colley Cibber. It presented Southerne as the bard best fitted to rescue the stage from the plague of harlequins, jiggers, and chattering monsters that infested it; and it bowed gracefully in the direction of Southerne's staunch adherents in the theatre, the ladies.

> But the bold *Briton* ne'er in earnest dines
> Without substantial haunches, and sirloins.
> . . . .
> Instead of light desserts, and luscious froth,
> Our poet treats tonight with *Spartan* broth;
> To which, as well as all his former feasts,
> The ladies are the chief-invited guests.

Major Richardson Pack's[9] moralizing epilogue spoke of this daughter of the author's muse as "The Hopes and Joy of his declining Age," and warned women not to marry such wretches as Cleombrotus:

copy has Ms. notes by Malone, and written into the title-page are the words "By Mr. Dennis." [R.G.H.]

[8] At least, in 1721 Chetwood printed an edition called the fifth—the first to which was added "the 400 Lines omitted in the Representation." This edition was in 12mo., 80 pp.+ii. The first three were in 8vo.; of the fourth I can find no record. The first Dublin edition was published by G. Grierson, 1720, 8vo.

[9] 1682–1728. Miscellaneous writer; entered the army; saw service in

> May poor *Celona's* wrongs a warning prove,
> And teach the Fair with dignity to love,
>
> . . . .
>
> Receive no daemon to an angel's arms.
> Success can then alone your vows attend,
> When Worth's the motive, Constancy the end.

We have advanced far into the morality of a chastened stage since Congreve's brilliant satire in the Epilogue to *Oroonoko!*

The history of the vicissitudes which *The Spartan Dame* underwent before it finally reached the stage is extremely interesting to trace, revealing as it does the thin-skinned political sensitiveness of England under William and Anne, when the slightest suspicion of invidious allegory made a play suspect as Jacobite propaganda.

The play was begun, Southerne himself tells us in the Preface to the first edition, a year before the Revolution of 1688. Four acts were completed at that time. Then, "many things interfering with those times," he laid it by until 1704, when he showed it to William Cavendish, first Duke of Devonshire.[10] Cavendish told him that he saw no reason why it might not have been acted the first year of the Revolution. Let Southerne tell the rest of the story: "I then finished it, and, as I thought, cut out the exceptionable parts, but could not get it acted, not being able to persuade myself to the cutting off those limbs which I thought essential to the strength and life of it: But since I found it must pine in obscurity without it, I consented to the operation; and after the amputation of every line, very near the number of four hundred, it stands on its own legs still, and by the favour of the town, and indulging assistance of friends, has come successfully forward upon the stage."

Spain, 1710, and was promoted to the rank of major. Curll printed several works by Pack between 1719 and 1729. *Cf. D.N.B.*, XV, 27.

[10] Southerne had dedicated *Oroonoko* to him. *Cf.* above, p. 130.

In his Preface to the little-known 1713 collected edition of his plays, Southerne had plaintively mourned his *Spartan Dame's* eclipse: "Eight Plays, I must own, are a numerous Issue for one Man to Father: And yet I have another, which, I am told, might be pleaded in Abatement of the Faults of the rest, a Tragedy, call'd, *The Spartan Dame,* which I should have been glad to have seen among 'em for the Support of the Family: But she has not been allow'd to appear in Publick, even in the Person of Mrs. Barry: So wanting the Recommendation of the Stage, that Play is contented to lye by, and wait upon the Leisure of Peace, and the Humanity of the Great Men in Power, to be permitted at one time or another to try its Fortune in the World."[11]

It is not surprising that the court of William and Mary looked unfavorably on the tragedy. Its main situation, which concerned a queen whose loyalties were divided between her father who had been dethroned and her husband who was the usurper, was altogether too much like the position of Mary between James, her exiled father, and William, her royal husband. Moreover, however directly the plot had been taken from Plutarch, Southerne's characterizations had been extended to make Leonidas, whose fate was the same as James's, a noble, high-minded monarch wrongfully deposed; while Cleombrotus, who in the allegory would be William, was treacherously ambitious and cruel. Small wonder that Southerne's ingenious disclaimers could not offset the direct political implications of his play!

The deletions that he was forced to make before its pro-

[11] To this 1713 edition of his plays Southerne prefixed the long congratulatory poem addressed to him by Elijah Fenton (see above, p. 21), with the comment: "The Hunger of Praise is very craving, I confess: But I have satisfied that craving, by printing at the Head of my Plays, Mr. Fenton's Excellent Poem, where he says finer things of the *Spartan Dame,* than, may be, the Town would come up to, if they had her among 'em."

duction were thoroughgoing. All passages developing the idea that Cleombrotus's revolt was against the king his father-in-law were cut out, as were all lines emphasizing the uprising of the people, their inconstancy, their being "saucy censurers of sovereign sway"—in short, all portions that made Cleombrotus a usurper and that showed the people supporting him. Not a little of the play's force is lost with these excisions.

When Southerne made in 1719 one more attempt to have his tragedy produced, he was aided generously by William Congreve, who wrote the following letter to Thomas Pelham Holles (1693–1768), Duke of Newcastle, and Lord Chamberlain since 1717:

My Lord,
By y^r Graces direction, m^r Southern has don[e] me the honour to read his tragedy to me. I cannot but think that it has been a wrong to the town, as well as an injury to the Author, that such a work has been so long witheld from the Publick. This I say with respect to it as a Play.

Whatever may have been supposed or suggested against it on the score of Politicks is in my Opinion absolutely groundless. I can see no shadow of an Objection to it upon that account, tho I have attended to it very precisely even in regard to that particular in Justice to Mr Southern and in Obedience to y^r Graces Commands. I am thus plain in my thoughts on this occasion. I am always with the greatest respect

My Lord
Y^r Graces most Obedient
humble Servant
Wm Congreve.[12]

The bread that Southerne had cast upon the waters when, many years before, he had helped Congreve's first play to the stage, was returning to him after many days.

It is difficult to determine, at this date, how accurate is Southerne's claim that the play was begun without any political allegory in mind, and that before the Revolution nearly

---

[12] Summers's edition of Congreve's *Works*, I, 97.

four acts were written "without any view, but upon the subject, which I took from the Life of *Agis* in *Plutarch*."[13] In a way, circumstantial evidence is against him: the play and the contemporary political situation dove-tail very neatly. Again, *The Loyal Brother,* in 1682, had glorified James. Southerne was in 1687 in James's army under James's natural son, the Duke of Berwick, who, we are told,[14] commanded him to begin the play. Moreover, the characterizations are changed from what they were in Plutarch to fit a Jacobite's conception of James's integrity and William's illegal assumption of the throne. Even if the play had been begun before the Revolution, as Southerne declares, still it is not impossible that he might have made dramatic material of a political situation that all England knew was potentially possible. Southerne's later attempts to deny a political intent would be understandable enough under this theory, for he himself, in the interim, had deserted the cause of James and was now cultivating with all assiduity the friendship of those men of rank who were strong anti-Jacobites. He even dedicated the play to Argyle, a former enemy of James's.

In spite of all this, I am inclined to grant Southerne his point. The intensification, beyond Plutarch, of the evil nature of Cleombrotus and the incorruptibility of Leonidas is a heightening that could be entirely justified by dramatic necessity. Most important of all, the logic of the situation is on Southerne's side. It is hard to believe that any poet would throw into dramatic form a political allegory which, if it were to represent events as they actually crystallized in England (and to have any political point at all, that is what it would have to do), would be automatically denied any hope of production. More concretely: the tragedy, supposing that it indicated Mary divided in her allegiance, James a hero, and William altogether unlovely, would have to be staged under the very noses of William and Mary. That would be obviously

[13] Preface. [14] Preface.

impossible—and Southerne was not interested in writing closet-drama. The situation as I conceive it is this: Southerne began the play in good faith, taking from Plutarch a situation with admirable dramatic possibilities. Even before he finished it, the Revolution descended, and he saw that Plutarch paralleled with uncanny exactness the England of 1688. Therefore, "many things interfering with those times" indeed, he regretfully laid it by until a new political day would dawn. Even so, it was thirty-two years before, by dint of vigorous cutting, he could convince the authorities that the play held no political gunpowder.

Nor is there any reason to argue, as does Friedrich on grounds of style, that the play must have been written after the Revolution.[15] The edition of Plutarch's *Lives* called Dryden's had been completed in 1686.[16] What would be more natural than that the young playwright should turn to it at once as a source of tragic material? To be sure, in spite of some passages of heroic weakness reminiscent of *The Loyal Brother,* the play as a whole represents Southerne at the maturity of his poetic and dramatic powers. But is it not reasonable to assume that any man grooming for production a play that he had only partially completed thirty years before, would subject it to careful revision? As a matter of fact, there is evidence to show as much. John Duncombe tells of a Mr. John Allen who advised Southerne as early as 1694 that *The Spartan Dame* would never succeed, but who, on reading it in 1719, "found it very different (he said) from what it was then."[17] No, lacking direct evidence to the contrary, we must take Southerne's assertions at their face value. But be-

---

[15] *Thomas Southerne als Dramatiker,* p. 64.

[16] Dryden did not translate the *Lives* in any part, but wrote for the edition a dedication and a *Life of Plutarch.* Some forty-one hands made the translation. *Cf.* Scott-Saintsbury, *Dryden,* XVII, 3.

[17] J. Duncombe: *Letters by Several Eminent Persons Deceased,* 3 vols., 2nd ed., 1773. I, 253 n. Duncombe's wife was Allen's youngest sister; so the note probably has authenticity.

cause the play is clearly shaped by his mature hand, it is discussed here in its place of chronological appearance.

The Story

CLEOMBROTUS, having falsely incensed the people of Sparta against their king, Leonidas, drives him into exile and assumes the throne. Celona, wife to Cleombrotus and daughter to Leonidas, does not allow her affection for her husband to blind her to the injustice perpetrated against her father, and she tells Cleombrotus plainly that she can be no queen to him, though she will still be faithful as his wife. Thelamia, Celona's sister, is married to Eurytion, who espouses the cause of Leonidas and follows him into exile. Cleombrotus, tired of his wife, lusts after his wife's sister; and when he is unable to win Thelamia by his pleas, he seduces her through a plot laid by his wicked henchman, Crites. Crites arranges for him to slip into Thelamia's bed in place of Eurytion, whose return Thelamia was expecting.

The energetic Crites, unknown to Cleombrotus, is also engaged in a political plot. Fearing that Celona will try to get her father back on the throne, he lures the exiled king back to Sparta by a false message to the effect that Celona is planning to kill her husband. It is Crites' plot to assassinate Leonidas when he appears in Sparta. But when Leonidas, who is too honorable to try to regain his throne by subversive means, hears that his daughter has been raped by Cleombrotus, he rises in righteous wrath and stirs the people to a counter-revolution. Cleombrotus, Crites, and the rest of their party flee to the Temple of Neptune. There they are besieged. Crites is killed by Cleombrotus on a false suspicion of treachery, and Cleombrotus himself is killed by the revengeful Eurytion, in spite of Celona's pleas that his life be spared. Thelamia takes poison. Leonidas is restored to his throne, while Celona retires to a life of broken-hearted seclusion.

Southerne's Use of Plutarch

SOUTHERNE drew on Plutarch's *Life of Agis* for the plot of *The Spartan Dame*. He has taken thence chiefly the political background and the main movement of events. The development of the characterizations and the added complications of the plot are all his own. Chelonis (with Southerne, Celona) is the only character whose motives and personality are indicated in Plutarch with anything like the fulness of Southerne's development. And even here the source differs from the play; when Leonidas is exiled, Chelonis resolves to leave her husband and follow her father, although, as with Southerne, she pleads for Cleombrotus's life when he is at last defeated.

To make the conflict of the rival kings more significant, Southerne makes Cleombrotus distinctly a villain, not only in his usurpation but in his treachery to his wife and to Thelamia. With Plutarch he is a colorless character about whom we are told little. Also, Southerne paints Leonidas, to whom Plutarch gave a distinctly unfavorable character, in glowing colors of impeccable integrity.

Chelonis is the only woman in Plutarch's story. There, her pleading for her husband's life is only the act of a woman true to her husband in political misfortune; in *The Spartan Dame* it is that of a wife loyal also to her domestic duty, even when her husband has betrayed her. The sub-plot of Cleombrotus's passion for Thelamia, and the character of Thelamia herself, are Southerne's own, as are the characters Eurytion and Crites.

Agis, who in Plutarch was co-king with Leonidas before his banishment, Southerne does not mention; the throne is not shared. With the loss of Agis there disappears much of Plutarch's political complication; for instance, the scheme for cancelling the people's debts and for a more equal distribution of property. The dethronement of Leonidas, his return and the resultant revolution in his favor, and the flight of

Cleombrotus to the temple are the same in both versions. In the source, however, Leonidas is moved to compassion by Chelonis's request for her husband's life, and so only sends him into banishment, whither Chelonis follows him.

As before, then, we see Southerne adapting freely his source material, changing it or adding to it as seems dramatically advisable. There are in *The Spartan Dame* no scenes that parallel, speech by speech, Plutarch's story, perhaps because Plutarch gives very few speeches.

Southerne's Spartans

EVEN today *The Spartan Dame* impresses favorably the reader who attempts to discover the secret of its contemporary success. The occasional flights of oratory that fitted the current conception of how the ancients talked and the well-integrated, single action cannot however hide the fact that the play's appeal rested on qualities other than those of neo-classic regularity. Southerne takes a classical story and translates it in terms of good, warm English action. Here is no Cato riding above the tumult, but a brisk conflict of human motive and character, glossed only superficially with Spartan calm. There is almost no attempt at local color, the lack of which induced Genest to call it "far from a capital play."[18] Southerne introduces such anachronisms as lictor and plebeian; Thelamia reads the story of the Roman Lucretia; Crites says that he has been with a set of men who railed on marriage, declaring that the institution was never made in heaven. "What Grecian ever dreamed that it was?" asks Genest, fairly enough. As in *The Fate of Capua,* the Grecian mobs might have come from Eastcheap. The ignorant rabble quibbles much in the manner of Shakespeare's plebeians. Crites voices his scorn of such a populace:

> Then they shake
> Their brainless coxcombs, rearing dirty palms,
> They snuffle out their fears.[19]

[18] III, 7.   [19] III, 1.

All that they lack to make the comparison complete is the sweaty nightcap. Most of all, in his crowded action, his spectacular climaxes, the bustle of his very energetic villains, and the taut emotionalism of his tragic crises, Southerne remained, as always, the heir of the Elizabethans. It is not as classical tragedy that we may approve *The Spartan Dame*.

Celona is the Spartan Dame, and the center of the tragic whirlpool. As daughter to the exiled king, wife to the usurper, and sister to her whom Cleombrotus rapes, she suffers betrayal as well as the pull of conflicting allegiances. With justice she could say to Thelamia: "If I may judge the cause, I'm injur'd most."[20] She is the very type of noble womanhood, loving her husband so tenderly that she can exclaim as she hears him speak:

> my list'ning soul is charm'd
> Into my ears, and dies upon the sound
> Of ev'ry word, soft as a lover's wish,
> And I cou'd hear you ever,[21]

and yet hating with all her honesty of heart his unscrupulous ambition:

> 'Tis therefore I abhor your tyranny,
> That base-born issue of unlawful might!
> Begot upon the fears of bad mens crimes,
> Or prostituted, slavish principles;
> Cradled in infamy, and rear'd in vice,
> Fatted with feasts of undeserved praise;
> Blown up with flattery to a giant size
> Of rapine, and oppressive insolence,
> To trample down the bounds of property,
> And seize the common birth-right, Liberty.
> This is the monster idol you set up,
> Which, in the pride of virtue, I despise . . .[22]

She can wither with scornful invective the hangers-on of Cleombrotus's party, who would like to win her approval:

[20] IV, 1.   [21] I, 1.   [22] II, 1.

> You brace of courteous, cringing sycophants!
> You double-hearted slaves, and double-tongu'd!
> Whose hollow flatteries would win me to
> Your rotten sides, only to prop your pride.[23]

Equivocation is not in her nature. Yet when Cleombrotus has at last fallen and faces imminent death, she stands staunchly by his side,

>   for he is mine,
> My husband still, however base and false.
> Tho' I am wrong'd in the most tender part,
> Most sensible of pain, I am his wife;
> That is the character I must maintain.[24]

Her stuff is that from which true heroines are cut. That she does not die at the end does not weaken the tragic effectiveness of the play. Her life is ruined by Cleombrotus's delinquency and death, but she must live on, destined to

>   bear this wretched load of life,
> But far remov'd, and shut out from the world,
> No more to be remember'd in my wrongs.[25]

Celona exhibits one quality altogether lacking in Isabella, Imoinda, and Favonia—a quality that adds to her stature as a tragic heroine—decisiveness. The issues at stake are never for an instant befogged in her mind; there is no blind groping toward a solution. That which the other heroines in a baffled way only pretended to do, she did; she envisaged circumstance and let play over it a stream of thought. In no uncertain terms she told Cleombrotus her exact opinion of his disloyalty; no less uncertainly, when it came time to cleave to him as wife to husband she accomplished the act with notable bravery and without compromising in any way her principles. It is refreshing to discover, after a series of heroines whose bewilderment was always stronger than their powers of decision, one whose fate was no less tragic but

---

[23] II, 1.   [24] IV, 1.   [25] V, 2.

who met it clear-eyed. To his usual effective portrayal of suffering femininity Southerne adds here a new strength of intellect that adds dramatic power to the customary enveloping pathos.

Yet the clear-sighted Celona, like all the other virtuous people in the play, is gulled by the most interesting villain in the whole range of Southerne's dramatic work. Crites is a character of Southerne's creation, necessary to the plot in that he makes possible Cleombrotus's betrayal of Thelamia and that he lures Leonidas back to a would-be assassination. I say that the conception of Crites is original with Southerne because he is not found in Plutarch. He is blood-brother to Iago, however, in many ways. For one thing, he is respected and trusted by those who should have known better. Leonidas believes in him;[26] Thelamia calls him a "faithful, honest friend";[27] Celona believes him "an honest-hearted man;[28] even Eurytion addresses him as "thou truly loyal man,"[29] and when he has to leave Sparta, entrusts Thelamia to Crites' care, thus making it possible for her to be ruined. Like Iago, Crites takes a genuine relish in his intrigues, and is not without a certain cynical wit. He is an accurate judge of human nature: when he writes the letter to Leonidas declaring falsely that Celona is planning the murder of Cleombrotus, his fellow-conspirator Agesilaus supposes that Leonidas will return joyfully to re-capture his crown. Crites knows Leonidas more thoroughly, and prophesies correctly

> That when the letter tells him that his daughter
> Intends her husband's murder, he will fly,
> To save her from the sin.[30]

As a villain he does not deceive himself; no "motiveless malignity" is his. Quite frankly he declares his code of ethics:

[26] III, 1. [27] III, 2. [28] II, 1.
[29] I, 1.   [30] III, 1.

> But he who makes his fortune in this world,
> Must sometimes do what he would blush to name.[31]

Another reminiscence of *Othello* lies in the relationship between Crites' wife Bizanthe and Thelamia. She is companion to Thelamia, against whom her husband was plotting, just as Emilia was servant to Desdemona.

That we may at least despise him whose genial ingenuity makes him hard to hate, Southerne reveals Crites in the last act as a physical coward; and he dies a villain's death as he is flung headlong from the temple walls by Cleombrotus, who mistakenly suspects him of betraying the cause to the besiegers.

There is small need to discuss the other characters in any detail. They are portrayed directly and clearly without attaining any degree of complexity or subtlety. Although Thelamia is an entirely passive character, her distresses are made very real. Particularly effective is her apprehension just before she welcomes to her arms in the darkness the man she believes to be her husband.[32] Eurytion plays a slight but important part as his wife's avenger. Cleombrotus and Leonidas are thrown into broad contrast, the one as the personification of perfidy, the other of honor. Leonidas betrays a peculiar trait that is yet of some dramaturgic value, leading on two occasions to the creation of scenes melodramatic if not strictly dramatic. When he has any bad news to break, he likes to test his patient by first creating a fiction worse than the reality; then, if that proves bearable, to reveal the truth. In this way he tries Celona's valor by telling her that he has killed Cleombrotus, before he delivers his real information—that he has been told that she is plotting against Cleombrotus's life. Later it becomes his duty to tell Eurytion of Thelamia's rape. He first declares that she is dead, and when Eurytion stands up under that, he tells him the lesser truth.

[31] II, 1.
[32] Southerne here makes tragic application of a motive long familiar to comedy.

Fate enters but slightly into the tragedy of *The Spartan Dame*. The clash is that of character against character instead of character against circumstance as in *The Fatal Marriage* and in the love-plot of *The Fate of Capua*. Southerne lines the good characters up against the bad and paints them in unmistakable colors. Nevertheless, he has written into the part of Celona a conflict that is within instead of without, and that accumulates thereby a good degree of tragic power.

Dramatic Technique

OF all Southerne's tragedies, *The Spartan Dame* has the most closely woven action. To the political plot taken from Plutarch he adds a complication of betrayed love, but that very betrayal proves to be the deed which precipitates in turn the political crisis. Cause and effect follow each other with undeviating certainty. It is worthy of note that while *The Fate of Capua,* Southerne's other "classical" tragedy, has eighteen scenes, *The Spartan Dame* has but nine.

Yet the stage success of Southerne's tragedies depended more on theatrically effective situations than on well-wrought plots. Such a situation is that which displays the nervous apprehension of Thelamia as she reads the story of Lucretia and compares it with her own situation, just before she is tricked by Cleombrotus. Another is the scene in which she reluctantly tells Celona of her rape. The most spectacular scene of all is the last one in the play, before the Temple of Neptune. The party of Cleombrotus and Crites has been routed by Leonidas and driven to the Temple for a last refuge. There is much business of battering in the gates, a surprise attack from within, and Cleombrotus hurling Crites from the walls. Just before Eurytion forces his way into the Temple through a secret underground passage and surprises the defenders, Cleombrotus brings to the edge of the walls Leonidas's third daughter, Euphemia, an inmate of the temple. Unless Leonidas will withdraw his forces immediately, he threatens to have his slaves rape Euphemia and then kill her. Such scenes as these load every rift with the ore of excitement.

In the Preface to the 1721 edition of the play Southerne first made an acknowledgment that also appears in the 1774 edition. "I have now an opportunity of doing justice to the dead," he says, "by acknowledging that the last scene of the third act, was almost all written by the honourable *John Stafford,* the most excellent father of the present most worthy Earl of *Stafford.*"[33] With unnecessary modesty, Southerne calls it "the best scene in the play." It is that in which Leonidas tests Celona by reporting the murder of Cleombrotus. The poetry here is of an inferior quality and serves only to throw into favorable contrast with it Southerne's own poetic virtues. Southerne's verse may sometimes come too trippingly from the pen, sometimes it diverges into bombast or descends to dulness; still, one excellence it maintains with unusual evenness—lucidity. The thought may not be profound, but it is always clearly stated. Stafford's poetry, on the other hand, is confused as well as inflated. It represents the efforts of a mediocre talent to attain the dignity of "sceptred palls" and the like. Four lines will illustrate the tone of much of it:

> The spirit that inflam'd the *Belides,*
> Has been too boasting late in hell, too vain,
> And rouz'd the honour of some bolder fiend,
> To show transcendent damning to their shades.[34]

The Spartan Dame was Southerne's last tragedy, and except for one weak comedy, at which we shall now glance, it

---

[33] "The present most worthy Earl of Stafford" was William Stafford-Howard (1690–1733), 2nd Earl of Stafford, who succeeded his uncle, Henry Stafford, 1st Earl, in 1719. William was the eldest son of John Stafford, who in turn was second son to Sir William Howard, 1st Baron and Viscount Stafford. John is listed in Burke's *Peerage* as "John, of Stafford Castle." Of the reputation that Southerne ascribes to him as "so masterly a writer" I can find no record.

[34] III, 4.

marked the close of his career as a dramatist. Its unusual popularity proved his ability to succeed in the form that he had tried and in which he had failed with *The Fate of Capua*. There is no record, however, that *The Spartan Dame* was revived later. It belonged to *The Fatal Marriage* and *Oroonoko* to keep Southerne's name fresh in the memory of the eighteenth century.

CHAPTER XI

MONEY THE MISTRESS

It requires some skill to know when to leave off writing.
Letter of Broome's to Pope concerning *Money the Mistress.*

IT is inevitable that any chronological history of Southerne's art should end on a note of anti-climax. The imagination that had produced *The Fatal Marriage* and *Oroonoko* had pretty well consumed itself by 1700.[1] Yet the habit of writing still remained, and from the ashes there rose in 1726 the somewhat bedraggled Phœnix of *Money the Mistress.* This last play of our author's represents a valiant effort to translate into terms of the new drama the comic spirit that had informed the comedies of 1690–93; actually, it is the sere and yellow leaf of his dramatic genius. The form remains, but it lacks the impregnation of vitality that had given the earlier plays their lease on life. Nevertheless, a certain charity becomes the historian at this point; the play, in spite of its weakness, is no disgraceful exhibition of senility. Southerne was sixty-six years of age at the time, and our wonder is, not that his last dramatic attempt should be ineffective, but that, like Dr. Johnson's dog walking on its hind legs, it could be done at all.

Money the Mistress was first performed at Lincoln's-Inn-Fields Saturday, February 19, 1725/6,[2] lingered for one or two more performances, and then passed into oblivion. From the first, Southerne's friends had been doubtful of the experiment, though they were inclined to humor him somewhat

---

[1] It must be remembered that *The Spartan Dame* was the completion and revision of a play partially written over thirty years before its production.

[2] See *Genest* III, 179, and Nicoll's hand-list of plays, *Early Eighteenth Century Drama,* p. 356.

as the Nestor of living poets. Even those who had "gone a great way in commendation of this . . . at the same time believed it would not take with the Town," Southerne tells us.³ Leonard Welsted⁴ wrote a Prologue in which he admitted that much

> Is wasted of his fire and wonted strength.
> The suns decay; the brightest lustre wains;
> Nor is he all he was in former reigns.

For one last time an appeal for support was made to the women, whose mothers had taken Isabella and Imoinda to their hearts.

> To you, ye fair, for patronage he sues:
> O! last defend, who first inspir'd his Muse!
> In your soft service he has pass'd his days,
> And gloried to be born for woman's praise:
> Deprest at length, and in your cause decay'd;
> The good old man, to beauty bends for aid;
> That beauty, he has taught so oft to moan!

Southerne had asked William Broome for an Epilogue. On Jan. 2, 1725/6 Broome writes thus to Pope:

> Mr. Southerne wants an epilogue, and will oblige me to write it. I am sorry he brings his play on the stage. His bays are withered with extreme age. From what I heard of it with you at Sir Clement Cottrell's, it cannot bear water, and the lead of my epilogue fastened to the end of it will add to its alacrity in sinking. Mr. Southerne's fire is abated, and no wonder, when philosophers tell us that the warmth and glory of the sun abates by age. It requires some skill to know when to leave off writing.

> N.B. Let Mr. Fenton and you take notice that I write this epilogue upon this express condition, that it shall not be spoken, if Mr. Southerne can procure one by another hand; if not, I will do myself the honour to attend the old bard, and hold up the train of his comedy in Drury.⁵

³ Dedication.
⁴ Welsted (1688–1747) was a poet, and author of the comedy *The Dissembled Wanton* (1726).
⁵ Pope's *Works,* ed. Elwin-Courthope, VIII, 111.

Instead of Broome's Epilogue, one by George Jeffrys[6] was spoken, which emphasized the fact that the faithless lover in the play was a Frenchman and that therefore Southerne's endeavor was "to brand a foreign vice."

> And, ladies, is it not extremely clever,
> He leaves your *English* sparks as true as ever.

The last lines of Broome's Epilogue were later included in his *Poems on Several Occasions*.[7]

In his letter to Broome Fenton said of Southerne and his play, "Because I could not counterfeit a transport, he has looked a little cold upon me ever since."[8] With typical stubbornness, Southerne refused to grant that *Money the Mistress* deserved failure. In his Dedication he expressed his belief that "with some skill and address" the story had been "brought by me into the unity of the scene and the compass of a play. . . . If the tale be good, the plot well laid, and digested into the strength and support of the whole; the disposition of the business natural and easy; the incidents proper and prepared; the sentiments honorable and virtuous, and the writing able to speak for itself, all which I hope I have secured in this piece, I shall think I have done my part." In explanation of its lack of success, he hurls a side-long

---

[6] Jeffrys (1678-1755) was author of numerous poems and two plays. On the second night of his *Merope* (1731), the audience was dismissed without his play being produced. (See *D.N.B.* X, 721.)

[7] 2nd. ed., 1750, p. 164.

> There was a time, when in his younger Years,
> Our Author's Scenes commanded Smiles or Tears;
> And tho' beneath the Weight of Days he bends,
> Yet, like the Sun, he shines as he descends:
> Then with Applause, in honour to his Age,
> Dismiss your veteran Soldier off the Stage;
> Crown his last Exit with distinguish'd Praise,
> And kindly hide his Baldness with the Bays.

[8] Pope's *Works*, VIII, 112.

shaft at pantomime and ballad opera: "Since the palate is vitiated, let those answer who have depraved it."

We prefer to remember Southerne, however, by the flash of quick humor with which he met the hisses of the audience on the first night. Benjamin Victor, who was present at the scene, tells the story:

> I happened to be behind the Scenes the first Night of this Comedy, and was very sorry to find that the Audience did not take the Age, as well as the great Merit of this Author, into their Consideration, and quietly dismiss this last weak Effort to please them. When they were hissing dreadfully in the fifth Act, Mr. *Rich,* who was standing by Mr. *Southern,* asked him, if he heard what the Audience were doing? His Answer was, *"No, Sir, I am very deaf."*[9]

In dedicating his play to John, Lord Boyle, Southerne acknowledged gratefully the favors that had come to him from the house of Orrery. John's father, Charles, had been Southerne's chief patron in the past, and the son was one of the best friends the poet was to have during his remaining twenty years of life.[10]

Story and Source

SOUTHERNE sets *Money the Mistress* in Tangier, a seaport of Morocco on the Strait of Gibraltar, formerly in England's possession.[11] Genest says optimistically that "the play would have had a better chance of success, if it had been brought out during the time that Tangier was in the hands of the English—in 1726 the majority of the audience probably did not know much about Tangier."[12] It is to be feared that a knowledge of Tangier would not have made the play any more appealing than it was. Even the international flavor of

---

[9] *History of the Theatres of London and Dublin,* 3 vols., 1761-71, II, 152.

[10] See above, pp. 15-17.

[11] Ceded to England by Portugal on the marriage of Chas. II in 1662. Abandoned by the English to the Moors in 1684.

[12] III, 181.

the characters—English, French, Spanish, Moor, and Jew—did not help to bring success to a play essentially ineffective.

The story runs as follows: Mariana, daughter to the covetous old Davila, is beloved by Warcourt and Mourville, both of whom are in the English army, which is at present repelling an attack of the Moors on the town. Mourville is young and dashing, Warcourt somewhat older and rich. Mariana favors Mourville, although her father, eager for a fortune, is trying to force her to marry Warcourt, who, however, will not marry the girl unless of her own consent. Mourville is captured by the enemy, and Mariana, together with her energetic friend Harriet, who plans the adventure, goes to the Moorish camp to try to arrange his release. Harriet thinks of a plan whereby Mariana takes Mourville's place as prisoner, secure in the knowledge that her father will ransom her. Harriet then goes away with Mourville, taking with her some valuable jewels that had been a present to Mariana from Warcourt, and that Mariana had entrusted to her friend's keeping. This false friend tells Mourville how she loves him, and convinces him that a marriage with her would be a more profitable procedure than one with Mariana, whose father, it has just been reported, has lost all his fortune with the capture of his merchant vessels. The two are married secretly. Warcourt comes to Mariana's rescue and ransoms her. Harriet pawns the jewels to give money to her new husband, who does not suspect the source of their wealth; and this pawning provides the clue whereby Harriet's dishonesty and Mourville's treachery are eventually uncovered, much to the shame of the latter, for whom it must be said that he is weak rather than iniquitous. It develops that the ships of Harriet's father, rather than of Mariana's, had been sunk. Warcourt repeats his honorable pleas for Mariana's hand and is told that he will be accepted.

A sub-plot concerns the attempt of Don Manuel, a Spanish captain of horse, to seduce Diana, wife to Marsan, who is in the English army. Diana reveals to her husband the unwelcome attentions of this rake, and a plot is laid whereby the lecherous Spaniard is utterly discomfited. This minor action enters the play only spasmodically towards the end, and is dismissed with a couple of scenes.

In his earlier comedies Southerne, drawing his situations from the open stock of Restoration comedy, was responsible to no particular source for his plots. Here, however, he takes his story directly from a romantic and sentimental travel-book of the Comtesse d'Aulnoy, *The Ingenious and Diverting Letters of the Lady . . . Travels into Spain.*[13] The plot of the play is essentially that of the novel, though it amplifies for dramatic purposes hints undeveloped in the original. Thus Davila is reduced to a grasping covetous person, and Southerne invents the effective episode of his leading, unawares and for a consideration, his own daughter to the Moorish camp. With unconscious irony, Davila addresses her as "my daughter." Mendez (with Southerne Mourville) remains about the same in both versions; he is progressively jealous, faithless, and repentant. Southerne motivates his desertion of Mariana more certainly by changing Henrietta (Harriet) from a timorous girl into a resourceful adventuress who instigates the trip to the Moors, suggests the substitution of Mariana for Mourville, and lures Mourville on to marry her by dangling the stolen jewels before his eyes. The jewels, which enter but slightly into the novel, are made much more of in the play, and finally precipitate the dénouement. All of the sub-plot, relating to Don Manuel, is Southerne's own.

Comedy of a New Order

Money the Mistress is not important enough to call for any very close examination here. It will be sufficient for our purposes to look briefly at some of the characterizations and then

[13] A reprint of the second (1692) edition was printed in 1899 by A. M. Huntington, London. The episode that forms the basis of Southerne's play is found there on pp. 173–241.

to consider in some detail the one point of interest that the play has for the student of Southerne—the dramatist's attempt to adapt his theory of comedy to the changing tastes of the age. The theatre of 1726 was not the theatre of 1690; new manners and new morals were demanded of its comic heroes, and in Southerne's somewhat fumbling efforts to put on the cloak of Cibber and speak with the voice of Steele we can read the measure of the distance between *Sir Anthony Love* and *Money the Mistress*.

Southerne calls his drama simply "a play," and certainly it is not comedy in the sense that those were which he had written in his early manhood. It is a play of romantic adventure, the very title of which points a moral. The basic idea of the play, the power of gold over the motives of men, is driven home in a number of characterizations.

Thus Mourville sells his honor in love for a pearl necklace and a diamond buckle. Davila's chief desire is to marry his daughter to a competence—it is his lust for money that makes him undertake the task of escorting to the Moorish camp the woman whom he did not suspect to be his daughter. Moluzza, the Moorish captor, will be moved by no pleas that are not backed up by a ready purse—"Money will find me, and a welcome at all times," he declares. Harriet has no compunctions about stealing the jewels that Warcourt had given Mariana. Of all these rascals, the most lively is Harriet. She has that buoyant resourcefulness characteristic of Southerne's villains, who are sometimes inclined to be more interesting than his heroes. The faithfulness and honesty of Mariana and the sensitive gentlemanliness of Warcourt shine more brightly, of course, in contrast to the ignobility of those to whom money is mistress.

Money the Mistress is a moral comedy, written to expose the futility of greed and reveal the charms of generous righteousness. Like the other sentimental plays of the time that were entrenching themselves more and more firmly in the theatre, it proposes to instruct even more than to entertain.

Southerne plumed himself on his success in making "the sentiments honourable and virtuous . . . the manners instructive of youth."[14] Years before, Dryden had compared Southerne with Terence, and now the old dramatist claims for himself the Terentian manner. The play "is framed on the model of *Terence*," he says, "and as Comedies ought to be, not to do harm."[14] As in 1694, "the present humour of the town"[15] was the line to which Southerne hewed, but that humour was decidedly not the same as that which had dictated the comic sub-plot of *The Fatal Marriage*.

Warcourt is a character new in Southerne's anthology—the faultless hero of honest intent and ready moralization. His utterances mark him off as one of the generation that, touched ne'er so lightly, exudes lofty sentiments. His wooing of Mariana is eminently post-Collier: "For I have long observ'd, and admir'd the gentleness of your disposition, which, in my estimation, is the nursing-mother of content in private life."[16] Again, "I have not that mint in my mouth for the coinage and utterance of false vows and oaths, which have passed current on many a virgin, ruined and undone, before the discovery of the baseness of the alloy."[16] Banter has disappeared before an access of sensibility.

Mariana is a heroine fit for such a hero, and in her characterization Southerne was on more familiar ground. Even Harriet grants that she is "well-natur'd, gentle-condition'd, beautiful."[17] Sententiousness comes readily from her lips: "Reputation! the reward of virtue, the voluntary tribute of all good people, paid to it, in commendation and esteem."[18] Deceived by Mourville, she finds a just shelter in the arms of Warcourt, the predestined protector of such innocence and purity.

As might be expected, the play closes in a very flood of poetic justice. Harriet reaps the fit reward of her deceit,

[14] Dedication.
[15] Dedication to *The Fatal Marriage*.
[16] I, 2.   [17] III, 1.   [18] II, 3.

exposed to the world as a betrayer of friendship and facing poverty with her pusillanimous husband. Mourville himself suffers the pangs of remorse for his weakness; of his fate he says "'Tis just upon me; I deserve it all."[19] Southerne could say with justice, "I have punished infidelity in the lover, and falseness in the friend."[20] To Warcourt and Mariana are granted the benison of success, financial and romantic, that marks the path of those whom sentimental comedy delighted to honor. The Governor closes the whole with an instructive aphorism:

> These patterns lay before our female youth,
> The sure effects of gallantry, and truth.

In the sub-plot, the comedy of manners and intrigue gives a last despairing gasp. Don Manuel is the ghost of the Restoration rake. Old, frothing, amorous, he gives himself to the one business that such as he knew best. Pseudo-witty phrases resembling those of his Restoration forbears are his, but in keeping with the morality of the day, he is not allowed success in his adventures. He who in his halcyon days would have mocked the virtuous is now in turn made the butt of much merriment by the upright. His plots against Diana's chastity end in his confusion, and he is laughed off the stage. After all, Don Manuel was out of his element—he had lived too long.

It is clear, then, that at the end of his long dramatic career, Southerne was embracing, albeit somewhat gingerly, the Sentimental Muse. There is evidence in his earlier work to show that the transition is no surprising one. He was not at ease in the new form, but that may be laid as correctly to a general disintegration of dramatic power as to an inability to adjust himself to a fresh comic pattern. It is a testimony to his energy that at sixty-six, and free from the necessity of replenishing his pocketbook, he was actively engaged in the

---

[19] V, 3.   [20] Dedication.

theatre, rubbing shoulders with a new generation of playwrights. Like his friends who loved him we had best draw the veil quickly over this deserved failure, *Money the Mistress,* and urge with Welsted in the Prologue:

> Nor let the wreath from his grey head be torn;
> For half a century, with honour worn.

CHAPTER XII

CONCLUSION

In him the poets' Nestor *ye defend!*
Great Otway's *peer, and greater* Dryden's *friend.*
—Prologue to *Money the Mistress.*

THOMAS SOUTHERNE emerges from a candid appraisal of his life and work with a greater importance in the history of the English theatre than he has hitherto been granted by the critics who have touched him only in passing. The new evidence that this study has brought together to show the esteem in which the poet's work was held by his contemporaries, as well as the unexpectedly long and continuous stage history of his two best plays, would alone support such an estimate. Moreover, his most effective work bears the test of a close critical scrutiny. This is not to say that such an examination reveals in Southerne unsuspected depths of genius, yet it is significant and not a little surprising to find how closely the quality of his most enduring drama approaches the best of its kind. But lest his advocate be accused of a critical myopia not unknown to special pleaders, it is advisable to draw together here the threads of Southerne's activity, and to place them in perspective against the background of the Restoration and eighteenth-century theatre. Thus it will be possible to illuminate with greater clarity his successes and his failures, and more importantly, to indicate his place in the development of English drama.

A "Practical" Dramatist

WE find Southerne a man capable, beyond most of his fellow-craftsmen, of adapting himself to a difficult age. His dramatic activity extended over a span of forty-four years, and the history of his artistic life in that period is one of lightly-poised sensitiveness to public taste and opinion. Politically and professionally he was an opportunist; if such a philosophy reflected invidiously on his artistic integrity, it at least brought him financial competency and a high degree of theatrical success. Nor was any taint of hypocrisy his; a character singularly honest and straightforward in its personal relations brought him to his grave as full of honor as of years. He conquered the environment that had beaten down Lee and Otway, greater geniuses than he, and had checkered even Dryden's life with disappointment. That Southerne succeeded where better artists failed makes him a fascinating object of study against the background of the Caroline and Orange theatre.

Not the least of his good fortune came from an ability to find harbor with generous patrons, a feat which he accomplished by sailing with the prevailing political wind. He began his career on the stage as a loyal Jacobite. *The Loyal Brother, or The Persian Prince* (1682) was a spirited defense of James and a thinly-veiled attack on Monmouth's ambition. On the accession of James to the throne, Southerne entered the king's army and was on the verge of preferment when the Revolution swept down and destroyed all such hopes. When he returned to the theatre, discretion seemed the better part of political wisdom for an ambitious young dramatist. *The Wives' Excuse,* therefore, he dedicated to Thomas Wharton, who had voted for the Exclusion Bill in 1680 and had been named privy counsellor and comptroller of the household as soon as William became king. In 1695, with *Oroonoko,* he sued for the patronage of William Cavendish, Duke of Devonshire, who had also been active in advocating the Exclusion Bill and was privy counsellor under William and Mary. Such trimming to the wind of patronage did not escape the eye of contemporary satire. In some verses purporting to represent *The Last Will and Testament of Mr. Tho. Brown,* published in *A Letter From the Dead Thomas*

Brown, to the Living Heraclitus (1704), Southerne is attacked for his inconstancy:

> Item. To S---rn, who for Gain
> And Place of Trust, turn'd Cat in Pan
> And a good Cause declining left,
> Because of present Pence bereft,
> I give my Inconstancy of Temper,
> To prove that he's not *Idem semper,*
> But with each Point of Mind can vary,
> And several hooks at several Seasons carry.[1]

The Tryal of Skill, or, a New Session of the Poets, published the same year, satirizes his opportunism in the same manner:

> Tom S-- Petition'd the next, and besought
>   The Court, that he must be preferr'd,
> For he two Fat Places already had got,
>   And most grievously wanted a Third.
>
> When the Judges amaz'd at his Temper and Suit,
>   Remanded him back to *White-hall,*
> And declar'd, who had lost his Esteem and Repute,
>   Was not fit for their Business at all.
>
> . . . .
>
> Such a Question as this drew the Blood into's Face,
>   And away from the Querists he ran,
> Well knowing how near it came up to his Case,
>   That so lately had turn'd *Cat in Pan.*

The theatre, so hard a task-master to many a starving playwright, proved rich in financial reward to this fortunate Irishman. From the very first, when he "raised the price of prologues" by paying Dryden twice as much as had ever been given for one, he was active in obtaining the highest possible returns for his labors.[2]

The changing morality in Southerne's play is another evi-

---
[1] p. 25. [R.G.H.]
[2] See detailed discussion of this above, pp. 24-27; 29-30.

dence of his sensitiveness to new dramatic fashions. Between 1690-93, when the comedy of manners was still the accepted comic tradition, he turned out in rapid succession three plays that were conventionally ribald in conception and execution. He wrote them with a pen dipped in the common well of Restoration cuckoldry and wenching. *Double-entendre,* cynical attacks on the church, fifth-act victories for *debauchées,* a sparrow-like concentration on the one all-important business of sex—these were there in abundance. Even the sub-plots of *The Fatal Marriage* and *Oroonoko* were comedies of manners in miniature. By 1695 Southerne had written five plays all stamped with the formula of lubricous wit. It was the fashion.

Then in 1698 the storm of Collier's *Short View* descended on this infected stage and sent the worried playwrights scurrying for shelter. The extent of their baffled rage may be determined by anyone who will examine Vanbrugh's or Congreve's disconcerted replies to the indictment. Accepting tacitly the parson's premise that "the business of *Plays* is to recommend Virtue and discountenance Vice,"[3] they found his position impregnable, and went down to a fore-doomed argumentative defeat. To be sure, the stage was not reformed overnight—some of the most brilliant examples of the comedy under fire came after 1698—but Collier had brought to the surface purgative tendencies that had been running underground for over a decade, and were ultimately to result in a drama made safe for sensibility. For us, the important thing is Southerne's reaction to the dispute.

Collier does not include Southerne in his survey of iniquity. Our poet was as liable as any to attack, but Collier was gunning after bigger game. For his share of the general abuse Southerne had to wait until 1719, and Arthur Bedford's *Serious Remonstrance In Behalf of the Christian Religion, Against the Horrid Blasphemies and Impieties which are still*

[3] Introduction to the *Short View.*

used in the English Play-Houses, etc. In this strident and extravagant book—the *reductio ad absurdum* of Collier—Southerne is included with the other innumerable heretics. Chapter and verse of *The Fatal Marriage* are cited to show "The Devil honour'd by the profane Cursing of the Stage," and "The Scriptures perverted to the Honour of the Devil." Type examples selected for anathema are such phrases as "Confusion," and "The Devil is in it." But in spite of the fact that he was not singled out by Collier for attack, Southerne sensed that a new scale of values was entering the theatre, and forthwith he gave up comedy, turning instead to a form least likely to give offense—classical tragedy.

Southerne's acceptance of the new code is pointed out in Charles Boyle's Prologue to *The Fate of Capua.*

> But he despairs of pleasing all the nation,
> 'Tis so debauch'd with whims of reformation.
> He's done his best: here is no wanton scene
> To give the wicked joy, the godly, spleen.
> Not one poor bawdy jest shall dare appear,
> For now the batter'd, *veteran* strumpets, here
> Pretend at least to bring a modest ear.

By 1726 the reformation was almost complete, and in *Money the Mistress* Southerne gave himself over to moralized comedy, where the sentiments were "honourable and virtuous" and the manners "instructive of youth."[4]

Even if Southerne had not declared his purpose to write down to the public taste, a survey of his plays in chronological order would show his progressive attempt to adjust his methods to popular demand. When he began to compose plays in 1682, the heroic wave, whose crest had just broken with Dryden's rejection of rhymed tragedy, was still strong, and a heroic manner seemed the most logical for a young dramatist to adopt. In two years he followed *The Loyal Brother* with *The Disappointment,* a curious medley of in-

[4] Dedication.

trigue, comedy, and sentiment, which showed him fumbling
for a suitable medium and at the same time anticipating in a
striking way the drama of sensibility. Then, after six years of
silence, there came the rapid succession of his comedies of
manners, each run from the same mold. Then a turn to tragedy and within two years *The Fatal Marriage* and *Oroonoko,*
tragi-comedies similar in mood and effect. The mingling here
of a serious and a humorous action was in accordance with
what Southerne considered the popular demand[5] and with
Dryden's pronouncement in his Preface to *Sebastian, King of
Portugal* (acted 1689): "the Genius of the *English* cannot
bear too regular a Play . . . the *English* will not bear a
thorow Tragedy; but are pleas'd, that it should be lightned
with Under-Parts of Mirth."[6] Between *Oroonoko* in 1695
and *The Fate of Capua* in 1700, however, came Collier, and
an increasingly strong aversion on the part of the critics to
tragi-comedy. So Southerne's next two plays, *The Fate of
Capua* (1700) and *The Spartan Dame* (1719), were written
to fit not only the changed morality but also the taste for
more regular tragedy of critics who were bending more and
more to French neo-classicism. And then, in 1726, the final
comedy, this time a complete capitulation to the school of
sentiment. From first to last, Southerne was trying desper-
ately to interpret the taste of the town and to reflect that
taste as accurately as possible in his plays.

[5] Dedication to *The Fatal Marriage.*
[6] To the "unities" of time and place, as well as of action, Southerne
gave short shrift. In the Prologue to *The Fatal Marriage* he scorns
those who affect them:

> There are some others too who offer battle,
> And with their time and place, maul *Aristotle.*
> Ask what they mean, and, after some grimace,
> They tell you, twelve's the time; and for the place,
> The chocolate-house, at the looking-glass.
> To please such judges, some have tir'd their brains,
> And almost had their labour for their pains.

Influences Operating on Southerne

LIKE any writer of importance, Southerne stands in a double relation to the history of his art. There were bearing in upon him easily recognizable forces from the drama of the past; on the other hand, the drama that followed him carried the imprint of his influence. Before we can attempt to place him historically, we must trace these threads of artistic continuity. Since Southerne's later reputation in the theatre depended upon two of his tragedies, it is natural that such a discussion should center for the most part on the two plays that gave him an important place in the history of English drama: *The Fatal Marriage* and *Oroonoko*.[7]

Southerne's earliest indebtedness was to the heroic drama. His first play, *The Loyal Brother,* is entirely within the heroic tradition, drawing its plot from a French romance, hinging its conflict on the opposing forces of love and honor, and filling the mouths of its characters with inflated speeches. The influence of Dryden appears particularly in the use of the short line and the substitution of blank verse for rhyming couplets. Sooner and more completely than might have been expected, though, Southerne rid himself of the heroic incubus. In none of his later plays does he apply the Drawcansir method. The old manner returns occasionally in a passage of elevated declamation or in scattered bursts of rhetorical bombast, but never again does it color character or situation with more than a touch of the familiar extravagance. Another and a softer temper brought him fame.

---

[7] Southerne's comedies owe little to the influence of any one dramatist. Their characters and situations may often, as we have seen, be paralleled in both earlier and later Restoration plays, but for the most part they belong to the artificial conception of comedy that was part of the times. Of those who wrote before him, Southerne reflects faintly in his witty dialogue the grace of Etherege. Nowhere does he approach the bitter cynicism of Wycherley. One feels that he is not so much critical of his characters as appreciative of their humorous idiosyncrasies.

Conclusion

More deeply important to Southerne's art was the Elizabethan drama, the influence of which is writ large over the whole of his dramatic achievement. A note of Jacobean horror and frenzied emotion is not infrequently heard in the midst of the falling cadences of a more modern sentimentality.[8] Madness brings its quota of terror. Gross comedy elbows itself to the side of tragedy in utter neglect of the unity of action. The abundance of incident and the rapidly changing scenes, with their concomitant use of the inner stage, are Elizabethan too. Even in his last tragedy, *The Spartan Dame*, which is avowedly "classical" in theme and treatment, the large number of characters, the bustle of action, and the use of spectacular scenes mark it as stemming from the main branch of English dramatic tradition. Southerne was never more than superficially under the rule of the new criticism; the passion and intensity of his best scenes owe nothing to French theory and everything to the vitality of a dramatic inheritance strictly British.

As might be expected, Shakespeare, of all the old dramatists, throws the largest shadow on Southerne's page. This is evident not only in the shaping of situation and the determining of character, but in frequent verbal echoes. Here Southerne shared in the general revival of interest that Shakespeare had enjoyed in the last twenty years of the seventeenth century. Before 1678 only *Measure for Measure*, *Macbeth*, and *The Tempest* had been altered to suit the Restoration palate; between 1678–82 ten more Shakespearian alterations reached the stage.[9] Southerne made no claim, as did

---

[8] See, for instance, the exaggerated scene of Sunamire's throwing herself, as she thinks, on the body of Tachmas (*Loyal Brother*, V, 3), and the torture of Pedro on the rack (*Fat. Marr.*, V, 4). Southerne does not, however, make as undisciplined a use of horror as Lee, for example, in *Caesar Borgia* (1679).

[9] *Cf.* Thorndike's *Tragedy*, p. 264. G. C. Odell names eight alterations between 1678–82. See *Shakespeare from Betterton to Irving*, 2 vols., New York, 1920. I, ch. 2.

Rowe, to write in imitation of Shakespeare, but he is in no small sense the great dramatist's inheritor. Yet the continuation of the Elizabethan tradition, important as that might be, is not Southerne's most important contribution to Restoration drama. The search for that contribution brings us to the heart of our study.

Southerne's Place in Restoration and Eighteenth Century Drama

SOUTHERNE'S place in dramatic history is linked with the emergence of sentimental drama, which has been so variously defined and whose origins have been tracked by almost every critic to a different source. A. W. Ward finds the root of sentimental drama in pity, and its first appearance in the subplot of Steele's *Lying Lover* (1704).[10] Professor Bernbaum sees it distinguished chiefly by a certain confidence in the goodness of human nature, and takes as its starting-point Cibber's *Love's Last Shift* in 1696.[11] With Professor Nicoll, the presentation of a moral problem first began to mark off sentimental drama from the rest, and he traces its beginnings as far back as 1680.[12] Even behind this, he says, it was hinted in the comedies of Dryden, Mrs. Behn, and Crowne; later, in Ravenscroft and D'Urfey, and "by 1676 [with *The Plain Dealer*], the age was moving steadily in the direction of sentimentalism."[13] Further back than Dryden in Restoration drama it would be hard to go.

The early appearance of sentimental tendencies in comedy, as Professor Nicoll would be the first to admit, was decidedly ephemeral, limited to a few chance moralized phrases or the inclusion in a typical comedy of manners of a character whose sensibilities were in advance of his time. Southerne do-

[10] *History of English Dramatic Literature*, III, 495.
[11] *Drama of Sensibility*, p. 76.
[12] *Restoration Drama*, pp. 227 and 252.
[13] *Ibid.*, p. 227.

nated his portrait to such a gallery in the character of Mrs. Friendall in *The Wives' Excuse*—a wife consciously moral and virtuous, repelling with elevated utterances the siege against her chastity.[14]

But it appears to have gone unnoticed that as early as 1684 Southerne wrote a comedy in which the entire main plot expressed the moralized emotions later known to sentimental drama. In *The Disappointment* were anticipated the characters that Cibber and Steele were to make famous: the loyal wife whose virtue triumphs in the end; the man and maid whose love was untouched by any cynical contempt of marriage; the faithful friend; the spurned mistress who is at last married to her former lover; and the rake purged just in time for the fifth-act curtain. Pathos is stronger here than wit, human nature is found to be fundamentally good, and aroused sensibilities find issue in an emotion altogether moral. The history of sentimentalism in England cannot afford to ignore this early appearance of a play that adumbrates, perhaps more clearly than any original comedy prior to *Love's Last Shift,* the approach of the new drama.[15]

Comedy, however, was not Southerne's chief gift to the stream of sentiment. In the later history of the theatre comedy came to encroach more and more on the province of tragedy, until Sir Fretful Plagiary in Sheridan's *Critic* could cry out: "A Dext'rous plagiarist may do anything.—Why, sir, for aught I know, he might take out some of the best things in my tragedy, and put them into his own comedy."[16] In the course of time, theatre-goers attended a comedy in

---

[14] Another virtuous wife appears, almost anachronistically, in the comic sub-plot of *The Fatal Marriage.* Julia is true to the jealous Fernando despite the efforts of Carlos to make her otherwise. Here, however, the situations are given no sentimental coloring.

[15] Mrs. Behn's alteration as *The Town Fop,* in 1676, of George Wilkin's Elizabethan play *The Miseries of Enforced Marriage,* though hardly a comedy, is of a clear sentimental appeal. Cf. Bernbaum: *Drama of Sensibility,* p. 50.

[16] I, 1.

order that they might weep. In view of this it seems to me reasonable to emphasize a little more than has been done the contribution that sentimental tragedy has made to the development of the drama of sensibility.[17] And here *The Fatal Marriage* and *Oroonoko* become of major significance.

Southerne's place in dramatic history depends largely upon these two plays and their influence in extending the borders of domesticated and sentimentalized tragedy. Domestic tragedy had entered English drama in Elizabethan times with *The Yorkshire Tragedy, Arden of Feversham,* and Heywood's *English Traveller* and *Woman Killed With Kindness.* But generally in Elizabethan drama, as later in Restoration, tragedy had been synonymous with the fall of kings or princes and had concerned itself with the affairs of state or court. *The Fatal Marriage,* however, is virtually a domestic tragedy. Its interest does not derive from the noble station of the protagonists; no crowns fall and no kingdoms totter. It is domestic drama on a rather high plane, to be sure; the atmosphere is not yet consciously bourgeois. But the emphasis is on the common humanity of the people concerned, and the distresses are those that might have come to any husband and wife. Isabella, Biron, and Villeroy are presented simply on the basis of the personal tragedy in which they were involved. It was still a long step to *George Barnwell* and the apotheosis of the London apprentice, but once the barrier of rank was removed the evolutionary process could be accelerated.

A surge of tearful pathos is at the center of Southerne's tragedy. His appeal is to the feminine emotion of pity, tragic terror standing meanwhile at a distance. One does not wonder that Southerne's staunchest supporters in the theatre were the women, for it was they who were glorified in all his

---

[17] Professor Nettleton has already touched on this: "Perhaps the real origin of sentimental comedy should be sought not simply in the moralized comedy of Cibber but in the somewhat sentimentalized tragedy of Otway and Southerne." *English Drama of the Restoration and Eighteenth Century,* p. 155.

tragedies. Semanthe, Isabella, Imoinda, Favonia, Celona—each was a main figure in a tragic action. Each was a plaintive sufferer under an unjust fate; each was pure and faithful to the undeservedly bitter end. In most instances, these heroines were incapable of battling with the overwhelming odds against them, and tragic conflict therefore dissolved into an orgy of pathos. It is not meretricious pathos, nor is it sentimental in the sense that the emotions are aroused only that they may be indulged; nevertheless it is a softening down of the elements necessary to tragedy if it is to evoke in its spectators anything more powerful than a passive contemplation of distress. The whole tone of these plays was one calculated to appeal to a later generation for whom the shedding of tears was the end of tragedy.

Southerne was no originator of the new tendency. Otway had preceded him in the construction of tearful situations replete with pathetic emotion. The domestic theme, the elevation of the heroine to the place of chief importance, and the appeal to compassion had been written into tragedy with *The Orphan* in 1680, and all that Southerne did was to strengthen an element already introduced. Inevitably, Southerne must come into comparison with his predecessor in the field of pathetic tragedy. His contemporaries had noted the likeness between the two; indeed, the greatest praise that Southerne received was to be called by Dryden another such poet as Otway. Criticism, however, has always been just in granting the supremacy to the earlier dramatist. Southerne could approximate Otway's tenderness, even at times his intensity, but the depth of passion and the inflection of great poetry that brings Otway into the borders of tragic genius were well beyond the other's lesser powers. At his best, Otway fuses intellect and emotion, while Southerne, striving for profundity, comes always short of it, and must be satisfied with the lesser reaches of pity. Yet within these limits he is second only to Otway.

The drop in poetic power from Otway to Southerne may be taken as the measure of the men. The verse of *The Fatal*

Marriage lacks the flexibility of that in *Venice Preserved*. There is as much use of enjambement, but the pauses are less subtly varied and the regularity of Southerne's lines beat more monotonously on the ear. We are surprised to find that Otway uses at least four times as many feminine endings as Southerne. It would be obscuring the level adequacy of Southerne's verse, nevertheless, to ignore the aptness of its adjustment to the tragic themes which it expressed. Tragedy, subsequent to as well as prior to Southerne, meant too often bombastic diction and artificial sentiments. Southerne had the merits attendant on simplicity, and it is noteworthy that his purity of diction drew both contemporary and eighteenth-century approval. Motteux, in 1693, commended his "purity of Diction."[18] Gildon found in him a "Purity of Language, which few of our Poets observe,"[19] and declared that "very few exceed him in the Dialogue . . . his Diction is commonly the best part of him . . ."[20] Davies, asserting that "the passion of love is no where so tenderly or ardently expressed" as in *Oroonoko*,[21] places him with Otway in excellence of language: "Without going into the usual method of censuring the style of our modern tragedies, I believe every man will agree with me, that the language of Otway and Southerne cannot be mended or improved:—through them nature speaks, and speaks with equal freedom and force."[22]

One need make no extravagant claim for Southerne to say that he was a powerful force on the side of naturalness in the contemporary theatre and that next to Otway he was the Restoration dramatist most active in determining the course of eighteenth-century tragedy. Between the death of Otway and the appearance of Rowe[23] he was the chief exponent of

[18] *Gentleman's Journal,* January 1692/3, p. 28.
[19] Gildon's Langbaine's *Lives,* p. 136.
[20] *A Comparison Between the Two Stages,* p. 30.
[21] *Dram. Miscellanies* (1785), III, 449.
[22] *Ibid.,* III, 237.
[23] Southerne was almost as superior to Rowe in poetic power and

the moral, problem tragedy to which a sentimental age was to give the benediction of its tears. His influence, as we have seen in our discussion of *The Fatal Marriage* and *Oroonoko*, was evidenced in the shaping of certain specific eighteenth-century plays, but his chief contribution to later drama was rather in the tone of pathetic sentiment which he helped to popularize and of which he was a chief continuator.

Historically, then, Southerne stands as the strongest link between Restoration and eighteenth-century tragedy—more specifically, between Otway and Rowe. The tragedy of all three was concerned preeminently with piteous love; it was inclined to be domestic, feminine, and emotional; in it the Elizabethan influence was strong. Like Otway and Rowe, Southerne softened the tragic conflict to one of pity, and thus prepared the way not only for the later prose, bourgeois drama, but for the final triumph in comedy of the Sentimental Muse.

dramatic energy as he was inferior to Otway. Rowe was still softer and more lachrymose than Southerne and even less cogent than he. His verse is smoother and at the same time more relaxed. And pathos in *The Fair Penitent* (1703) and *Jane Shore* (1714) assumes a still larger proportion; the moralizing tendency, too, is there pushed to further extremes.

APPENDIX

SOUTHERNE'S WILL

P. C. C. Edmunds, 191.

Thos Southerne.

In the Name of God Amen The Sixth day of November in the Year of Our Lord 1731 and in the ffifth Year of the Reign of His Majesty King George the Second I Thomas Southerne of Saint Margarets Parish Westminster Gent[1] being of sound mind and memorie and in perfect health of Body doe make and declare this my last Will and Testament in manner following Imprimis I willingly resign my Soul to God who gave it and my Body to be interred in the Churchyard of the parish where it happens to fall And for the distribution of my Temporal Estate and the settlement of all such Goods and Chattels debts Judgments and Mortgages as I shall die possessed of or entitled to in England or Ireland I doe give bequeath and dispose of the same in manner and form following that is to say I will and devise that my dear daughter Agnes my Executrix doe well and truly pay or cause to be payd all my Just and lawfull debts in convenient time and defray my ffuneral Expences which I desire may not exceed Twenty pounds I doe constitute and appoint the abovesaid Agnes whole and Sole Executrix of this my last Will and Testament And I doe hereby Revoak all former Wills and Testaments by me at any time made, declaring this to be my last and only Will and Testament In Witness whereof I have hereunto sett my Hand and Seal the day of the date above mentioned written by my own hand Tho: Southerne. Sign'd Seal'd and publish'd by the said Tho. Southerne as his last Will and Testament in our presence and Subscribed by us in the Presence and at the request of the said Testator Hester Turner daughter of Mr Webb late Attorney at Glouster William Powell son of Mr Symonds of Pengethly in Herefordshire Richd Browne my Landlord in little Aumary near Deans Yard Westminster.

This will was proved at London the Third day of June in the Year of Our Lord One Thousand Seven Hundred and fforty Six before the Worshipfull Robert Chapman Doctor of Laws Surrogate to the Right Worshipfull John Bettesworth Doctor of Laws Master Keeper or Commissary of the Prerogative Court of Canterbury lawfully constituted by the Oath of Agnes Southerne Spinster the daughter of the deceased and Sole Executrix named in the said Will To whom Administration was granted of all and singular the Goods Chattels and Credits of the said deceased being first sworn duly to Administer.

BIBLIOGRAPHY

THIS bibliography is selective rather than exhaustive. When I have had occasion to refer to a work only once, the edition and the reference are given in the note and are not duplicated here. On the other hand I have several times included books which were not quoted but which proved valuable as sources of general information. The bibliographies of *The Fatal Marriage* and of *Oroonoko,* however, are as complete as I have been able to make them, because never before has there been any attempt to trace the history of their published editions. Unquestionably there are some printings of these plays that I have missed, but the total of 53 for the former and 57 for the latter is rather startling testimony for their continued popularity.

There have been three collected editions of Southerne's plays:

1. Two volumes, London, 1713. 12mo. Printed for Jacob Tonson, Benjamin Tooke, and Bernard Lintott. There are eight plays in this edition, neither *The Spartan Dame* nor *Money the Mistress* having been written by 1713.
2. Two volumes, London, 1721. 12mo. Printed for J. Tonson, B. Tooke, M. Wellington, and W. Chetwood. Includes all the plays except *Money the Mistress.*
3. Three volumes, London, 1774. 12mo. Printed for T. Evans and T. Becket. Prefaced with a *Life* of Southerne by Evans and dedicated to David Garrick. This remains the only complete edition of the plays.

Editions of The Fatal Marriage

The / Fatal Marriage: / or, the / Innocent Adultery, / A / Play, / Acted at the / Theatre Royal, / by / Their Majesties Servants. / *Written by* Tho. Southerne. / *Pellex ego facta mariti.*—Ovid. / London, / Printed for *Jacob Tonson,* at the *Judges Head* near / the *Inner-Temple-Gate* in *Fleetstreet,* 1694.

Bibliography 221

Quarto, pp. viii+79+i; consisting of title-page (with verso blank), pp. i–ii; the Epistle Dedicatory ("To Ant. Hammond Esq; of Somersham-Place"), pp. iii–v; verses "To Mr. Southerne, on his Play," etc., signed "W.S.," p. vi; prologue, p. vii; list of "The Persons Represented," p. viii; text of the play, pp. 1–79. Upon the unnumbered reverse of p. 79 is the epilogue. There are headlines throughout, each verso being headed *The Fatal Marriage: Or,* and each recto *The Innocent Adultery.* The signatures are A – – L (eleven sheets, each four leaves). No half-title.
Yale Copy. First Edition.

1713	In the first collected edition of Southerne's plays, Vol. II.
(1719)	The only record I find of this edition is an advertisement on the title-page of *The Spartan Dame* (1719): "A correct Edition, just Publish'd, of Mr. *Southern's Fatal Marriage,* or the *Innocent Adultery.*"
1721	In the second collected edition of the plays, Vol. II.
1732	London. Printed for J. Tonson. pp. 83.
1735	London. J. Tonson. pp. 95.

(Garrick's version, *Isabella,* from here on.)

1757	London. J. and R. Tonson. First edition of Garrick's adaptation. pp. 58.
1758	London. J. and R. Tonson. Second edition of Garrick's adaptation. pp. 62.
1769	Dublin. P. & W. Wilson & W. Sleater. pp. 62.
1773	Edinburgh. Printed for John Wood.
1774	In the third collected edition of the plays, Vol. II. (Published in the original form.)
1774	London. In Garrick's *Works,* 2 vols., Vol. II.
1776	London. In Vol. XII of the *New English Theatre.*
1776	London. Bell's *British Theatre,* Vol. V.
1777	London. C. Bathurst. pp. 57.
1779	London. J. Harrison, etc.
1780	London. Bell's *British Theatre,* Vol. V.
1783	London. In Vol. XII of the *New English Theatre.*
1784	London. "Marked with the variations in the manager's book." C. Bathurst.
1785	Dublin. W. Sleater & T. Wilkinson. pp. 52.
1789	London. J. Christie. First edition to include all of the prompter's notes of James Wrighten.
1790	London. C. Lowndes. Has Wrighten's notes.
1792	London. J. Bell.

1792	London. W. Lowndes.
1797	London. Bell's *British Theatre,* Vol. V.
1800	London. No. 11 of "Roach's British Theatre."
1803	Dublin. (Deposited in the Trinity College Library. I have no description of this edition.)
1804	London. Sir Walter Scott's *Modern British Drama,* Vol. I, pt. 2.
1804	London. In Sharp's *British Theatre,* Vol. III.
1806	London. "Printed from the prompt book." With remarks by Mrs. Inchbald.
1808	London. Inchbald's *British Theatre,* Vol. VII.
1808	London. Matthews & Leigh. With biographical anecdotes, etc.
1811	Edinburgh. "Adapted for theatrical representation," etc.
1811	New York. Published by the Longworths at the Dramatic Repository Shakespeare Gallery in November.
1814	London. John Miller. Revised by J. P. Kemble.
1815	London. In *The London Theatre,* 1815, etc. Vol. XXII.
1815	London. Printed at the Chiswick Press for Whittingham & Arliss. "Correctly given, from copies used in the theatres, by Thomas Dibdin."
(1817)	London. C. Cooke. *British Drama,* Vol. I.
1821	London. In *English Theatre,* Tragedies.
1824	London. *The British Drama,* etc. Vol. I, 1824, etc.
(1824, etc.)	London. *London Stage,* Vol. I.
1826	Philadelphia. *Acting American Theatre,* Vol. II.
(18—?)	Edinburgh. Oliver and Boyd.
(1829, etc.)	London. Cumberland's *British Theatre,* Vol. IX.
(1830?)	London. The Penny National Library, etc. Vol. V.
1831	London. "Revised by J. P. Kemble, with prefatory remarks by W. Oxberry, comedian." In *New English Drama,* 1818–32. Vol. XXII.
(183–)	Philadelphia. A. R. Poole & Ash & Mason. Lopez and Wemyss' edition, *The Acting American Theatre.*
1832	Philadelphia. J. J. Woodward. *British Drama.*
1834	London. *The Acting Drama,* etc.
(1850, etc.)	London. Lacy's *Acting Edition of Plays,* etc. Vol. XCIV.
(185–)	London. Printed from the acting copy, with remarks by D.G. (Re-issue of Cumberland's *British Theatre,* No. 58, Vol. IX.)
(1864, etc.)	London. J. Dick. *The British Drama,* Vol. II.
(1883)	London. (J.) *Dick's Standard Plays,* No. 46.

Translations of The Fatal Marriage

1749   L'Adultère innocent, comi-tragedie. *Le Théâtre Anglois.* Tome VIII.
(1788, etc.) Die unglückliche Heurath. Ein Trauerspiel . . . Nach dem Englischen des Southerne. Von Schröder. 1792. Deutsche Schaubühne. Bd. 45.

Editions of Oroonoko

Oroonoko: / A / Tragedy / As it is Acted at the / Theatre-Royal, / By His Majesty's Servants. / Written by Tho. Southerne. / —*Quo fata trahunt, virtus secura sequetur.* Lucan / *Virtus recludens immeritis mori / Cœlum, negatâ tentat iter viâ.* / Hor. Od. 2. lib. 3. / London: / Printed for *H. Playford* in the *Temple-Change. B. Tooke* / at the *Middle-Temple-Gate.* And *S. Buckley* at the / *Dolphin* against St. *Dunstan's* Church in *Fleetstreet.* / MDCXCVI.

Quarto, pp. viii+84+ii; consisting of title-page (with verso blank), pp. i–ii; the Epistle Dedicatory ("To his Grace William Duke of Devonshire," etc.), pp. iii–vi; prologue, pp. vii–viii; list of "Persons Represented," p. viii; and text of the play, pp. 1–84, followed by an unnumbered leaf carrying, recto and verso, the epilogue. There are no headlines, the pages being numbered centrally in Arabic numerals within round brackets. The signatures are A--M (twelve sheets, each four leaves). M4 is a blank. No half-title.
Yale Copy. First Edition.

1699   London. "The second edition . . . Printed for H. Playford . . . and B. Tooke." pp. vi+62. 4to.
1699   London. 4to. (This is distinctly another edition, although it has been confused with the one above. This is printed for H. Playford, B. Tooke, and A. Bettesworth. pp. viii+80. It is not called "the second edition," as is the other.
       This edition exists in two forms, the same but for the title-page. One issue has "R" Bettesworth instead of "A" Bettesworth on the recto. The "R" issue lacks the "newly-published" list of books at the bottom.)
1711   London. Collection of *Best British Plays,* Vol. V.
1712   London. Printed for T. Johnson.
1713   London. In first collected edition of Southerne's plays, Vol. II.

1721	London. In second collected edition of the plays, Vol. II.
1721	London. B. Motte.
1722	Dublin. G. Grierson.
1735	London. W. Feales, etc., pp. 106.
1736	London. W. Feales. Engraved frontispiece by Van der Gucht.
1739	Dublin. "4th edition corrected." P. Crampton. (This "corrected" edition follows exactly the 1721 edition.)
1740	London. "Printed for the booksellers in town and country." pp. xii—193-274—ii. (Evidently paginated for some volume of plays. I possess only the single, unbound play.)
1744	London. C. Bathurst, etc. pp. 84.
1749	London. C. Hitch.
1750	Dublin. Wilson. pp. 78.
1751	London. C. Hitch. pp. 84.
1756	Glasgow. W. Duncan, junior.
1759	Edinburgh. A. Donaldson.
1759	London. C. Bathurst. Altered by Hawkesworth. pp. 60.

(Except where the notation is to the contrary, the following editions are in Hawkesworth's alteration.)

1760	London. A. and C. Corbett. Altered, 600 lines added (by an unknown hand).
1760	Glasgow. Robert and Andrew Foulis. Altered by Francis Gentleman. Acted at Edinburgh.
1768	Edinburgh. Martin and Witherspoon. *Theatre*, Vol. VI. (Original version.)
1774	London. In the third collected edition of the plays.
1775	London. C. Bathurst. pp. 64.
1776	London. C. Bathurst. "Marked with the variations in the manager's book." pp. 84. (Prints the whole play.)
1776	London. In the *New English Theatre*, Vol. VI.
1776	London. In J. Bell's *British Theatre*, Vol. VI.
1777	London. Bell's edition. "Regulated from the prompt-book . . . by Mr. Wild, Prompter." (Prints the whole play.)
1778	London. J. Wenman. pp. 20. (With slightly abbreviated subplot.)
1785	London. In the *New English Theatre*, Vol. VI. (Prints the whole play, with inverted commas around portions omitted in the representation.)
1785	London. "Printed for the Proprietors and sold by R. Randall . . . and all Booksellers in England, Scotland, and Ireland."
1785	London. C. Bathurst. pp. 83.

1791	London. J. Bell. (Prints the whole play, with inverted commas around portions omitted in the representation.)
1797	London. J. Bell's *British Theatre,* Vol. XIX.
1804	London. J. Sharpe, in Sharpe's *British Theatre,* Vol. XI.
1804	London. Edited by Sir Walter Scott in *Modern British Drama,* Vol. I.
(1806)	London. Longman, Hurst, Rees, and Orme.
1808	London. In Inchbald's *British Theatre,* Vol. VII.
1811	London. *Modern British Drama,* Vol. I.
1815	London. In Dibdin's *London Theatre,* No. 50. (Sub-plot retained in abbreviated form.)
1816	London. In *The London Theatre,* 1815, etc., Vol. XV. pp. 67. (Sub-plot retained in abbreviated form.)
1817	London. Cooke's edition in *British Drama,* Vol. XI. (Sub-plot retained in abbreviated form.) With critique by Sir Richard Cumberland.
(1820?)	London. T. Hughes. pp. 70.
1824	London. In a new edition of Inchbald's *British Theatre,* Vol. III.
1824	London. In *The British Drama,* Vol. I.
1824	London. In *The London Stage,* Vol. II. (Sub-plot only slightly abbreviated.)
1829	London. In Cumberland's *British Theatre,* Vol. XXV.
(183–?)	London. The Music Publishing Co. (On cover, "Cumberland's British Theatre, 179.")
1832	Philadelphia. J. J. Woodward, *British Drama.* (Sub-plot retained in abbreviated form.)
1834	London. *The Acting Drama,* etc.
1850	Philadelphia. *The British Drama,* Vol. I.
1883	London. (J.) *Dick's Standard Plays,* No. 122.
1928	Oxford. Edited by B. Dobrée in *Five Restoration Tragedies.*
n.d.	Edinburgh. Oliver and Boyd.
n.d.	London. Cooke's edition. pp. viii+81.
n.d.	London. John Cumberland, Camden New Town.

Works Useful for Reference

Alumni Dublinenses, ed. G. D. Burtchaell and T. U. Sadleir, London, 1924.

Behn, Mrs. Aphra, *The Works of,* ed. M. Summers. 5 vols. London, 1915.

Bernbaum, Ernest, *The Drama of Sensibility.* Boston and London, 1915.

Biographica Dramatica, or, a Companion to the Playhouse . . . Originally Compiled, to the year 1764, by David Erskine Baker. Continued thence to 1782, by Isaac Reed, F.A.S. And brought down to the End of November 1811 . . . by Stephen Jones. 3 vols. in 4. London, 1812.

Calendar of State Papers, Domestic Series. London.

Cibber, Colley, *An Apology for the Life of,* ed. R. W. Lowe. 2 vols. London, 1889.

Cibber, Theophilus (and other hands), *The Lives of the Poets of Great Britain and Ireland, To the Time of Dean Swift.* 5 vols. London, 1753.

Companion to the Playhouse [D. E. Baker]. 2 vols. London, 1764.

Comparison Between the Two Stages, A [Charles Gildon]. London, 1702.

Congreve, William, *The Complete Works of,* ed. M. Summers. 4 vols. London, 1923.

Dalton, Charles, *English Army Lists and Commission Registers, 1661–1714.* 6 vols. London, 1892–1904.

Davies, Thomas, *Dramatic Miscellanies.* A New Edition. 3 vols. London, 1785.

Dibdin, J. C., *Annals of the Edinburgh Stage.* Edinburgh, 1888.

Dictionary of National Biography, A, ed. Leslie Stephen and Sidney Lee. Revised edition. 22 vols. London and New York, 1908–09.

Doran, John, *Annals of the English Stage.* 2 vols. New York, 1865.

Downes, John, *Roscius Anglicanus, or, An Historical Review of the Stage from 1660–1705.* Fac-simile Reprint of the Rare Original of 1708. Ed. Joseph Knight, London, 1886.

Dryden, John, *The Works of,* ed. Scott and Saintsbury. 18 vols. Edinburgh, 1882–93.

——, *Critical and Miscellaneous Prose Works of* . . . *with an Account of the Life and Writings of the Author,* ed. Edmond Malone. 3 vols. in 4. London, 1800.

Friedrich, Karl, *Thomas Southerne als Dramatiker.* Inaugural-Dissertation. Nürnberg, 1914.

Genest, John, *Some Account of the English Stage from the Restoration in 1660 to 1830.* 10 vols. Bath, 1832.

[Gentleman, Francis], *The Dramatic Censor, or Critical Companion.* London, 1770.

[Gildon, Charles.] [See *Comparison Between the Two Stages.*]

Ham, Roswell G., *Otway and Lee.* New Haven and London, 1931.

Hamelius, P., *Thomas Southerne's Loyal Brother.* Liége, 1911.

Hotson, Leslie, *The Commonwealth and Restoration Stage.* Cambridge, U.S.A., 1928.

[Jacob, Giles], *The Poetical Register: or The Lives and Characters of all the English Poets.* 2 vols. London, 1723.
Johnson, Samuel, *Lives of the English Poets,* ed. G. B. Hill. 3 vols. Oxford, 1905.
Langbaine, Gerard [and Gildon, Charles], *The Lives and Characters of the English Dramatick Poets.* London [1699].
Malone, Edmond, *Historical Account of the English Stage.* London, 1800. [See also under Dryden.]
Molloy, J. F., *Romance of the Irish Stage.* 2 vols. London, 1897.
Motteux, P. A., *Gentleman's Journal, or The Monthly Miscellany.* London, Jan. 1691/2—Oct./Nov., 1694.
Nettleton, George H., *English Drama of the Restoration and Eighteenth Century.* New York, 1914.
Newspapers and Periodicals. Daily Courant, Daily Journal, Daily Post, London Chronicle, London Gazette, St. James's Evening Post, Critical Review, Gentleman's Magazine, London Magazine, Monthly Review.
Nicoll, Allardyce, *History of Restoration Drama, 1660–1700.* Cambridge, 1923.
——, *History of Early Eighteenth Century Drama, 1700–1750.* Cambridge, 1925.
Nuck, Richard, *Über Leben und Werke von Thomas Southerne.* Berlin, 1904.
Odell, G. C. D., *Annals of the New York Stage.* 7 vols. New York, 1927–31.
Orrery Papers, ed. Countess of Cork and Orrery. 2 vols. London, 1903.
Otway, Thomas, *The Works of,* ed. M. Summers. 3 vols. London, 1926.
Periodicals. [See *Newspapers.*]
Pope, Alexander, *The Works of,* ed. Elwin and Courthope. 10 vols. London, 1871–89.
——, *The Works of,* ed. Warburton. 9 vols. 1751.
Seilhamer, G. O., *History of the American Theatre.* 3 vols. Philadelphia, 1888–91.
Term Catalogues, 1668–1709, The, ed. Edward Arber. 3 vols. London, 1903–06.
Thaler, Alwin, *Shakespeare to Sheridan.* Cambridge, U.S.A., 1922.
Thorndike, A. H., *Tragedy.* Boston and New York, 1908.
Ward, A. W., *A History of English Dramatic Literature to the Death of Queen Anne.* New and Revised Edition. 3 vols. London, 1899.
——, *Thomas Southerne,* in the *Dictionary of National Biography,* XVIII, 688–90.
Wood, Anthony À., *Athenæ Oxonienses,* ed. Bliss. 4 vols. London, 1813–20.

INDEX

Absalom and Achitophel, 37.
Addison, Joseph, 26, 114 n., 115.
Aesop, 128.
Albion and Albanius, 37.
All for Love, 40.
Ambitious Slave, The, 99.
Amends for Ladies, 61.
Arden of Feversham, 214.
As You Find It, 8.
Aulnoy, Comtesse d', 199.
Aureng-Zebe, 41.

Barry, Mrs. Elizabeth, 77, 90, 98–99, 100, 163.
Beaux Stratagem, The, 86.
Bedford, Arthur, 207.
Behn, Mrs. Aphra, 36, 103–06, 131–38, 212.
Bernbaum, Ernest, 105, 212, 213 n.
Betterton, Thomas, 48, 77, 163.
Biographica Dramatica, 13, 27 n., 28.
Blackmore, Sir Richard, 22.
Booth, Junius Brutus, 162.
Boswell, James, 154–55.
Boyle, Charles, 6 n., 8, 15–16, 163, 165 n., 197, 208.
Boyle, John, 11, 15, 16–17, 197.
Bracegirdle, Mrs., 64, 77, 90, 99.
Broome, William, 195, 196.
Brown, Thomas, 205–06.
Buckingham, Duke of (See Sheffield, John).
Butler, James, Earl of Ossory, 48 n.

Caius Marius, 35.
Careless Husband, The, 25.
Cavendish, William, Duke of Devonshire, 130, 179, 205.

Charles II, 34, 37.
Cibber, Colley, 1, 19, 25, 51, 64, 70 n., 86, 176, 178, 212.
City Heiress, The, 36.
City Politicks, 37.
Cleomenes, 14, 26.
Collier, Jeremy, 164, 207–08.
Colman, George, 118.
Confederacy, The, 72.
Congreve, William, 3, 18, 99, 130, 181.
Constant Couple, The, 25.
Cooper, Anthony Ashley, 29, 34, 35 f.
Cowley, Abram, 75.
Critic, The, 213.
Crowne, John, 37, 61, 212.
Cutter of Coleman Street, 75.

Davies, Thomas, 216.
Decameron, The, 110.
Defoe, Daniel, 12–13.
Dennis, John, 19 n., 20, 177–78.
Disappointment, The, or The Mother in Fashion, 4, **48–62**, 208–09, 213.
Dissembled Wanton, The, or, My Son Get Money, 75.
Dobrée, Bonamy, 158.
Don Quixote, 49, 60–61.
Double Dealer, The, 99.
Downes, John, 100, 163–64.
Drummer, The, 26.
Dryden, John, 1, 13, 22, 24, 26, 27, 29, 34, 35, 37, 40, 41, 78–79, 99, 100, 205, 209, 212.
Duncombe, John, 183.
D'Urfey, Thomas, 36, 74 n.

Election of a Poet Laureate in 1719, The, 23.

English Traveler, The, 214.
Estcourt, Richard, 25–26, 86.

Fair Example, The, 25–26, 86.
Fair Vow-Breaker, The, 103.
Farquhar, George, 4, 25, 86.
Fatal Love, or The Forced Inconstancy, 34.
Fatal Marriage, The, or The Innocent Adultery, 26, **98–127**, 143, 145, 148, 171, 172, 191, 207, 209, 214, 216–17, 220–23.
Fate of Capua, The, 8, **163–75**, 191, 208, 209.
Female Prelate, The . . . Life and Death of Pope Joan, 34.
Fenton, Elijah, 8, 17, 20–21, 178, 196.
Ferriar, J., 155.
Field, Nathaniel, 61.
Fitzjames, James, 5.
Fletcher, John, 109, 149.
Friedrich, Karl, 134 n., 183.

Garrick, David, 120–22, 153, 160.
Gay, John, 12.
Gentleman, Francis, 118, 154–55.
Gentleman's Journal, The, 77 n., 79 n., 89, 99, 118, 216.
Gentleman's Magazine, The, 10, 19 n.
Gildon, Charles, 4, 109, 132, 216.
Gould, Robert, 22.
Gray, Thomas, 10.
Griffin, Benjamin, 124.

Hamelius, Paul, 32.
Hamlet, 57, 58 n., 118.
Hammond, Anthony, 100–01.
Harwood, Thomas, 156.
Hawkesworth, John, 150–51, 155.
Henley, Anthony, 20.
Heywood, Thomas, 214.

Holles, Thomas Pelham, 181.
Hopkins, Charles, 12, 25.
Hughes, John, 20.
Humours of Purgatory, The, 124.

Isabella, or The Fatal Marriage, 120–22.

James, Duke of York, 4–5, 37, 38 f.
Jeffrys, George, 196 n.
Johnson, Dr. Samuel, 21, 152–53.

Kean, Edmund, 161.
Kemble, Fanny, 124.
Kendrick, Dr. Daniel, 23.
Killigrew, Thomas, 75.

Lamb, Charles, 73.
Lancashire Witches and Teague O'Divelly, The, 35.
Lee, Nathaniel, 24, 42, 205.
Lennox, Charles, Duke of Richmond, 30.
Liberty Asserted, 20.
Limberham, or The Kind Keeper, 35, 78 n.
Little Thief, The, 109.
Lives of the Poets, The (Theo. Cibber), 9, 27, 70 n., 100 n.
Livy, 168, 173–75.
London Magazine, The, 11 n.
London Merchant, The, or The History of George Barnwell, 111, 214.
Love for Love, 72, 74, 75, 101.
Love's Last Shift, 19, 51, 86, 212, 213.
Love Triumphant, 99.
Loyal Brother, The, or The Persian Prince, 4, **28–47**, 58, 60, 182, 210.
Lying Lover, The, 25, 51, 212.

Madden, Samuel, 21-22.
Maid's Last Prayer, The, or Any Rather Than Fail, **89-97.**
Malone, Edmond, 3, 26, 99.
Mariamne, 20-21.
Married Beau, The, or The Curious Impertinent, 61.
Measure for Measure, 58.
Money the Mistress, 8, 16, **194-203,** 208.
Monmouth, Duke of (See Scott, James).
Monsieur Thomas, 149.
Montford, Mrs. Susannah, 63, 64 n., 65, 77, 90.
Montford, William, 64, 77.
Morton, Thomas, 157.
Motteux, P. A., 79 n., 89, 99, 118, 216.
Moyle, Walter, 12 n.

Negro Slaves, The, 156-57.
Nettleton, George H., 103, 214 n.
Newcastle, Duke of (See Holles, Thomas Pelham).
New Session upon the Poets, Occasion'd by the Death of Mr. John Dryden, A, 23.
Nicoll, Allardyce, 96 n., 128 n., 163 n., 212.
Night-Walker, The, or The Little Thief, 109.
Noble Slave, The, 156.
Norton, Richard, 19, and n.
Nun, The, or The Fair Vow-Breaker, 103.
Nun, The, or The Perjured Beauty, 103.

Old Bachelor, The, 18, 89.
Oldfield, Nance, 178.
Oldys, William, 9-10.
Oroonoko (Southerne's play), **128-62,** 205, 207, 209, 217, 223-25.
Oroonoko, or The Royal Slave (Mrs. Behn's novel), 131-38.
Orphan, The, 107 n., 215.
Othello, 56-7, 171.
Otway, Thomas, 24, 26, 35, 42, 44, 107, 110, 113, 205, 215-16, 217.

Pack, Major Richardson, 178.
Parson's Wedding, The, 75.
Pausanias, the Betrayer of his Country, 19.
Payne, Nevil, 35.
Plain Dealer, The, 74, 95, 212.
Playhouse, The, A Satyr, 22.
Plutarch, 182, 185-86.
Pope, Alexander, 12, 14-15.
Porter, P., 31-32.
Prince of Angola, The, 155.
Provoked Wife, The, 86.

Rawlinson, Dr. Richard, 3-4.
Recruiting Officer, The, 75.
Relapse, The, 55, 72, 86, 128.
Religio Poetae, or A Satyr on the Poets, 7.
Revenge, The, 26.
Roscius Anglicanus, 100, 164 n.
Rowe, Nathaniel, 44, 107, 176, 216 n., 217.
Royalists, The, 36.

Satyr Against Wit, A, 22.
Scott, James, 37, 39.
Scott, Sir Walter, 124.
Sebastian, King of Portugal, 209.
Second Maiden's Tragedy, The, 61.
Settle, Elkanah, 34, 99.
Sexes Mis-Match'd, The, or A

New Way to Get a Husband, 149.
Shadwell, Thomas, 34–35.
Shaftesbury, First Earl of (See Cooper, Anthony Ashley).
Shakespeare, William, 42–44, 56–58, 117–18, 166, 186, 211–12.
Sheffield, John, 23.
Siddons, Mrs., 125–26.
Siege of Constantinople, The, 35.
Siege of Damascus, The, 20.
Sir Anthony Love, or The Rambling Lady, 25, 63–76, 148.
Sir Barnaby Whig, 36.
Skipwith, Thomas, 64.
Slave, The, 157.
Smith, William, 101.
Southerne, Agnes, 7, and n.
Southerne, Francis, 2.
Southerne, George, 3.
Southerne, Thomas, biographical sketch, **1–27**; his will, 218–19.
Spanish Fryar, The, 34.
Spartan Dame, The, 5, **176–93**, 209, 211.
Stafford, John, 54, 192.
Steele, Richard, 4, 25, 51, 176, 212.
Summers, Montague, 61 n., 103, 148 n.

Swift, Jonathan, 8, 17.

Terence, 14, 201.
Themistocles, 21.
Tryal of Skill, The, or, a New Session of the Poets, 206.

Vanbrugh, John, 72, 86, 128.
Venice Preserved, 29, 34, 36, 107 n., 216.
Verbruggen, Jack, 129, 163.
Verbruggen, Mrs. Susannah, 129–30.
Victor, Benjamin, 197.
Victorious Love, 156.

Walker, William, 156.
Ward, Sir A. W., 212.
Way of the World, The, 74.
Welsted, Leonard, 75, 195.
Wetenhall, Edward, 3.
Wharton, Thomas, 205.
Wives' Excuse, The, or Cuckolds Make Themselves, **77–88**, 205, 213.
Woman Killed With Kindness, A, 214.
Wycherley, William, 95.

Yorkshire Tragedy, The, 214.
Young, Edward, 26.

YALE STUDIES IN ENGLISH

I. The Foreign Sources of Modern English Versification. CHARLTON M. LEWIS, Ph.D. $0.50. (*Out of print.*)
II. Ælfric: A New Study of His Life and Writings. CAROLINE LOUISA WHITE, Ph.D. $1.50.
III. The Life of St. Cecilia, from MS. Ashmole 43 and MS. Cotton Tiberius E. VII, with Introduction, Variants, and Glossary. BERTHA ELLEN LOVEWELL, Ph.D. $1.00. (*Out of print.*)
IV. Dryden's Dramatic Theory and Practice. MARGARET SHERWOOD, Ph.D. $0.50.
V. Studies in Jonson's Comedy. ELISABETH WOODBRIDGE, Ph.D. $0.50.
VI. A Glossary of the West Saxon Gospels, Latin-West Saxon and West Saxon-Latin. MATTIE ANSTICE HARRIS, Ph.D. $1.50.
VII. Andreas: The Legend of St. Andrew, translated from the Old English, with an Introduction. ROBERT KILBURN ROOT, Ph.D. $0.50.
VIII. The Classical Mythology of Milton's English Poems. CHARLES GROSVENOR OSGOOD, Ph.D. $1.00. (*Out of print.*)
IX. A Guide to the Middle English Metrical Romances Dealing with English and German Legends, and with the Cycles of Charlemagne and of Arthur. ANNA HUNT BILLINGS, Ph.D. $1.50.
X. The Earliest Lives of Dante, Translated from the Italian of Giovanni Boccaccio and Lionardo Bruni Aretino. JAMES ROBINSON SMITH. $0.75. (*Out of print.*)
XI. A Study in Epic Development. IRENE T. MYERS, Ph.D. $1.00.
XII. The Short Story. HENRY SEIDEL CANBY, Ph.D. $0.30. (*Out of print.*)
XIII. King Alfred's Old English Version of St. Augustine's Soliloquies, Edited with Introduction, Notes, and Glossary. HENRY LEE HARGROVE, Ph.D. $1.00.
XIV. The Phonology of the Northumbrian Gloss of St. Matthew. EMILY HOWARD FOLEY, Ph.D. $0.75. (*Out of print.*)
XV. Essays on the Study and Use of Poetry by Plutarch and Basil the Great, Translated from the Greek, with an Introduction. FREDERICK MORGAN PADELFORD, Ph.D. $0.75.
XVI. The Translations of Beowulf: A Critical Bibliography. CHAUNCEY B. TINKER, Ph.D. $0.75. (*Out of print.*)

XVII. The Alchemist, by Ben Jonson, Edited with Introduction, Notes, and Glossary. CHARLES M. HATHAWAY, JR., Ph.D. $2.50. Cloth, $3.00. (*Out of print.*)

XVIII. The Expression of Purpose in Old English Prose. HUBERT GIBSON SHEARIN, Ph.D. $1.00. (*Out of print.*)

XIX. Classical Mythology in Shakespeare. ROBERT KILBURN ROOT, Ph.D. $1.00.

XX. The Controversy between the Puritans and the Stage. ELBERT N. S. THOMPSON, Ph.D. $2.00. (*Out of print.*)

XXI. The Elene of Cynewulf, Translated into English Prose. LUCIUS HUDSON HOLT, Ph.D. $0.30. (*Out of print.*)

XXII. King Alfred's Old English Version of St. Augustine's Soliloquies, Turned into Modern English. HENRY LEE HARGROVE, Ph.D. $0.75.

XXIII. The Cross in the Life and Literature of the Anglo-Saxons. WILLIAM O. STEVENS, Ph.D. $0.75. (*Out of print.*)

XXIV. An Index to the Old English Glosses of the Durham Hymnarium. HARVEY W. CHAPMAN. $0.75. (*Out of print.*)

XXV. Bartholomew Fair, by Ben Jonson, Edited with Introduction, Notes, and Glossary. CARROLL STORRS ALDEN, Ph.D. $2.00. (*Out of print.*)

XXVI. Select Translations from Scaliger's Poetics. FREDERICK M. PADELFORD, Ph.D. $0.75. (*Out of print.*)

XXVII. Poetaster, by Ben Jonson, Edited with Introduction, Notes, and Glossary. HERBERT S. MALLORY, Ph.D. $2.00. Cloth, $2.50.

XXVIII. The Staple of News, by Ben Jonson, Edited with Introduction, Notes, and Glossary. DE WINTER, Ph.D. $2.00. Cloth, $2.50.

XXIX. The Devil Is an Ass, by Ben Jonson, Edited with Introduction, Notes, and Glossary. WILLIAM SAVAGE JOHNSON, Ph.D. $2.00. Cloth, $2.50. (*Out of print.*)

XXX. The Language of the Northumbrian Gloss to the Gospel of St. Luke. MARGARET DUTTON KELLUM, Ph.D. $0.75. (*Out of print.*)

XXXI. Epicœne, or the Silent Woman, by Ben Jonson, Edited with Introduction, Notes, and Glossary. AURELIA HENRY, Ph.D. $2.00. Cloth, $2.50.

XXXII. The Syntax of the Temporal Clause in Old English Prose. ARTHUR ADAMS, Ph.D. $1.00. (*Out of print.*)

XXXIII. The Knight of the Burning Pestle, by Beaumont and Fletcher, Edited with Introduction, Notes, and Glossary. HERBERT S. MURCH, Ph.D. $2.00. (*Out of print.*)

XXXIV. The New Inn, by Ben Jonson, Edited with Introduction, Notes, and Glossary. GEORGE BREMNER TENNANT, Ph.D. $2.00.

XXXV. A Glossary of Wulfstan's Homilies. LORING HOLMES DODD, Ph.D. $1.00. (*Out of print.*)
XXXVI. The Complaint of Nature, Translated from the Latin of Alain de Lille. DOUGLAS M. MOFFAT, M.A. $0.75.
XXXVII. The Collaboration of Webster and Dekker. FREDERICK ERASTUS PIERCE, Ph.D. $1.00. (*Out of print.*)
XXXVIII. English Nativity Plays, Edited with Introduction, Notes, and Glossary. SAMUEL B. HEMINGWAY, Ph.D. $2.00. Cloth, $2.50. (*Out of print.*)
XXXIX. Concessive Constructions in Old English Prose. JOSEPHINE MAY BURNHAM, Ph.D. $1.00.
XL. The Tenure of Kings and Magistrates, by John Milton, Edited with Introduction and Notes. WILLIAM TALBOT ALLISON, Ph.D. $1.25. (*Out of print.*)
XLI. Biblical Quotations in Middle English Literature before 1350. MARY W. SMYTH, Ph.D. $2.00.
XLII. The Dialogue in English Literature. ELIZABETH MERRILL, Ph.D. $1.00. (*Out of print.*)
XLIII. A Study of Tindale's Genesis, Compared with the Genesis of Coverdale and of the Authorized Version. ELIZABETH WHITTLESEY CLEVELAND, Ph.D. $2.00.
XLIV. The Presentation of Time in the Elizabethan Drama. MABLE BULAND, Ph.D. $1.50.
XLV. Cynthia's Revels, or, the Fountain of Self-Love, by Ben Jonson, Edited with Introduction, Notes, and Glossary. ALEXANDER CORBIN JUDSON, Ph.D. $2.00.
XLVI. Richard Brome: A Study of His Life and Works. CLARENCE EDWARD ANDREWS, Ph.D. $1.25.
XLVII. The Magnetic Lady, or Humors Reconciled, by Ben Jonson, Edited with Introduction, Notes, and Glossary. HARVEY WHITEFIELD PECK, Ph.D. $2.00.
XLVIII. Genesis A (Sometimes Attributed to Cædmon), Translated from the Old English. LAWRENCE MASON, Ph.D. $0.75.
XLIX. The Later Version of the Wycliffite Epistle to the Romans, Compared with the Latin Original: A Study of Wycliffite English. EMMA CURTISS TUCKER, Ph.D. $1.50.
L. Some Accounts of the Bewcastle Cross between the Years 1607 and 1861. ALBERT STANBURROUGH COOK. $1.50. (*Out of print.*)
LI. The Ready and Easy Way to Establish a Free Commonwealth, by John Milton, Edited with Introduction, Notes, and Glossary. EVERT MORDECAI CLARK, Ph.D. $1.50.
LII. Every Man in His Humour, by Ben Jonson, Edited with Introduction, Notes, and Glossary. HENRY HOLLAND CARTER, Ph.D. $4.00.

LIII. Catiline, His Conspiracy, by Ben Jonson, Edited with Introduction, Notes, and Glossary. LYNN HAROLD HARRIS, Ph.D. $2.00.
LIV. Of Reformation, Touching Church-Discipline in England, by John Milton, Edited with Introduction, Notes, and Glossary. WILL TALIAFERRO HALE, Ph.D. $2.00. (*Out of print.*)
LV. Old English Scholarship in England from 1566 to 1800. ELEANOR N. ADAMS, Ph.D. $2.00.
LVI. The Case Is Altered, by Ben Jonson, Edited with Introduction, Notes, and Glossary. WILLIAM EDWARD SELIN, Ph.D. $2.00.
LVII. Wordsworth's Theory of Poetic Diction: A Study of the Historical and Personal Background of the Lyrical Ballads. MARJORIE LATTA BARSTOW, Ph.D. $1.50. (*Out of print.*)
LVIII. Horace in the English Literature of the Eighteenth Century. CAROLINE GOAD, Ph.D. $3.00.
LIX. Volpone, or The Fox, by Ben Jonson, Edited with Introduction, Notes, and Glossary. JOHN D. REA, Ph.D. $2.50.
LX. The Mediæval Attitude toward Astrology, Particularly in England. THEODORE OTTO WEDEL, Ph.D. $2.50.
LXI. Purity: A Middle English Poem, Edited with Introduction, Notes, and Glossary. ROBERT J. MENNER, Ph.D. $3.00.
LXII. Ann Radcliffe in Relation to Her Time. CLARA FRANCES MCINTYRE, Ph.D. $1.50.
LXIII. The Old English Physiologus: Text and Prose Translation by ALBERT STANBURROUGH COOK; Verse Translation by JAMES HALL PITMAN. $0.80.
LXIV. The Life and Work of Joanna Baillie. MARGARET S. CARHART, Ph.D. $2.00.
LXV. The Influence of Robert Garnier on Elizabethan Drama. ALEXANDER M. WITHERSPOON, Ph.D. $2.00.
LXVI. Goldsmith's Animated Nature: A Study of Goldsmith. JAMES HALL PITMAN, Ph.D. $2.00.
LXVII. The Riddles of Aldhelm: Text and Verse Translation, with Notes. JAMES HALL PITMAN, Ph.D. $1.00.
LXVIII. The American Indian in English Literature of the Eighteenth Century. BENJAMIN BISSELL, Ph.D. $2.00.
LXIX. The Life and Poems of Nicholas Grimald. L. R. MERRILL, Ph.D. $4.50.
LXX. Christ and Satan: An Old English Poem, Edited with Introduction, Notes, and Glossary. MERREL DARE CLUBB, Ph.D. $2.00.
LXXI. Oliver Goldsmith's The Citizen of the World: A Study.

HAMILTON JEWETT SMITH, Ph.D. $2.00. (*Out of print.*)
LXXII. St. Erkenwald: A Middle English Poem, Edited with Introduction, Notes, and Glossary. HENRY L. SAVAGE, Ph.D. $2.00.
LXXIII. Eastward Hoe, by Chapman, Jonson, and Marston, Edited with Introduction, Notes, and Glossary. JULIA HAMLET HARRIS, Ph.D. $2.00.
LXXIV. The Life and Poems of Richard Edwards. LEICESTER BRADNER, Ph.D. $2.00.
LXXV. The Life and Works of Edward Moore. J. HOMER CASKEY, Ph.D. $2.00.
LXXVI. Sir Walter Scott's Novels on the Stage. H. A. WHITE, Ph.D. $2.50.
LXXVII. Nathan Field, The Actor-Playwright. ROBERTA FLORENCE BRINCKLEY, Ph.D. $2.50.
LXXVIII. Thomas Heywood: A Study in the Elizabethan Drama of Everyday Life. OTELIA CROMWELL, Ph.D. $2.50.
LXXIX. Melanthe: A Latin Pastoral Poem of the Early Seventeenth Century. JOSEPH S. G. BOLTON, Ph.D. $2.50.
LXXX. The Dramatic Work of Samuel Foote. MARY MEGIE BELDEN, Ph.D. $2.50.
LXXXI. Thomas Southerne, Dramatist. JOHN WENDELL DODDS, Ph.D. $2.00.